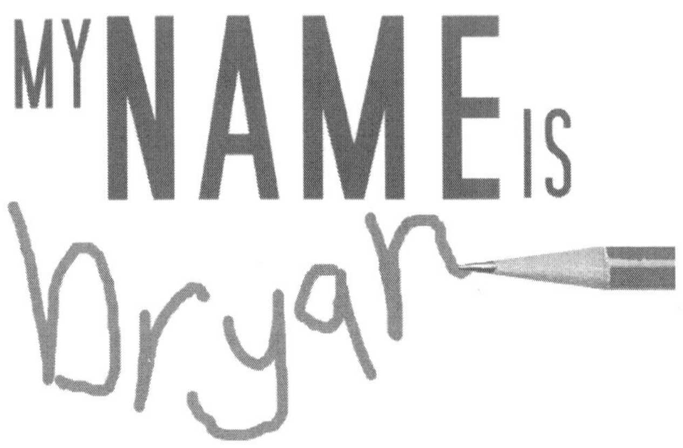

STACY LYNN CARROLL

Based on a True Story

ISBN: 978-0-9908041-0-9
LCCN: 2014950849

This book is based very closely on actual events. Names of the family, places, and events have not been changed. Other names have been changed to protect their identities. Dialogue has been added to help move the story along, but the people in this book and the things they have gone through are very real. Any trademarks, product names, or named features or places are assumed to be the property of their respective owners, and are used only for reference. The quotes in this book are used with permission from the individuals (still living). In allowing the author to use their quotes, they are not endorsing this book.

Dedicated to Grandpa Mayo Carroll, Glenn Carroll, and Glenda Carroll Jennings. They may no longer be with us physically, but will always remain a part of our lives through heart and spirit.

Other books by author Stacy Lynn Carroll:

The Princess Sisters trilogy:
~*The Princess Sisters*
~*Frogs & Toads*
~*Forever After (coming soon)*

CHAPTER ONE

"Hardships often prepare ordinary people for an extraordinary destiny."

\- C.S. Lewis

June 1979

"Cliff jumping. You in?" Bryan's smile widened as he watched his best friend's eyes light up.

"Absolutely! When?" Greg asked.

Bryan threw his large duffel bag into the opening under the bus. "I don't remember. I think my dad said it's toward the end of the trip. But apparently we get to conquer some pretty big rapids first."

"Sweet! This trip totally beats what we did last year."

"Yeah, no kidding."

Bryan and Greg stepped away from the bus, wandering across the parking lot to settle under a large oak tree.

"Hey, man, you ready?" Another lanky teenage boy came up to the pair.

"Yeah, my dad was telling me about some cliffs we can jump off during the rafting trip." Bryan could hardly contain his excitement.

"Oh yeah? How high?"

"Not sure," Bryan said, looking around as some other guys approached. "But it sounds awesome."

"What sounds awesome?" one of them asked.

"Cliff jumping," Greg chimed in.

"Seriously? Sweet!"

"Are the leaders going to let us?"

"Yeah, Duane is the one who told my dad about them," Bryan said.

"Hey, looks like we're loading now." Greg pointed at the line of teenagers snaking their way through the parking lot and onto the bus.

Bryan and his friends were the last to get in line.

"Oh, man, that means we're probably sitting up front."

"Loser seats. Right behind the . . ." Bryan trailed off as they climbed the three steps and found the last two empty rows were directly behind the chaperones, just as he had feared. "Parents," he sighed.

Carol Jean turned around in her seat and flashed her son a huge smile. Bryan tried to return the grin, but it came across as more of a grimace. It was bad enough his parents were on the trip, but now he had to sit by them?

"Oh, Bryan," Carol Jean laughed. She rolled her eyes and turned to her husband, Glenn. "Have you ever seen a more sullen teenager?" she asked.

Glenn turned in his seat and smiled. "Well, he is stuck with all us old fogies. Poor kid can't catch a break. First his boss doesn't want him to come, then he has to travel on his last youth conference trip with both his parents and his sister. Maybe we should start planning his pity party now."

"Okay, thank you," Bryan waved his parents off and turned to Greg.

"Your boss didn't want you to come?" Greg asked, putting on his black aviators and leaning back in his seat. "How come?"

"Summer is the busiest season for pouring concrete, as I'm sure you can imagine," Bryan explained. "My boss couldn't find a replacement so he didn't want me to come." Bryan shrugged. "I was able to talk him into it eventually though."

Greg nodded.

Bryan lay his head back against the soft, grey headrest and closed his eyes. He wasn't tired enough to sleep, but after working hard labor outside every day, it felt nice to just sit and relax with his eyes closed. His thoughts traveled to Jana and he wondered what she was doing at that moment.

As if reading his thoughts, Greg asked, "So how are things going with Jana?"

Bryan opened his eyes and smiled. "Really great! She's amazing and lots of fun."

"So what're your plans? You gonna keep pouring concrete?"

"For now. At least until I can get a job at a garage somewhere."

"Still no college?" Carol Jean asked, trying to hide the disappointment in her voice. She had been eavesdropping from the row in front of them.

"What would I do with college? If I'm going to be a mechanic, the best schooling I can get is in a garage."

"Have you found a garage to take you on as an intern yet?" Glenn asked, trying to turn around in his seat.

"No. I thought it would be better to start applying after this trip. I didn't want to get on somewhere only to tell them I needed a week off."

Glenn nodded his head in agreement. Bryan watched as his dad quickly put his focus back on the driver and the road. His dad had a map in his head and could get anywhere without a problem. He always preferred the scenic route to reaching his destination quickly. Bryan knew it drove him crazy to just sit back and watch as the driver sped past several attractive pullouts. His dad constantly said, "Life is about the journey," before turning down a dusty little side road. But they always ended up right where they needed to be. Bryan smiled as he watched Glenn's lip twitch. He knew it was killing him not to say anything.

Bryan looked down the long row of seats toward the back of the bus, catching his sister's eye. He smiled, but Becky returned to her conversation without acknowledging him. The game was on. Bryan stared, unblinking at the side of Becky's face. His eyes bore into her cheek until it started to turn pink. His eyes narrowed, but still he didn't blink. Becky's mouth twitched at the corners, until she finally broke into a smile. Bryan laughed and turned around in his chair. He had won.

The drive was peaceful, especially compared to family vacations. With four younger sisters, road trips were anything but quiet. There was always fighting over seats or music or screaming at each other to stop touching.

"If both your parents are here, who has your other sisters?" Greg asked.

"Brenda is at a junior rangers camp, and both Glenda and Jenny are staying with a cousin."

"So this must be a nice week off for you, huh, Mrs. C?" Greg asked, leaning forward.

"I'm not sure I'd call rafting through rapids a relaxing week off, but I'm sure we'll have fun."

Several hours later, the bus jostled Bryan awake as they drove over loose gravel, nearing the San Juan River. He hadn't even realized he'd fallen asleep. Once they reached the river and everyone climbed off the bus, they split into smaller groups of ten or so to a raft, and each raft had a chaperone in charge. Duane walked to the front of the group and welcomed them enthusiastically.

"How's everyone doing this morning?" he asked.

"Fabulous, marvelous, and wonderful!" Glenn's response was louder than any of the kids in the group. Several of them turned toward him and smiled. His enthusiasm increased the excitement around them.

Once everyone was quiet again, Duane gave a small lesson on rowing and had the kids all practice smooth, strong strokes together. Once food and supplies were safely loaded, the kids climbed aboard the big yellow rafts and pushed off.

They spent the first two days on the water for a good portion of the day. They pulled off occasionally to eat or explore but spent most of their time working together to row through the brownish green water. They had little time for floating, as the water moved quickly over the large rapids. When they did get moments of calm, the kids got in water fights with the other rafts or jumped in the water to swim and cool off. They had to travel so many miles each day to ensure they'd make it to the next camp site and that the trip would end on time.

Having already turned eighteen, Bryan was one of the oldest kids in the group. He was even in charge of his own raft since there weren't enough adults to go around. He took this charge seriously and watched over his group as he guided them down the smooth river.

On day three, some of his group began to get restless so Bryan devised a plan. They slowed down and waited for Becky's raft to come into view, and then they pulled up alongside it to ambush her and her friends. Several boys jumped aboard, grabbing the screaming girls and throwing them into the water. The girls squealed and tried to get away, but the ambush worked in the end. They not only emptied their opponent's raft, but they were saved from boredom as well. Becky grabbed onto the side of her brother's raft, gasping, and asked Bryan for help. He grabbed her by the lifejacket to pull her aboard, when two other girls popped up from the water and grabbed Bryan, yanking him in. The cold water rushed into his face, burning his nose and eyes. He sputtered and coughed, and then broke his head through the waves, chuckling.

On the last night of the trip, as their raft neared Slickhorn Canyon, Bryan and his friends began talking excitedly about the anticipated cliffs.

"Did Duane say how tall the cliffs are?"

"No. You wanna take bets?"

"Twenty feet."

"Fifty feet."

"One hundred feet!"

Bryan and his friends laughed as two of them jumped into the waist-high water to help pull their raft ashore. Bryan slowly got to his feet and wiped the sweat from his brow. Leaping from the raft and pulling it the rest of the way up the bank, he held the yellow beast steady so his passengers could climb out. Duane appeared at their sides, a glint in his eye as he whispered, "You boys ready?"

They nodded enthusiastically. "Let's do it!"

They hoisted the raft further up the bank. Dinner was underway and several groups of teenagers relaxed around the bank where they had made camp. Excited at the aspect of exploring the canyon and finding the cliffs to jump from, Bryan definitely wasn't ready to be done for the day. A stream flowed into the canyon, forming several smaller ponds. Duane led the way, following this stream past the surrounding area.

"I'll catch up to you guys in a minute," Bryan called. Duane nodded. The boys hooted in excitement as they followed closely behind him, making their way up the steep, red rocks. Bryan had to get his raft secure for the night before he could go. Since he was in charge, it was his duty every night to make sure the raft was tied down and their supplies were safe. Once everything was carefully placed in the shade of some nearby trees, Bryan ran to join the others.

He began hiking in the direction the other guys had gone. He hiked nearly a mile and was about to turn back when he saw them jumping off a ledge that overlooked the water. The crimson cliff stood before him like a towering giant, with arms stretched up toward heaven. A smile spread across his face and he lunged at the overhang; David was ready to take on the mighty Goliath. Bryan could hear laughter growing closer as he climbed higher and higher. His long legs made the ascent easy, and as he grabbed the last dusty ledge, he heaved himself up and over the top. Spending the last couple months working hard outdoors had seriously increased Bryan's muscle mass, so he was able to climb up to the rocky ledge with relative ease. As he watched the other jumpers, some hit the water with pencil-straight legs while others bent their knees, looking as though they were sitting mid-air. A couple of the guys started doing flips off the cliff edge into the water. It seems inevitable that when a large group of guys get together, they try to outdo one another. Bryan watched another buddy flip off the ledge and land feet first in the water below, and then jump up out of the ripples and shake the water from his hair, laughing as he made his way back to the shore to try it again.

Bryan didn't want to do a flip. That just seemed stupid. It's harder to control the way you land, and he was nervous about clearing enough space to keep his head from hitting rocks. He couldn't really just jump either. After the flippers, that would make him look like a pansy. Bryan spent the majority of his life living near a pool, and he spent a large number of weekends on a lake with his family's boat. He was a seasoned swimmer. He had no doubt in his mind that he could show up these boys.

Bryan stepped closer to the edge and looked down, waiting for the others to clear out of his way. With perfectly straight arms raised above his head, he bent his knees slightly for momentum and jumped. A huge smile spread across his face as he sailed through the air, the wind caressing his cheeks as the water neared. Bryan knew he had done a perfect swan dive. He only wished he could have seen how beautiful it must have been to the onlookers. His fingertips touched the cool liquid first, his body forming a flawless straight line behind them. But something was wrong. He was sailing through the water, and the river floor was coming too fast. His hands hit the sand hard. His elbows buckled. Bryan's head smashed into the bottom and with a loud POP, he knew his life would be changed forever.

CHAPTER TWO

"The past is set in stone.
We cannot change that.
The only thing we can
change is our future, which
is as moldable as clay."

- Jaime Heiner

Bryan could no longer move. Every inch of him wanted to panic. He wanted to scream, he wanted to cry out for help, but he couldn't feel his body and there was nothing he could do. A voice inside him told him to be calm and wait. If he panicked, he would run out of air. If he waited, then he at least stood a chance.

His body didn't float to the top or sink to the bottom. Bryan remained suspended in the river, waiting for someone to come and get him. It was a good thing he was such a seasoned swimmer, or he would surely have lost consciousness by now. He looked up and saw light from the sun bouncing off the surface. Then he saw a hand in the water reaching out for him. Bryan waited but the hand didn't move. It seemed to be floating in the water like a dead fish, just above his head. *Why don't they just grab me?* he wondered. Then Bryan noticed the arm connected to the hand extended from his own body. His own hand floated toward the surface, and he couldn't even make it move. Bryan knew he shouldn't panic or he would run out of air that much faster. Instead, he remained completely calm and concentrated on his breath, trying not to focus on the ghost hand that drifted next to him.

Bryan had always heard when faced with death, your life flashes before your eyes. He never believed it until this moment. As his throat became smaller and his lungs burned, Bryan felt suspended, watching his memories play out as if on a giant movie screen.

"It's a boy!" The nurse placed the small blue bundle in Carol Jean's arms. Bryan looked up at his much younger mother as she lay in a hospital bed. She stared down into his soft, pink face, tracing his cheek with her finger. His mom's face had a glow about it as she softly stroked his little arms, counting each finger as she smelled and touched every inch of his miniature body.

The door opened and his dad rushed to her side. Bryan stared up at his younger father whose eyes were moistened with emotion as he kissed his mother tenderly.

"What should we call him?"

"Bryan," his mom whispered. "Let's name him Bryan."

KNOCK!

KNOCK!

KNOCK!

The grip tightened around his three-year-old fingers while she knocked with her other hand. Bryan cringed with each pounding of wood, knowing he would get it if the new baby woke up. The door swung open, his mom looking frazzled and tired. Her face quickly changed from annoyance to surprise when she saw Bryan standing there.

"I think this belongs to you." Her neighbor smiled sweetly. "I found him wandering down the street."

Carol Jean's face flushed pink. "Oh my goodness, thank you so much!" She stared at the defiant face on her blond little boy. "Bryan! How did you get out?"

Bryan marched past her and sat on the couch, his arms folded, his chin thrust out. "I'm not tired." His mom was too exhausted to be furious. He watched as she looked back to her neighbor helplessly.

"Bryan and Becky have been squabbling all morning. I finally got both Becky and Brenda down for naps. I told Bryan he needed to lay down too, but he told me he's too old for naps. I left him in his room, thinking he'd fall asleep. I went in my room and laid down, hoping I'd catch a few minutes at least before one of them woke up. I must have fallen asleep more soundly than I thought. I really don't know how he got outside without my hearing! I've just been so tired since Brenda was born. I don't think I've slept in three months . . ."

His neighbor put a hand up to stop the explanation. "Carol Jean, you have three children under the age of three, including a newborn. You don't need to explain anything to me. Have a nice day." She slipped out the front door before his mom could utter another word.

She walked over to the couch and plopped down beside Bryan. "You, mister, are in big trouble! You know better than to leave the house by yourself!"

"I'm not tired," he said unapologetically. He slid from the couch and began pushing his cars around on the floor.

"Bryan, time to come in for dinner!"

His mom stood at the back door of their new home, watching as Bryan's glove closed around the baseball with a *thump!* He grasped the white leather in his hand and threw it again without even glancing at his mom.

"Bryan! Come in NOW!"

"Come on, Mom, just a few more pitches. Please?" He continued to throw and catch the ball with his grandfather, the leather making a satisfying smacking sound each time they connected.

Carol Jean let out an exasperated breath. "Mayo, can you give me a hand, please?"

Grandpa Carroll chuckled. "All right, Bryan, you need to listen to your mom. We can play more tomorrow."

Reluctantly, Bryan dropped his glove and shuffled toward the house. He squeezed past his mother's large belly and went inside to wash his hands.

"Do you want to stay and eat?" Carol Jean offered.

"No thank you. I'm sure Thelma has dinner for me at home."

"Can I at least offer you a glass of water before you leave? You two were working pretty hard out there."

"Sure, thank you." Grandpa Carroll looked at Bryan and added, "He really is a good boy, ya know."

Carol Jean let out a large sigh. "I know. But he might also be the death of me. He is the sole cause of this," she added, holding up a section of greying hair.

Grandpa Carroll smiled. "So does that mean you're hoping for another girl?" He nodded toward her growing belly.

"I don't really know. Some days I hope for another boy, so he can have a brother. Then he lights something on fire and I think maybe another girl wouldn't be so bad."

Bryan pretended he couldn't hear them and began piling food onto his plate.

"Wait for your father, please."

Bryan rolled his eyes and slumped back in his chair.

"Bye, kiddo. I'll see you later."

Bryan jumped to his feet. "But if I eat real fast, can't we go back out tonight?"

"It's already getting dark. Besides, your Grandma will wonder where I am." Bryan's face fell. "Oh, come now, enjoy dinner with your family and I'll see you tomorrow." With that, Grandpa Carroll waved goodbye and shut the door behind him.

The door opened again a moment later and Glenn entered the kitchen. "Sorry I'm late," he said.

"Daddy!" Becky and Brenda came screaming into the room and each wrapped themselves around one of his legs. He laughed and lifted one leg at a time, depositing the girls into their chairs. Then he ruffled Bryan's hair and leaned over to give Carol Jean a kiss.

"How was your day?" she asked.

Glenn looked tired but he responded in the same way he always did. "Fabulous, marvelous, and wonderful." He looked down at Bryan. "Grandpa says you're getting better at catching."

"Yeah, I am! I didn't drop the ball one single time!"

"Wow. I don't think I was that good at catch when I was seven. You must be practicing really hard."

"Just until Mom makes me come inside." He made a face.

"I know you like playing outside, buddy, but if you don't eat, you won't have enough energy to be an athlete."

Bryan began spooning mounds of food into his mouth until his plate was clean.

"Nahw ca I gow pway ouside?" he asked around a mouthful of food.

His sisters giggled as mashed potatoes sprayed out over the table.

"No, it's too dark. You can play again tomorrow."

Bryan was ready to argue when the doorbell rang. He swallowed his last chunk of food and raced for the door. "I'll get it!"

A little boy from down the street stood on his porch, holding a wind-up train in his hands. "Hi, Bryan. Danny told me you fixed his record player. I was hoping you could help me with my train, too? It won't go anymore."

Bryan reached for the train, his eyes lighting up as he looked it over. He twirled the small wheels with his thumb and then tried winding it himself. "I can look at it tonight. Why don't you come back tomorrow and see if I have it fixed by then."

"Gee, thanks, Bryan!"

Bryan immediately carried the train into the living room and began dismantling it with care. He loved fixing things! His reputation was starting to grow among the other kids in the neighborhood. He hadn't yet found a toy he couldn't fix. Soon the train was scattered all over the floor and he was still fiddling with the pieces when Carol Jean came in and told him it was time for bed.

The next morning Bryan woke up and raced into the living room to finish his project. He was startled to see his grandparents sitting on the couch.

"Good morning, Bryan." In response to his confused face his grandpa laughed and added, "Your mom had the baby last night."

He nodded and then waited expectantly for what he was afraid to hear.

"It was another girl. They named her Glenda."

Bryan sighed and slumped down to the floor. He picked up two pieces of the train and began fitting them together again. They heard a cry from the girls' room and his grandma got up to take care of his sisters. Grandpa Carroll carefully slid off the couch and grunted as he tried to squat beside Bryan on the floor.

"So what are you working on?"

"It's a train. It got broken, so I'm fixing it."

"You sure are good with your hands. Do you want to show me how it works?"

Bryan began pointing out the different pieces to his grandpa while he screwed them back together.

"You're not very happy about having another sister, are you?"

Bryan just shrugged and continued working.

"You know, having all sisters isn't so bad."

He scrunched up his nose and made a face.

Grandpa Carroll chuckled before continuing. "They will all look up to you. I already know Becky and Brenda follow you around everywhere."

"Yeah, it's annoying."

"They only do that because they love you and they want to be just like you. You're their big brother, their protector. It's a very important job. Do you think you can handle it?"

Bryan thought for a moment and then nodded.

"Good boy. Now when you're finished with that, what do you say we head back outside and throw the ball around some more?"

Bryan's mom usually had to pry him out of bed on Sunday mornings, but not today, not when candy was involved. Bryan grinned as he hopped out of bed and quickly moved down the hall. He couldn't wait to see what the Easter Bunny brought. His mouth began to water as he thought about all the eggs he would find during the hunt later. As Bryan came around the corner, he stopped dead in his tracks. His mom's mom sat on their sofa, looking tired and reading a book.

"Grandma?" Bryan whispered.

She looked up and smiled warmly, inviting him to come hug her with outstretched arms. He moved slowly towards her, his heart racing.

"Where are Mom and Dad?" he asked.

Grandma patted the cushion beside her. Bryan sat and looked up into her eyes, searching for answers.

She wrapped one arm around his shoulders and placed her other hand on top of both of his. "I'm really sorry to tell you this," she started, and Bryan held his breath. "Your Grandma Carroll passed away last night. Your parents are at the hospital with Grandpa Carroll right now."

Bryan continued to stare at her, unable to fully process the words. "She . . . died?" he finally asked.

Grandma gave his hand a squeeze and nodded.

"But . . . it's Easter."

"I know, sweetie. I'm sorry. Your parents have been gone most of the night."

"But, are they coming back for the Easter egg hunt?"

"No, dear. No baskets or egg hunts this year. Why don't you go get dressed now? I'm taking you and your sisters to church."

Bryan sat, unmoving for several minutes. "How is Grandpa?"

"I'm not sure, sweetie. You'll have to ask your parents when they get home."

All Bryan could think about for several days after was Grandpa. He just wanted to see him, but was always told that Grandpa was busy with funeral arrangements. The day of the funeral finally arrived and Bryan still found he couldn't reach Grandpa. He was too surrounded by a long line of family and friends, offering their love and support.

Once the funeral ended and everyone went home, Bryan turned back around and ran out the front door. He jumped on his bike and flew down the block, forgetting that he wasn't wearing any shoes. He kept going until he arrived at his safe haven: Grandpa Carroll's house. He paused only briefly to stare at the huge wooden door. Once he caught his breath, Bryan reached for the handle and opened the door slowly. He walked quietly through the house until he found Grandpa Carroll sitting in his den, staring silently at the golf game on TV. Bryan carefully climbed up beside him on the bright, floral couch and laid his head against Grandpa Carroll's drooping arm. Without a word spoken between them, Grandpa Carroll reached over and covered both of Bryan's hands with one of his own. They sat together and watched golf until Grandpa Carroll fell asleep.

>♦< >♦< >♦<

Bryan stared out the front window at the large, white ambulance which sat parked in his driveway. He waited eagerly to see Becky's reaction as she walked up the front steps. He was disappointed when Becky simply rolled her eyes and marched into the house. Bryan waved from the family room, a big grin spread across his face as the paramedics bandaged his leg. "What did you do now?" she asked.

"I was just climbing a tree." Bryan shrugged.

"All right, Bryan, you're good to go," one of the paramedics said. "Just be a bit more careful from now on."

Carol Jean laughed. "If only I had a nickel for every time I said those same words to him . . ." She looked at Bryan's impish grin and shook her head. Bryan loved building fire-moats around his castles in the sandbox, he loved leaping off the roof to feel like he was flying, he loved trying stunts on his bike and skateboard, and he definitely didn't plan on giving up his favorite activities any time soon.

As soon as the paramedics finished their work and began packing up, Bryan leaped to his feet.

"Can I go visit Grandpa now?"

Carol Jean nodded without looking up, her head in her outstretched hand, massaging the migraine that threatened to appear. She thanked the men profusely for coming.

Bryan slammed the door behind himself and picked up his fallen bike from the sidewalk.

Bryan's leg prevented him from pedaling very fast, which he found annoying, but he was still able to move with barely an issue. He burst through Grandpa Carroll's unlocked door and walked straight over to the game cupboard. He slid checkers under his arm, grabbing two apples off the counter as he passed through the small kitchen. He walked into the living room and set up the small, brown TV tray right in front of Grandpa's chair. He pulled up a folding chair and set the pieces out, reserving the red for himself.

"So whad'ya do this time?"

Bryan looked down, having forgotten about his leg already. "Oh, I was just climbing the tree in our yard. Brenda said when I fell, I was knocked out for ten whole seconds!" he said, beaming with pride.

Grandpa Carroll chuckled. "Shouldn't the bandage be on your head then?"

"No, I didn't hurt my head at all! I just scraped my leg when I was coming down, I guess."

Bryan threw a snowball at Becky, who squealed and threw one back. Bryan laughed and ducked just in time for the snowball to hit little Glenda square in the face. She began to scream and cry. Bryan and Becky both stopped laughing and ran over. Bryan scooped her up in his arms and bounced her until she calmed down.

"I'm sorry, Glenda. Do you want to help us build a snowman?"

She nodded through her tears and Bryan gently placed her back on the powdery ground. He began to form a tight ball of snow in his hands and then showed Glenda how to help him push it through the snow until the ball was too big to roll anymore. Becky and Brenda pushed over the ball they had been working on. Brenda ran inside to look for a carrot while Becky and Glenda scoured the ground for stones that could make up the eyes and mouth. Bryan quickly rolled a small ball of snow for the head and had to stand on his tippy-toes to get it safely on top of the snowman's middle. Brenda ran back outside, waving a carrot above her head.

"Mom and Dad want to talk to us inside. They said to come in when the snowman is done."

"What for?" Becky looked up from her search.

"I dunno." Brenda shrugged.

They all looked to Bryan. "What? I didn't do anything, I swear!"

Becky and Glenda gave up on their search for pebbles, only finding two. They used those for the eyes and ended up using a stick to create his lopsided smile. They all trudged inside, shaking the snow from their coats as they peeled off the extra layers with their frozen fingers.

Glenn and Carol Jean were seated at the kitchen table, mugs of hot cocoa ready and waiting for the kids as they walked in.

"What's the matter?" Bryan asked.

"Nothing's the matter," Carol Jean said with a smile.

"Then why do you look so serious?" Becky asked, pulling her mug closer as she sat down.

Their parents looked at each other and smiled.

"We're going to have another baby!" Carol Jean announced. She reached down and picked up Glenda, who waited with outstretched arms.

The older three remained speechless. They just stared at their parents waiting for the inevitable, "Ha ha! April fools!" But it didn't come.

"Ummm, congratulations," Brenda finally said, standing up and giving her mother a half-hearted hug.

Becky did the same, but Bryan continued to stare. His eyebrows smoldered together as he glared at his parents, trying to wrap his head around this news. His anger finally broke through the surface. He slammed his fist into the table and then stalked from the room.

Over the next nine months Bryan spoke very little about the baby. Even though his mother continued to grow in size, he still went about his life and spoke to her as though she weren't pregnant. He wanted nothing to do with helping his parents in preparations for the new addition.

As the pregnancy neared the end, Carol Jean became increasingly tired and uncomfortable. She often needed more rest during the day and had to sit on the couch with her feet up. She continued to get bigger, but the baby still did not come. Late one night, Carol Jean finally went into labor, two weeks past her due date. The baby only lived eight hours. They named her Beverly.

Glenn returned home from the hospital the next day, empty-handed and broken-hearted. Carol Jean had become septic from the long pregnancy and difficult delivery, and was to remain at the hospital for several more days. Grandpa Carroll came over and played with the kids so Glenn could get some rest and try to plan the small funeral. He walked up the stairs, his eyes misting as he tried hard to be strong for his other children. Glenn thanked his dad for coming, his eyes red and swollen, his face grim.

The girls started fighting so Grandpa Carroll turned on a movie for them and sank into the couch. Glenda climbed up in his lap and was soon fast asleep. Bryan slowly got up from his spot on the floor and sat down next to his grandpa. He leaned his head on Grandpa's shoulder and began to cry.

"I'm sorry," he whispered

"For what?" Grandpa asked.

"I didn't want the baby, but I didn't want her to die!"

"Oh, Bryan, this is not your fault. It's just one of those things . . ."

"Why did she die?" he looked to Grandpa Carroll with round, swollen eyes.

"Well, it seems your sister waited too long to come. Babies can't stay inside their mommies forever or they start to get sick."

Bryan didn't really understand, but he nodded anyway.

"The neat thing to remember is now you have a guardian angel who is watching over you in heaven."

Bryan mustered half a smile, but then his face quickly became serious again. "Is Mom going to be okay?"

"She will. With time."

"Is she going to be able to come to the funeral?"

Grandpa let out a long, slow sigh. "It's not looking like she will."

Bryan's eyes grew wider.

"Your mom will be okay," Grandpa assured him, patting his leg. "Her body has been through a lot and it will take some time to heal. We'll just keep praying for her to come home soon."

Bryan nodded to Grandpa and then immediately bowed his head and folded his arms in silent prayer.

One year later, Bryan found himself a big brother again. He stood over Jenny's basinet, watching her sleep.

"Can I hold her?"

Carol Jean looked at him, surprised. "Of course," she said. "Why don't you sit down?"

"Oh, come now, the boy is eleven years old. He doesn't need to sit," Glenn said, placing the baby into Bryan's outstretched arms.

Bryan looked at his sister's tiny, pink face. She slowly opened her eyes and smiled up at him, and he smiled back.

"She likes you!" Carol Jean said.

Bryan grinned at his mom and then looked at Jenny again. "I like her, too."

"Byan, Byan, way fo me!"

Bryan pushed the towel up on his shoulder and turned around. Little Jenny ran as fast as her two-year-old feet would carry her, trying to catch up. She was stripped down to just her diaper, her pudgy little hands wrapped around a blue float ring. She finally caught him and smiled up into his face.

Bryan returned the grin, scooping her up into his arms. "Does Mom know you're out here? I'm going to the pool." He pointed toward the community pool entrance, which stood only two doors down from their house. "I really can't play with you right now."

"We're right here." Carol Jean emerged from the house with a large tote bag filled with towels and pool toys. "She just wanted to walk with you."

"Mom, come on, I thought you said I could go to the pool by myself," Bryan said, setting Jenny back down on the sidewalk.

"Sorry, sweetie, but your sisters saw you getting ready and wanted to come."

Bryan grumbled but continued to walk, his four little sisters trailing behind him in a line. Once they were splashing and playing in the water, Bryan forgot about his frustrations and had fun swimming with Brenda and Becky. Bryan loved that he could cream his sisters every time they raced. He could hold his breath under water the longest, too. He'd sit at the bottom of the pool, looking up and watching as Brenda started squirming right before her head broke through the water. Becky followed shortly after, slapping the water with the palm of her hand when she realized she'd been beaten again. Bryan's lungs burned for oxygen, but he remained under the water until he feared he might pass out. Then he'd kick off the bottom, his head bursting through the water like a shot from a cannon.

Bryan could hear screaming inside the house before he even got his keys into the lock. He rolled his eyes and brushed his shaggy hair from his forehead. "Oh, the joys of having four sisters," he mumbled. He leaned his broad shoulder into the door and pushed it open.

Glenda stood in front of the piano, screaming at it, her face purple with rage.

"Get out here now, you little brat!"

Bryan thought she looked insane until he heard the faint, defiant reply.

"No!"

Bryan walked up behind Glenda and placed a hand on her shoulder. She turned with a start, her eyes glowing like fire.

"She won't come out!" Glenda held her hand up, displaying the piano for Bryan. "She got mad and climbed back there, and now mom will get home and I'll be in trouble!"

"How did she even get back there?"

Their family piano sat along the railing by the top of the basement stairs. The back of the piano was against the banister and had the sheer drop off down the stairs directly behind it.

"She climbed over the banister and walked along the ledge." Glenda's voice seemed to be calming a little. "I even called next door, and Mrs. Wright couldn't get her to come out either. This is my first time babysitting alone. Mom's going to kill me if she finds out I let her walk along that ledge."

Bryan knelt down by the side of the piano and peeked behind it. Two little, blue eyes looked back out at him. "Jenny," he coaxed in a soothing voice. "Hey, Jenny, you wanna go for a car ride with me?"

Jenny giggled and crawled out from her hiding spot. She lunged at Bryan, who caught her mid-jump and tickled her in the air.

Glenda grunted angrily and stormed away.

"Tell Mom we went for a ride," he yelled. Jenny squealed and threw her arms around Bryan's neck, hugging him tightly.

He walked back outside to his green Pinto, placing Jenny on the front sit before going around and sliding in behind the wheel. It was warm even though the sunlight was fading. Bryan started the car and drove around the neighborhood. Jenny leaned out the car window, enjoying the thick summer breeze on her face. As Bryan stepped on the gas, Jenny's knee hit the door handle and the door swung open, with her still hanging on it. Jenny began screaming, and even though Bryan could feel his heart stop, he kept his calm. He carefully slowed to a stop and then got out to gently lift her off the door.

"Shhh, shhh, you're okay," he soothed. When Jenny stopped trembling, he put her back inside the car. As they started driving again, he made jokes about how silly she looked, hanging on like a little monkey. It didn't take long before they were both laughing about the whole thing.

They returned home about an hour later, Jenny clutching the stuffed musical bear Bryan bought her. All thoughts from their adventurous evening were forgotten.

"Did you have fun?" Carol Jean knelt down to hug Jenny, who nodded enthusiastically, and then ran to her room to make a bed for the new 'baby.' Carol Jean stood and smiled at Bryan. "Glenda told me what happened. Thanks for taking her out."

Bryan nodded. He walked past his mom into the kitchen for a snack.

"Don't eat too much; dinner will be ready soon."

"I'll be hungry then, too," he said, piling layers of ham onto his colossal sandwich.

Carol Jean grabbed a handful of blonde locks which hung past his ear. "It's time for a haircut," she said, making a face.

Bryan pulled out of her reach. "I like my hair long, Mom. Just let it go."

"But it looks so awful!"

"Everyone wears their hair like this. I'd look stupid if I cut it."

"He's right, Mom," Becky added, stepping into the kitchen.

Carol Jean threw her hands up in the air. "I give up!"

"Thanks," Bryan mumbled to Becky before heading downstairs to his bedroom. As he walked down the basement hallway, he pulled a pencil from his backpack and scribbled 'I hate Mom' on the clean, white wall.

Bryan stepped into the auto shop at school and paused in the open doorway. The loud clanging of tools on metal and the sharp whirring of an impact wrench might deter others from wanting to enter, but not Bryan. He took a deep breath, sucking in the fumes of motor oil and body sweat. Oh yeah, this was home. He grinned before stepping towards his project for the day, a Chevy that needed a stereo installed. He learned all the basics last year when he took auto shop—c hanging oil, rotating tires, the ins and outs of engines—but now that he was in his senior year, he could work on bigger projects alone. He rubbed his hand along the smooth orange paint, tracing the beauty and power of the car beneath his rough fingertips. He marched to the small booth that stood between the two shops. He selected the tools he would need for that day and checked them out before returning to the beauty that waited for him.

"Hi, Bryan!" Another student high fived him as he walked past.

"Hey, Bry, can you help me a sec?" A tall, skinny kid with glasses waved him over. Bryan paused and answered his question with ease, and then he wiped his slick hands off on his jeans so he could get to work. This was easily the best part of his day: no solving problems, no writing stupid poetry. The garage was where he belonged. Once the stereo was in place and all the wires connected, he cranked the volume to show off his completed work. Some of the other students wandered over to listen.

"You should install the sound system for the dance next weekend," one of them yelled.

"Yeah, right, like Bryan would leave the garage long enough to go out to a dance." Several of the boys laughed.

"So come on, Bryan, who asked you? Marsha?"

"Naw." Bryan threw his rag down on the hood. "You know my rule. We went out twice and all she wanted to do was shake my hand so . . ." He moved his thumb up over his shoulder. "She's history." The guys laughed some more.

"You really won't take a girl out on a third date if she hasn't kissed you yet?"

"I figure if she doesn't kiss by the second date, then she must not be interested." Bryan paused, looking thoughtful. "I forgot about the dance next weekend. But it's girl's choice so..." He shrugged.

The bell rang, signaling the end of the day. Bryan wiped the grease from his hands and gathered his book bag. As he drove home, he noticed his friend Sue trudging through the snow, alone on the sidewalk. He pulled over and offered her a ride, which she gladly accepted. They chatted easily the rest of the way to her house.

"This is it." She pointed out her window at the red, brick rambler when they arrived. "Hey, Bryan." She paused from opening her door. "Are you going to the Valentine's dance next weekend?"

"Nope, not yet. Why?"

"Really?" She sounded surprised.

"I haven't been asked. The dance is actually on my birthday this year, too. How's that for a downer?" he joked.

"My little sister doesn't have a date yet."

Bryan scrunched up his nose.

"No, she's really cute! And she's not that young, she's a junior this year."

"She's cute?"

"Yeah, I think you'd really like her!"

Bryan continued to look at Sue, uncertain.

"So . . . can I pass your name off to her?"

"Sure, I guess," Bryan answered.

"Great! Thanks for the ride!" She closed the door quickly and ran up the front steps, ducking her head against the biting wind.

Bryan shook his head as he pulled away from the curb and headed home. *Oh well,* he thought. *She probably won't call anyway.*

When he got home he grabbed a handful of cookies from the kitchen and ran down the stairs. He kicked his shoes off and was shuffling through his records, trying to decide which one to play when he heard the telephone ring. A short time later he could hear Brenda yelling for him down the stairs.

"What?" he shouted back.

"Phone!"

Bryan lifted the receiver off the wall and, stretching the cord as far as it would go, hid in the hall closet for privacy. He cleared his throat before putting the phone up to his ear.

"Hello?"

"Umm, hi, yeah, is this Bryan?"

"That's me."

She giggled. "Hey, I'm Jana, Sue's sister. Listen, she told me you didn't have a date for the dance yet, so I was wondering if you wanted to go?"

Bryan only paused briefly. "Sure."

"Great!" He could hear her smile through the phone.

"Do you want me to drive?" Bryan offered.

"Yeah, actually, that would be really nice."

"Okay, I'll pick you up at 7:00 for dinner. Does that work?"

"Sounds good. See you then!"

"See ya."

Bryan was nervous as he walked up her porch steps a week later. He checked his reflection in the glass on her door one last time, straightened the tie on his blue tuxedo, and knocked twice. He was excited when the door slowly opened and a really cute redhead stood there, waiting. Jana had curly auburn hair and blue eyes that seemed to sparkle when she looked at him and smiled. Bryan quickly introduced himself and held out the yellow carnation corsage he purchased for her. Bryan's hands shook as he pinned it to her long, purple, lacy dress. She pinned him in turn with a white boutonniere as they smiled shyly at each other. Bryan offered her his arm and they got in the car to go to dinner.

Bryan took her to a restaurant nearby called The Heather. Talking became easier and more natural as the night wore on. After dinner, when they went out and got in the car, it wouldn't start. After checking things out, Bryan discovered someone had stolen the cable that goes from the coil to the distributor. Fortunately, Jana's friends were nearby, and they gave them a ride to the dance. They had a good time at the dance and got along well. Bryan was impressed that the mishap with his car didn't seem to bother her. After the dance, her friends took Jana home first.

"Thanks for a great time," she said. She leaned over the seat and gave Bryan a kiss on the cheek before climbing out of the car. "And happy birthday," she whispered, with a smile.

Once home, Bryan told Glenn about his car and the two of them left again to retrieve it.

The next time Bryan saw Jana was several weeks later. They talked for a few minutes and arranged a time when they could meet up so he could give her the pictures from the dance. They ended up talking for almost an hour and that's when he decided to ask her to go to the next dance. The trick was deciding exactly how to do it. The practice of just asking somebody to go didn't seem to be good enough anymore. After much thought, he finally came up with the idea to do something like a message in a bottle floating in the ocean. Bryan bought a large fishbowl with a number of tropical fish. He found a small bottle shaped like a wine bottle. He rolled up a note in it, asking her to go with him to the dance.

The next trick was figuring out how to deliver it. He convinced a friend to drop it off, wearing tights and a cape. Bryan drove him over to Jana's house and let him out. He continued down the street, parking several houses away. His friend rang the doorbell then took off and hid until she came to the door. Bryan picked him up and waited for Jana's reply, which he received the next day. He took it as a good sign that she answered so quickly. They had a great time at the dance together, without any car problems this time, and dated pretty steadily from then on.

Just days before the trip, Bryan got home from work to find his dad out in the garage, a large circular saw buzzing in his hands. "Hey, Bryan, can you give me a hand?" he called.

"Whatcha doin'?" Bryan asked.

"Duane asked me to make some pack frames to fit in the rafts for our trip."

"Pack frames? For what?"

"To suspend all the packs and coolers so they don't just sit in the bottom of the raft and cause a tear or anything."

Bryan held onto the large, long piece of wood and held it steady while Glenn worked the saw, cutting it into a two foot by six foot board.

"So Duane tells me there's some great jumping cliffs about four days in on the river."

Bryan's eyes lit up. "Really?"

"Yes, really. You interested?"

"Heck yeah, I'm interested! How high are they?"

"He didn't say, he just told me where they are. It's off in a little canyon . . . uh . . . Slickhorn, I think he called it."

"Oh man, that sounds awesome! Can I tell the guys?"

"Of course. It's not a secret. Duane says he'll show us the way when we get there. Just don't tell your mom."

Bryan hefted the next plank against the stack that was forming against the wall. "Of course not. She'd just worry the whole trip."

"Exactly," Glenn said. "Exactly."

"Do you really have to go?"

Bryan kissed Jana tenderly, enveloping her with his muscular arms. "It's my last chance to go since I'm an 'adult' now." The toothy grin split his face as he used air-quotes for the word. He might have graduated high school, but he sure didn't feel like an adult yet.

"I just have a bad feeling about it."

"I think you're just going to miss me," he teased. Then his tone softened. "I'll miss you, too," he added, kissing her on the top of her head. "It's only five days. You'll see me again soon."

Jana shook her head, not wanting to let him go. She buried her face in his chest and let a few silent tears escape. She didn't want him to see her cry. She carefully wiped them away and looked up expectantly into his deep blue eyes. He obliged, kissing her one final time before letting go.

"I'll call you as soon as we get back."

"I love you, Bryan!"

He smiled. "I love you, too."

CHAPTER THREE

"Being deeply loved by someone gives you strength, while loving someone deeply gives you courage."

- Lao Tzu

At the top of the cliff, Bryan's friends stood laughing and pointing where Bryan entered the water. He had been the most daring of the group, the first to go in head first. They slapped each other on the back and dared one another to try it next. A minute passed. Then two. The laughter stopped, and their faces turned solemn as the boys looked to each other for what to do. In panicked voices, their words echoed what their eyes had been communicating. No one could jump in after Bryan for fear they would land on top of him. Finally, Robert, a boy on the ground who witnessed the whole incident, jumped into the water, his eyes scanning quickly for Bryan's body. He spotted him a few feet away, floating in the water. Their eyes locked and Robert moved swiftly through the water, grabbing Bryan around the middle and pulling him upward.

Bryan's head broke through the surface and he gasped for air, his lungs burning for sweet breath. Others who stood on the bank rushed to Robert's aid as they came out of the water. Several of them grabbed onto Bryan and helped get his limp body to shore. All of his friends who had been at the top of the cliff came running into view. Bryan was surrounded by people, each shooting similar questions at him.

"Are you okay?"

"Does it hurt?"

"Can you move?"

Bryan wasn't moving at all. Three of his friends rushed down the mountain path in search of his parents, while two of the EMTs from their trip followed closely behind them. The EMTs jogged the mile back to the riverside, grabbing one of the boards from out of a raft. They panted as they took turns carrying the solid wood back up the path and placed it under Bryan, to try and stabilize his neck. Bryan recognized the board as one he had cut himself just days before.

Back at camp, Becky and a couple of her friends heard about the group of guys who were jumping off the cliff. They wanted to check it out, so they were heading up the path when they ran into Bryan's friends who were rushing down it. Even though she normally didn't panic over her brother getting hurt, Becky felt a sense of dread as the boys spoke. She knew in her gut that this time was different. Becky began running the rest of the way to the water's edge where Bryan lay in the sand. Seeing his pale face and limp body on a plank of wood made her eyes burn. She grabbed Bryan's hand and sniffed the tears back in, knowing she had to be tough. It was weird seeing him like that. Her normally tall, muscular brother suddenly didn't look so big anymore.

Carol Jean and Glenn came running up a few minutes after Becky. Glenn spoke with the EMTs while Carol Jean knelt in the sand next to her son. His face was pale and his body motionless, but his eyes locked on hers and he actually smiled.

"You should have seen it, Mom. That was my best dive ever!"

Carol Jean chuckled as the tears rolled down her cheeks. "Oh, Bryan." She took his hand in hers and squeezed it lightly. She squeezed a little harder, but Bryan still did not respond. She panicked. "Bryan!"

"What, Mom?" He looked at her strangely.

"Can you feel this?" She squeezed his hand with all her might.

"Feel what?"

Carol Jean fell off her knees, into the sand. Her hand covered her mouth as she tried not to cry or scream.

Glenn turned around and came over to them. "We need to talk." He tried to make his voice seem light, but the look in his eyes was deadly serious.

"I'm not leaving his side, Glenn."

"Just tell me, Dad, do they think I'm going to die?"

Glenn sighed heavily. "They don't know. They're pretty sure your neck is broken, but we can't know anything for certain until we get you to a hospital. That's where the problem is. The only way to get to a phone is by finishing the river."

"But there's still seventeen miles left," Bryan spoke up.

Glenn only nodded.

Carol Jean looked back down the path they had come which led to the water's edge. "You mean..?"

"Yes. Duane and I are going to take several of the young men and row as fast as we can the rest of the way. Then we'll have to hike to the top of the mountain where the nearest ranger's station is and we'll call for a helicopter from there."

"A helicopter?" Carol Jean looked as white as her son.

Glenn glanced up at the surrounding mountains and high, sloping cliffs. "That's the only way we're going to get him out." He looked straight into Bryan's eyes. "You hang in there, you hear me? We'll get help as fast as we can. I want you to stay hydrated, and I'll see you in a couple hours, okay?"

Bryan nodded. Carol Jean stood to give Glenn a hug goodbye. "It will only take a couple hours?" she whispered in his ear.

"At least twelve," Glenn spoke quietly.

Carol Jean could barely get her next words past the lump rising in her throat. "Will he . . . make it that long?"

Glenn looked down at Bryan's still frame. He then looked directly into Carol Jean's pleading green eyes. "If someone doesn't come for you in eighteen hours, it means we couldn't reach help." Carol Jean looked as though she were about to crumple to the ground. Glenn put a firm hand on each shoulder, partly to be sure she heard him and partly to prevent her from falling over. "In eighteen hours, if no one has come, I want you to load Bryan onto a raft and finish out the river. I will be waiting for you at the end."

Carol Jean nodded very slowly. They exchanged a worried look, both knowing Bryan would never survive seventeen miles in a raft in his condition. Glenn kissed her quickly before he turned and ran back down the path with Duane and six of the strongest boys in the group.

As the sun faded into the night sky, Bryan started shivering. Several of the girls gathered some sticks and other kindling, while two of the other leaders began building a fire near him on the beach. Becky and her friends hiked back to the campground and retrieved Bryan's down sleeping bag from inside his tent. Everyone was eager to help. Standing around and waiting was agonizing.

Carol Jean had a small bottle of water by her side and occasionally dampened a clean sock with it. She'd then place the sock over Bryan's mouth so he could keep his mouth moist and suck, without drinking too much. The EMTs were worried about him eating or drinking too much, since they didn't know what would happen if he threw up. Their goal was to prevent him from vomiting. Bryan continued to suck slowly, though his body ached for moisture. He wanted nothing more than to guzzle an entire gallon of water. The group had to pack in their water for the entire trip, and since this was the last night, rations ran low. Carol Jean had to keep careful watch on how much he drank, to be certain he would have enough to get him through the next day.

Bryan was grateful he didn't feel any pain as he continued to lay on the stiff, hard board. His limbs would occasionally tingle, which kept affirming in his mind that he was still alive. Waiting felt strange. He was completely surrounded by people, every one of them at his beck and call, yet no one was really talking to him. It was like the entire camp waited in limbo to learn his fate.

When dinner was ready, the leaders encouraged the youth to get some food and settle down for the night. No matter the outcome, they all had to continue on the river tomorrow. It took a lot of convincing and prodding from the leaders to get the kids to leave Bryan and go back to camp. Becky and Carol stayed by Bryan's side, making sure he remained warm and continuing to keep his mouth moist with water. Bryan tried to joke, "I hope you didn't get that sock from my foot." This only reminded them that Bryan couldn't feel his feet and he wouldn't have known if they had.

A couple of Becky's friends brought them some plates of food. The plates sat on the sand beside them, getting cold. Bryan encouraged them to eat, but the ladies kept the plates on the ground, their mouths shut tight. The smell of beans and hot dogs made Bryan's stomach rumble with hunger, but they knew it might be dangerous to feed him, for fear he might choke or throw up. So they sat and listened to their rumbling tummies while the buns grew soggy from the beans and turned into a pile of mush on their plates.

The seconds ticked by slowly. The night air was still; the only sounds that could be heard were some chirping crickets and the slow, labored breaths coming from Bryan. Becky broke the silence by reminiscing their childhood.

"Remember that time we buried those Penny Savers in the gulley by our house?"

Bryan strained to smile. How could he ever forget? "Yeah, remember how much fun we thought it would be to deliver those papers to earn some cash?"

Becky nodded and made a gagging motion with her finger. "That was really stupid."

"No, the stupid part was getting caught. If we had gotten away with it, it would have been pure genius. Bury the papers in the dirt, then still get paid for delivering them. It was supposed to be a fool-proof plan."

"Until Grandpa Carroll caught us," Becky said. "That part was not so fun. I still remember how much he yelled."

"It wasn't the yelling that got to me," Bryan admitted. "I couldn't handle his disappointment. I never want Grandpa Carroll to look at me that way again." He shuddered at the thought.

Becky yawned, and stretched her stiff legs out into the sand in front of her. "What about that time you set the sandbox on fire?" she grinned.

"I didn't set the whole sandbox on fire." Bryan felt the need to clarify. "I built a sandcastle in the sandbox, then made the moat out of gasoline. Only the moat was on fire."

They both laughed as they continued to share stories. Carol Jean knew some of the stories, but other instances of mischief, she did not. Bryan chuckled at the horrified expression on his mom's face. "I'm so glad I didn't know about this back then," she said, rubbing her forehead.

Carol Jean finally encouraged a drowsy Becky to go to sleep.

"I can't leave. What if help comes? What if he needs me?"

"I promise I will wake you up if anyone gets here or anything changes. Neither of us are going to be much use to Bryan tomorrow if we don't rest."

"I'm fine. Why don't you go to sleep first?"

"Rebecca Carroll, go to your tent and sleep. I will see you in the morning." Her tone left no room for argument.

Becky squeezed her brother's cold, clammy fingers. "Good night," she whispered. Holding her flashlight high, she walked down the winding path to her tent.

Bryan watched as his mom's head began to bob and her eyelids tried to close. She was fighting sleep, but it kept threatening to come.

"Carol Jean?"

She jumped at the voice as it approached.

"Sorry," the man whispered.

"It's okay."

"Do you want to try and get some sleep? I can sit with Bryan for a couple hours."

"Thank you, but no. I'm his mom and I'm not leaving his side."

The other chaperone put his hands up in surrender and walked toward her slowly.

"Carol Jean, you are going to have a very long day tomorrow, and probably several days after. Please get some rest. You won't do Bryan any good tomorrow if you aren't functional."

Carol Jean looked back at her big, strong boy who was really a man now. The way he lay there, bundled in blankets and completely helpless, she was reminded of the same boy, significantly smaller. He was just a larger version of that perfect, little boy placed in her arms at the hospital eighteen years ago.

"How could this happen to my baby?" she whispered.

He placed a gentle hand on her shoulder and helped Carol Jean to her feet. Her legs tingled and burned from sitting in the same position on the hard ground for so long. She stood, unmoving.

"Mom, get some sleep. Pete and I can talk shop about cars and before you know it, morning will be here."

Carol Jean bent down and kissed Bryan's forehead, her lips singed with his growing fever. As she hiked back to camp, she looked up at the beautiful stars shining brightly in the night sky and prayed for a miracle.

Glenn watched the same stars as he rowed with everything he had left. They all panted, finding it hard to catch their breath, yet still they paddled on. Their legs cramped from sitting for so long, and their arms were on fire.

Their stiffened necks seared with pain. They finally reached a point where they took turns letting one boy sit out at a time. He would stretch his aching muscles and rest his shaking body for twenty minutes and then pass his break on to someone else. Glenn never took his turn.

"Come on, Glenn, you've got to rest or you're going to pass out from exhaustion." Duane spoke quietly.

"I'll pass out after we've reached the phone. Right now, I've got enough adrenaline to keep going and I'm afraid if I stop, it will go away. I can't stop. I won't stop," he mumbled.

The boys quit asking him and continued to break in silence, praying to God that they'd make it in time.

Becky lay awake in her tent, unable to sleep. How could her mom possibly think she would sleep? After tonight, she wondered if she would ever want to sleep again. Every mean thing she had ever said to her brother ran around her mind in circles. Every time she got him in trouble, every time she started a fight, every time she said something mean to his face or behind his back. Only a year apart, they were practically twins growing up. Why couldn't she have been a better sister? A better friend? She couldn't take it anymore and slipped out of her tent. She wandered around the trees for a little while before grabbing her sleeping bag and walking back to the beach. She didn't care what her mom said. If she were going to be grounded, or if she were going to get yelled at, she didn't care. She'd take it. Anything was better than lying in that dark tent, listening to the other girls breathe, and wondering how this could have happened. Bryan had always been so invincible.

As Becky stretched her sleeping bag out on the sand and laid down, Bryan didn't say a word. She reached across the bag and grasped his hand. They stared across the fire in the moonlight, wondering what would happen next.

A twig snapped and Becky jumped at the sound. Three of Bryan's friends appeared in the firelight, sleeping bags under their arms. They laid them out in the sand side by side and started talking about motorcycles, as if nothing were wrong. Two more girls from Becky's tent showed up. One had a book with her, and they took turns reading from it out loud to the group.

Glenn squinted his eyes in the moonlight for any sign that they were near the end of the river. Sweat dripped from every inch of his body. His arms were completely numb from overuse and he wondered if he'd ever regain feeling in them. His body seemed to be screaming in pain at him for the abuse he put it through all night. Duane sat on the edge of the raft, squinting in the moonlight toward the shoreline, trying to gauge where they were.

"This is it." Duane broke the silence. The boys all moaned as they pulled their oars from the water. The river was about to run into Lake Powell and at this point, they needed a motor to get them the rest of the way. Duane hoisted the heavy plank up and reached underneath for his outboard motor. He carefully attached it to the end of their raft and yanked hard on the chord. The motor rumbled to life, cutting through the silence that surrounded them.

"If only I'd known, I would have packed enough gas to get us the entire way."

Glenn placed a hand on Duane's shoulder and shook his head. "No one could have planned for this."

Carefully, Duane guided the raft through the murky water. Glenn almost couldn't believe his eyes when they saw the spot to pull out coming up. They made it!

Glenn leaped from the raft, grabbing the line and pulling the large yellow craft to shore. It bumped and scraped along the sand until it was inland enough for the boys to all climb out. They wanted nothing more than to collapse on the sand and sleep. Unfortunately, they still had a three mile hike to the top of the mountain where the phone was located. Glenn offered to let them rest a few minutes. He was surprised when they shook their heads and said, "Let's go. We'll have all day for resting after we reach the phone."

They began the steep climb, following the dark trail with the aid of a couple of flashlights. Out on the open water, the moon lit their way. But here, amidst the shade of the trees, it was harder to see. The boys lost their footing a couple of times. They kept close together, pushing and encouraging each other to press onward.

When the ranger's station came into view, the boys whistled and cheered. Glenn's team of troopers collapsed to the ground outside the station, finding different places around the building to lean against the walls. Glenn pushed the worn, wooden door open with his hand, his feet creaking on the floorboards as he entered. A large man dressed all in green sat behind a desk, his head resting against the mahogany desk. Glenn's shoes creaked with each step, causing the soft snoring to abruptly halt. The ranger sat up carefully, straightening his hat.

"What can I do you for?" he asked, yawning wide.

"I need to use your phone, please. There's been an emergency down at the river."

"Oh, I'm sorry, our phones are out of order."

Glenn's face fell and he feared he might actually pass out. He steadied himself by reaching out for the nearest chair to regain his balance.

"No, I'm just joshin' ya!" he joked. Upon seeing the seriousness of Glenn's face, his own face immediately went grim. "Here you go," he offered, sliding the black rotary across the desk and into Glenn's hands. Glenn picked up the receiver and dialed 9-1-1 with shaking fingers.

"9-1-1, what's the nature of your emergency?" The soothing voice had a calming effect on Glenn.

"We're at Slickhorn Canyon in Southern Utah and my son was cliff diving." Glenn choked up a little as he spoke. "I think his neck is broken."

Carol Jean shouldn't have been able to sleep with all the thoughts and worries churning around her mind, but the emotional overload completely drained her body. She fell asleep surprisingly quickly and slept soundly through the night. When she awoke the next morning, the events from the previous day came crashing back. She bolted out of her tent. As she drew near the beach, Carol Jean tripped over a sleeping bag left lying in the sand. She looked around and noticed the ground was completely covered in sleeping bags. Everywhere she looked, they lay in the hot sand, some filled with sleeping youth, others with kids sitting atop them. There had to be fifty kids sleeping and sitting around Bryan like a soft wall of protection. Carol Jean had to watch where she stepped to avoid fingers and feet as she made her way through the teenagers toward her son.

The sun was scorching now, with the temperature at 100 degrees and steadily climbing. Despite the heat, Bryan's face grew paler by the hour. His tongue felt swollen and rough, like sandpaper rubbing against the roof of his mouth. It was harder and harder for him to stay awake. His mom remained steadily by his side, waking him each time he began to doze. His friends continued to try and make him smile and laugh, but he didn't return the smile as easily. The waiting was pure agony. His body tingled occasionally, but it was becoming less and less frequent. He had been trying to get his foot, a finger, anything to move, but he was becoming increasingly tired and the concentration it required was exhausting. He had to stop thinking about his stationary limbs and focus his mind on staying awake.

Carol Jean looked at her watch for probably the millionth time. Glenn left seventeen hours earlier. She stared up at the bright blue sky, squinting into the sunlight, and straining her ears for any sign of hope. All she could hear were the voices of youth all around her and an occasional bird. She couldn't see even a cloud in the sky and pretend the helicopter was hiding behind them.

One of the EMTs approached her cautiously. "Do you want us to start preparing a raft?"

"I just . . ." She looked to the sky again and found nothing. "No, but yes."

The EMT nodded. "I'll have my guys start moving supplies around to make room, just in case."

Carol Jean waved him away and placed a hand on Bryan's forehead. His pale, clammy skin had become beet red and cracked in a matter of hours. Her palm seared from his touch. She grabbed her bottle and dripped the last remaining drops onto the crusty sock. Bryan's lips were cracked and stained with dried blood. He didn't even react to the sock being placed on his mouth. His eyes were closed, his breathing shallow. They were out of time.

CHAPTER FOUR

"Courage is not having the strength to go on; it is going on when you don't have the strength."

- Theodore Roosevelt

The low rumble of the helicopter brought silence to the camp. Everyone froze and stared at the dark bird as it sped across the sky toward them. All preparations to move Bryan halted. One of Bryan's friends screamed in triumph, his fist pumping into the air. Everyone began screaming and cheering. Becky's friends surrounded her, crying and hugging in a big huddle. Several boys ran down the path as fast as they could to direct them to where Bryan lay. The cliffs were high and menacing all around him. The only space large enough for a helicopter to land was back at their camp, near the river's edge. Bryan cracked his eyes open and watched as it neared and then seemed to disappear again behind the mountain.

Several minutes later, four men jogged toward him. The sea of kids split down the center and made room for Bryan's rescuers. The leaders started herding the kids back down the path, guiding them toward the river and the rafts where they had to climb aboard to finish out their trip. Bryan heard many well wishes yelled his way, but he concentrated instead on the men checking his vitals. They looked him over head to toe and began discussing the best way to get him back to the helicopter.

Becky pulled herself apart from the group and ran into Carol Jean's arms.

"Why can't I come with you?"

"There isn't enough room in the helicopter. You need to raft the rest of the river with everyone else. Dad will be waiting for you at the end."

Becky hugged her mom tight, afraid to let go. She knew she was too old to be clinging to her mommy like a little girl, but right now, she didn't care.

"You've got to go, sweetie."

Becky wiped her eyes with the back of her hand and approached Bryan. One of the rescuers tried to hold her off.

"Please," she begged. "He's my brother. I just want to say goodbye."

He stepped aside and let Becky approach. She kissed Bryan's cheek, leaving tear stains on his face. "I love you, Bryan."

Bryan opened his dry mouth to reply, but couldn't get the words passed his desiccated throat. Becky didn't need him to respond. The moisture in his eyes told her everything. She waved one last time as she followed her friends back down the rocky path, turning back several times until she couldn't see them anymore.

After carefully transferring Bryan to a bright orange stretcher, the rescue team tightened black straps across his ankles, just above his knees, over his thighs, his waist, his arms, his chest, and shoulders, and his forehead. They worked together seamlessly and efficiently, securing him in a matter of minutes. They then began attaching and tying ropes to each of the carabiners. Once everything was secure and in place, they worked carefully and gradually to lower Bryan back down the mountain. It was a slow process, taking nearly two hours to travel the one mile hike from the cliff where he fell to the riverside. Carol Jean followed quietly behind them. She had a hundred questions running through her mind, but didn't want to interrupt the progress.

When they finally neared the camp, the thrumming of the helicopter blades was almost deafening. Carol Jean was surprised to see the huge, green camo-painted copter instead of a smaller one with the medical symbol painted on the side. As if reading her mind, one of the rescuers spoke the answer loudly.

"There weren't any life flight helicopters available to come, at least not any that were near enough to get to you in time. The military base is much closer and they were willing to help out."

"I can still go with him, right?"

The man nodded and held out a hand to assist her into the helicopter. Once they had Bryan securely in place, the pilot checked around to be sure the area was cleared of people and readied for takeoff. As they started to rise into the air, Carol Jean screamed.

"Shut the doors! You forgot to shut the doors!"

One of the rescuers put a hand on her arm and shook his head.

Carol Jean trembled as she held onto the strap that dangled from the roof above her. She was terrified of heights. She glanced down as they flew over the river and saw the yellow dots that lined the water below.

"They're waving to you, Bryan," she said. As she looked at him, she screamed again. "What's wrong with his face?"

Bryan's face and arms had broken out in a deep red rash.

"He's suffering from heat stroke. We need to get to the hospital now!"

Another one of the rescuers broke into a box beside Carol Jean and pulled out several small white packets. He began to break and move them around in his hands until they became cold, and then he laid one on Bryan's forehead and another two on each of his arms. Bryan's body began convulsing as he dry heaved, but thankfully his empty stomach had nothing to throw up. When his body calmed again, one of the men spoke to him.

"Bryan, can you tell me how you're feeling?"

He could barely croak out two words. "Dizzy. Headache."

The men nodded to each other and continued to make every effort to cool Bryan's sweltering body.

Finally the helicopter began bouncing slightly as they prepared to descend. Another stretcher and several doctors and nurses stood ready on the ground, waiting for their arrival. The moment the copter touched the earth, both teams flew into action. Bryan's straps and belts were unfastened and they swiftly transferred him to the waiting stretcher. The rescuers shouted his vital numbers to the waiting medical team. The medical team then took flight, zooming Bryan through the double white doors and into the air conditioned building. Carol Jean had to run to keep up with them while another nurse shot questions at her.

Once inside, after making certain his neck was secure, they soaked Bryan in an ice bath until his body cooled and the rash went away. The doctors also hoped the cold from the bath would help the swelling in his neck go down. After laying on the beach for eighteen hours, his neck and spine were so swollen they feared they wouldn't be able to help Bryan right away. When he felt well enough, they whisked Bryan off to radiology for a series of x-rays. After what felt like an eternity, he was finally in a hospital gown, lying in a bed, awaiting his diagnosis. Carol Jean sat in a hard chair beside his bed, holding onto Bryan's hand when the doctor tapped on the door and came in. She searched his face for clues, but he gave away nothing.

"Hello, Bryan. How are you feeling?"

Bryan didn't know how to respond to that. He hadn't felt anything in two days. Instead he asked the question he'd been wanting to ask since his neck first popped when he collided with the sand.

"Am I paralyzed?"

"Yes."

His mom let out a tiny cry, which Bryan chose to ignore.

"Will I be able to have kids?"

"We don't know."

Bryan let the information sink in. The doctor had finally confirmed what they already knew, but thinking you're paralyzed and knowing it are two very different things.

The doctor went on. "We've done all that we can for you. Now that you're stable, you get to take one more helicopter ride to a bigger hospital with specialists who can help you go on from here. Do you feel up to that?"

"Yes," Bryan said.

"Good. Well, you've got two choices," he said, turning to Carol Jean. "We can send him up to the regional hospital here in Arizona, or we can send him to the University of Utah hospital in Salt Lake."

"Definitely send him to the U. That's not too far from our house."

"All right, I'll go make the preparations. You should be leaving within the hour."

"Thank you." Carol Jean stood to shake his hand.

"Any chance they will shut the doors on the helicopter this time?" Bryan asked. "That really freaked my mom out."

The doctor's eyes widened, his eyebrows rising into his hairline. "Well, your mom can't ride with you this time."

Carol Jean snapped her head back to him. "What do you mean?"

"I'm sorry, with the medical staff and equipment to keep your son alive during the flight, there just isn't room for any other passengers."

"How am I supposed to get home?"

"I'm not sure, Mrs. Carroll. I thought arrangements had already been made."

Carol Jean stared at him blankly.

"Clearly they have not. Well, I need to make some important phone calls to get Bryan out of here as soon as possible. I will send a nurse who can hopefully help you out with some options."

Carol Jean collapsed back into her chair beside Bryan's bed and held her head in her hands. "Now what?" She was met by a soft snoring sound and looked up to see Bryan had finally gone to sleep. He had been awake for over twenty-four hours. Still, she felt nervous and kept glancing at all the machines which surrounded him. They continued to beep happily, voicing that Bryan was still alive. She sighed and walked from the room. It was time to make some phone calls of her own.

A perky little nurse bounced down the hallway toward her. She had short, brown hair which bobbed as she walked.

"So, I hear we need to get you home," she said, showing off her tall, crooked teeth when she smiled.

Carol Jean sighed and nodded her head.

"Follow me this way. We'll make a few phone calls and get this thing figured out."

"Thank you so much." Carol Jean paused and looked back at Bryan's closed door.

"Don't you worry about a thing, hon. You aren't sitting on the hot sand anymore. If something changes with him, the machines will let us know." She put an arm around Carol Jean's waist and pulled her down the long hallway.

After several phone calls, Carol Jean had a bus ticket back to Salt Lake. She would be leaving the hospital shortly after Bryan. She had also called her sister to ask if Glenda and Jenny could stay for another day and if they'd be willing to pick Brenda up from her camp at the end of the day.

She picked up the receiver one last time and paused. She took several deep breaths before finally dialing, her fingers shaking.

"Hello?" Glenn's older sister answered the phone.

"Hi, Donna." Carol Jean could hear her own voice trembling. "There was an accident on the trip. Bryan . . . he . . . was diving and broke his neck."

Donna gasped. In response to a question Carol Jean couldn't hear, she said, "No, Dad, I'll talk to you in a minute. Please finish watching your golf game." Turning her attention back to the phone she asked, "So is he . . .?"

"He's . . . paralyzed from the neck down." It was the first time Carol Jean had spoken the word out loud. It felt too surreal. She kept waiting for this nightmare to end so she could go back to her normal life.

Donna sniffed as she whispered, "Oh, Carol Jean, I'm so sorry! What can I do?"

"Well, that's actually why I'm calling. Bryan and I are at a small hospital in Arizona, but they're getting ready to fly him to the University of Utah hospital. I can't fly with him. There's not enough room. Could you please meet him at the hospital so he's not alone?"

Donna didn't hesitate. "Of course."

Carol Jean breathed out a sigh of relief. "Thank you. Now please don't tell your dad. Not yet, at least. Be sure to keep him away from the newspapers, and don't let him watch the news. We don't want him finding out from anyone but us."

"I completely agree. I'll find something to keep him occupied, don't you worry. Just get here safe and I'll see you soon."

Donna hung up the phone and looked at her dad, snoozing in his big, brown armchair. He had moved in with her a couple months ago, although he swore up and down that he didn't need someone to take care of him. She looked at his peaceful face and watched as his chest rose and fell. He seemed to be sleeping pretty heavily.

She tiptoed past him and slowly lowered herself onto the green couch. The leather beneath her groaned. Donna squeezed her eyes tight, hoping he hadn't heard, but her dad snorted and sat up with a start. He looked around and saw his game still on the TV, so he sat back. Donna breathed a sigh of relief. Then he turned and looked at her.

"So who was on the phone?"

CHAPTER FIVE

"When you get to the end of your rope, tie a knot and hang on."

– Franklin D. Roosevelt

Donna rushed through the double white doors and looked around for which way to go next. She saw a small red arrow next to the letters ICU pointing upstairs. She raced to the elevator and waited impatiently for one of the doors to open. After what felt like forever and the moaning of an approaching lift, the doors to her left finally opened. She stepped inside. She smashed the number five with her thumb and waited again as the doors creaked to a close. The soft jingle of the elevator music was especially annoying as she watched the numbers climb with anticipation. The doors barely opened when Donna began pushing her way through them. She hurried off the elevator and glanced both directions, trying to decide which path to try first.

When she heard several voices and saw a gurney being wheeled quickly down the hall, her stomach flipped and she knew to follow. Seeing her tall, strong nephew covered in wires, unmoving on the bed, sent chills up her spine. She charged after the gurney and caught up in time so Bryan could see a familiar face looking out for him. She waved over the doctor's shoulder, catching Bryan's eye. He grinned and then closed his eyes.

Bryan barely slept in two days and wondered if he'd ever sleep again. With the constant poking, prodding, and questioning, even an hour-long nap seemed like a luxury.

After another round of X-rays, the doctors were happy to note that his spine was not severed. Pieces of his bone had crushed on impact and were now pushing into his spine. The biggest problem was still his swelling from lying on the beach for so long without treatment. The next step was to put him in traction to keep his neck in place while the swelling went down and the bones mended.

Donna was asked to leave the room for a moment, due to the gruesome nature of putting someone in traction.

"I will be right outside those doors, waiting for you."

Bryan tried to nod, but his head was already being held in place. He stared at the closed door, wondering when his mom and dad would get back in town. The doctor started with the right side of Bryan's head. He felt intense pressure on that side, and he heard the grinding of bone as they screwed the device into his skull. Bryan was very grateful he couldn't feel any pain as they screwed it into the other side and the pressure started all over again.

The head of the bed was raised slightly, with the traction device attached to the metal railing on the back of the bed. He wore the arched piece that screwed into his head on either side like a headband, with a long cord extending from the center and connecting to a weight that hung below his bed. The weight pulled his head and neck straight with about ten pounds of constant force.

The doctors also noticed Bryan had gotten a big bed sore on his underside from remaining in the same position in wet swim trunks. Their answer to this problem was to make Bryan's bed rotate from left to right. The constant rocking motion made it so he was never lying in exactly the same position for more than a few seconds, to give his sore time to heal and prevent new ones from occurring. Bryan found it extremely bizarre and irritating.

Donna came back into the room a short time later. She stood by Bryan's side and listened carefully while he regaled her with the entire story.

Becky sat quietly in her raft. She put her paddle in the water, and then got lost in thought and forgot to stroke. Her paddle started to drag in the water, pulling her arm with it. She quickly yanked up, splashing the two girls who were sitting behind her.

"Hey!"

"Oh, sorry," Becky mumbled.

The girls continued to stroke in silence. The mood in the raft changed drastically that day. No one dared laugh or talk. Instead of enjoying the smooth paddling and cool water, they were no longer traveling for fun. They were traveling to reach a destination. With determination, Becky picked up her pace, and the others followed suit.

The water began to move faster, a sure sign they were approaching a rapid. At the beginning of the trip, they would have been squealing and daring each other to ride the bull by sitting on the front of the raft. Instead, they rushed over the rocks and continued their somber journey.

When evening approached, Becky looked toward the banks, watching for their final place to pull out. As they came around a bend, they saw their bus waiting to take them all home. Never had a big, smelly bus looked so inviting. Relief washed over her when she saw her dad waving from the edge of the river.

The moment the raft stopped, she leaped over the edge and raced toward him, throwing her arms around his middle. Glenn wrapped his big arms around her, holding her tightly. Becky pulled away, wiping her eyes with the back of her hand.

"Let's go find your mom and brother," he whispered.

Becky nodded and followed him to the waiting bus. They had to wait several minutes for everyone to load their bags and climb aboard. Thankfully, everyone moved with a sense of urgency among them, for their sakes.

Carol Jean spent most of her night on a hot, crowded bus. She tried to rest, but couldn't get comfortable in the thinly padded seats. Every time she laid her head back, it bumped into the metal bar behind her, so she gave up trying. As she bounced along, her nostrils accosted by sweat and warm bodies, Carol Jean found herself longing for the open doors of the helicopter once again.

In the very early hours of the morning, the bus screeched to a stop in downtown Salt Lake City. Carol Jean leaped to her feet and stumbled forward, her feet numb and almost asleep from being stuck in the same position for so long. She carefully stepped down the three metal stairs and breathed a huge sigh when she saw her sister waiting for her on the bench at the bottom.

"You're here," Carol Jean sighed in relief.

"Of course I'm here. Where else would I be?"

Carol Jean gave her a hug and almost crumpled into her arms.

"Phew! Carol Jean!"

"I know. I haven't had a chance to shower in a couple of days. I still have smells from the river, helicopter, hospital, and bus on me."

"Well, let's get you a shower and a fresh pair of clothes, shall we?"

"No, we're not far from the hospital. Let's go check in on Bryan first."

"Come on, Carol Jean, I'll have you to the hospital within the hour."

"I'm going to see my son first. You can drive me there, or watch me walk. But I'd sure appreciate your help."

"All right, sis, you win. Let's go check on Bryan."

It took them longer to navigate the parking tunnels than it did to drive to the hospital. Once they secured a parking spot, they walked in the main entrance and looked around. Arrows pointed to each of the different departments, signs everywhere with names listed alphabetically, with the constant buzz of people passing by. Carol Jean stood frozen for several moments. This hospital was definitely bigger than the last one. She willed her feet to move forward and they obliged.

They approached a large, circular desk with a friendly woman sitting behind it answering phones. She seemed to know her stuff.

"Hi there!" she greeted them. "What can I do for ya?"

"Well, my son was brought in yesterday by helicopter. He has a broken neck."

The woman reached out and placed a hand on top of Carol Jean's, patting it gently. "Oh, honey, I'm so sorry to hear that. Well, he should be in the ICU. Just head straight down this way until there's a curve in the hallway. Follow along that curve 'til you come to the elevators and go to level five. Someone up there should be able to direct you to his room."

"Thank you." Carol Jean smiled politely and charged forward in the direction she had pointed.

They reached the elevators and she punched the number five with her finger. The doors creaked shut and the elevator jerked into motion, stopping twice to pick up more passengers on their way up. The doors squeaked open when they reached their destination. Almost immediately in front of them was another desk, this one much smaller. A younger girl with long brown hair pulled up in a tight ponytail stopped them.

"Who are you here to see?"

"Bryan Carroll."

"And what's your relation to the patient?"

"He's my son. Now can you please tell me where he is?"

"We don't usually allow visitors on the floor until 7:00 a.m."

"Look, he broke his neck while we were river rafting, he was stranded on the beach for a day and a half, they had to life flight him to a hospital in Arizona, and then they had to transfer him here. I couldn't fit on the helicopter, so I have been on a bus for the last ten hours. I've barely slept and I haven't showered in several days." Carol Jean's voice rose with each item on her list until it almost came out as a squeak. "Please! Let. Me. See. My. Son."

The nurse looked over Carol Jean's dirty clothes, her disheveled hair, and into her pleading eyes. "Just a minute. I'll be right back."

"Do you think she's going to go find a doctor?"

"Either that or security," Carol Jean retorted. She rested her head on her arm, which was leaning against the desk.

Her sister smiled and began rubbing her back slowly with her fingers.

A few moments later the young nurse returned, followed by a tall man wearing a long, white lab coat.

"Mrs. Carroll?"

Carol Jean looked up, grateful he had a stethoscope and not handcuffs. "That's me."

"I'm Dr. Jensen, Bryan's doctor." He extended his hand and motioned for the women to follow.

"This is my sister."

The doctor nodded his greeting and continued to lead the way down the hall. "Bryan seems to be responding very well."

Carol Jean froze. "You mean he's moving?"

The doctor's face fell. "No, no. I'm sorry, poor choice of words. He seems to be getting his color back and he is alert and doing well mentally." The doctor stopped abruptly outside a tall, white door at the end of the hall. "Before we go in, I should probably let you know that we've put Bryan in traction. It can be startling to see if you aren't expecting it."

"What's that?"

"Basically it's a brace we've screwed into his skull on either side to prevent his neck from moving and causing any further damage."

Carol Jean covered her mouth with her hand. *Screwed into his skull?* She took a deep breath and pushed the door open. Her first instinct was not to cry, as she feared, but she had to actually bite her cheek to prevent herself from laughing. The sight of Bryan rolling back and forth on the large bed like a giant, rocking baby cradle was too surprising to handle. He was somehow asleep, though. Maybe it really did work like a baby cradle. Carol Jean had the urge to laugh again. "I really am too tired," she mumbled.

Donna sat in a chair across from his bed, her head resting against the wall, snoring softly. She stirred as Carol Jean and the doctor continued to talk. Donna sat up a few minutes later, rubbing her kinked neck and looking around. She spotted Carol Jean and quickly got up.

"Oh, thank goodness you made it!" She hugged Carol Jean tightly.

"Barely." She returned the hug with just as much force. "Thank you for being here with him. I don't know what I would have done if he had to go through this alone."

"Of course. He's finally sleeping, as you can see."

"And how's your dad?"

"He's doing fine."

"Does he know about Bryan yet?"

Donna shook her head.

"Good. Glenn and I will come by and visit him, probably tomorrow." She sighed and looked up at the ceiling. That was not a visit she looked forward to. "So where does he think you are?"

"He knows a 'friend' of mine was in an accident and that I'm in the hospital visiting. It just seemed easier than lying."

Carol Jean agreed. Donna left a short time later to check on Grandpa Carroll and get some rest, but not before she made Carol Jean promise to call her day or night if she needed a hand with anything else.

Around 7:00 a.m., the doors opened and Glenn and Becky came bursting into the room. It was a bittersweet reunion. Carol Jean cried tears of both joy and sorrow into Glenn's shoulder as he held her close. Becky, still wearing nothing but shorts and a T-shirt over her swimsuit, collapsed into the chair Donna had vacated and watched her brother sleep.

"I'm going to sneak out now that Glenn's here and let you be together as a family."

Carol Jean thanked her sister as she hugged her goodbye. With a promise similar to Donna's, she slipped out the door. When the door clicked shut, Bryan's eyes peeked open and settled on Becky sitting up in the black, plastic chair.

"Hey, squirt," he smiled.

She stood and moved closer to his bed, Glenn and Carol Jean joining her on either side. "How are you feeling?"

"Fabulous, marvelous, and wonderful," he said, quoting Glenn. "What else?" He looked to his dad and smiled.

"Of course you are." Glenn smiled in return, tears springing to his eyes.

Becky scooted her chair closer. "So you got bored with all the ambulances and decided to move up to helicopters, huh?"

"Yeah, my plan worked so well I got to ride in two of them."

They all tried to smile, but it faded quickly. "So what have the doctors said?" Glenn asked.

"I'm paralyzed. I will be quadriplegic for the rest of my life."

Almost as if on cue, Bryan's hand jerked. Becky jumped to her feet. "Your hand moved! You're going to be okay!"

"It's just a muscle spasm," Bryan said. "The doctor said my arms and legs will probably twitch for awhile after the accident. I don't have any control over it. It's just the muscles dying out."

Becky sat back down. "Oh."

"So will you need surgery or anything?"

"No. The doctor is leaving tomorrow to go on sabbatical for four weeks. He wants me to stay in traction while he's gone and they'll decide what to do next after he gets back."

"What do you mean, he's going on sabbatical?" Glenn's voice echoed through the hospital room. "What's going to happen to you? Who will take care of you while he's gone?"

Before Bryan had a chance to answer, the door opened. All eyes turned and Dr. Jensen stepped in. "Well, good morning!"

Glenn scowled. "How can you go on sabbatical when my son needs you here?" Glenn approached the doctor until their faces were mere inches apart.

The doctor put a hand up to stop Glenn. When he spoke, his voice was calm and patient. "Your son needs to be in traction for four weeks, Mr. Carroll, whether I am here or not. There isn't much we can do until the swelling goes down, other than stabilize his neck. My nursing staff is phenomenal. He will be in very capable hands. Even if I were here in town, the nurses would be the ones caring for Bryan."

Glenn stepped back. "Sorry," he muttered.

"It's quite all right. These are stressful circumstances. I promise I am doing everything I can to help Bryan. Now, let's see how you're doing today," Dr. Jensen said, turning to Bryan. The doctor checked all of Bryan's vitals and made notes on his chart before stopping Bryan's rocking bed to check his sores. "They're looking much better today," he said, turning the bed back on, much to Bryan's dismay. "We'll get you in a regular bed in no time."

"So Bryan said he doesn't need surgery?" Carol Jean spoke up.

"That's right. Your son suffered from what we call an explosion fracture. Since he remained on the beach so long after the accident, everything swelled up around his injury. We've done several X-rays already, but unfortunately, the only thing we can do at this point is put him in traction. I'm leaving on sabbatical in the morning. For now, we will keep him in traction for four weeks and then see how everything is healing at that point, and go from there."

"And then what exactly does the traction do?"

"It keeps Bryan's head firmly in place so his neck can heal. Similar to putting a cast on a broken arm. We just want to be sure he's going to heal properly."

A light knock on the door sounded before it opened slowly. In walked a middle-aged woman with long, dark hair pulled back into a tight ponytail. She smiled at Bryan and his family, her face warm and friendly.

"Ah, here we are," Dr. Jensen said. "This is Christine, your occupational therapist. She will be working with you to help stretch and strengthen your muscles while you're here in traction. As I said before, I'm leaving on sabbatical, but I am leaving you in very capable hands." Dr. Jensen held out his hand to Christine and then slipped from the room.

"Hello," she said, holding out her hand and shaking hands with Glenn and Carol Jean while they made introductions. She approached Bryan and patted his arm. "It's nice to meet you, Bryan." She smiled again. "We're going to become good friends, I just know it."

Bryan's parents asked several questions as they tried to grasp the reality of their new situation. Christine politely and patiently answered all that she could as she explained the next steps they would take on his road to recovery.

"So there's no surgery or procedure we can do to help him?" Glenn asked. "We just have to wait it out for four weeks and hope he heals properly in traction? I just don't want to give up hope. Isn't there more we can do?"

"Mr. Carroll," Christine cut him off with a calm voice.

"Glenn."

"All right, Glenn, you need to understand your son suffered a very serious C4-C5 break. He's lucky it didn't kill him. I am going to work with him as much as possible to try and help him learn to do as much as he can for himself. But he will most likely need full time care and assistance for the rest of his life."

Christine noticed Carol Jean had begun crying and she stopped. Softening her voice even more, she continued. "I'm not telling you this to upset you or make you feel hopeless. I just want you to understand the severity of the situation before we move forward. You can choose to accept what has happened to your son, and help him continue to have as normal a life as possible, or you can deny it and waste time on trying to cure what has happened."

Glenn looked up at the bright, white hospital lights shining overhead. He sniffed a couple times, wiped his eyes, and then looked Christine square in the face.

"All right. What do we need to do?"

"Well, because Bryan's break was a C4-C5 and not a C4 complete, it is possible he could get partial function in his arms again."

"But you just said . . ."

Christine put a hand up to silence him. "I didn't want you to think he would be able to regain full functionality. He is still going to need daily assistance with life. He will not be able to use the restroom on his own, or bathe himself, or anything like that. With extensive physically therapy, he might be able to drive his own motorized wheelchair or wrap his arms around things to grasp them. The hope is that he'll be able to at least transfer himself from his bed to his chair, but we'll have to see how things go. Every break and every patient is different. We'll take it one day at a time and help Bryan regain as much functionality as possible. We do need to cone his fingers first, which we'll do in the next day or two."

"What does that mean?"

"It means we will use special braces to curl his fingers under, so his hands will look like they are permanently in a fist."

Carol Jean gasped. "Why would you need to do that?"

"Your son has no nerve feeling in his hands and fingers anymore. His tendons will tighten without use very quickly. It's best that we decide how we want them to tighten, so his hands can still be beneficial to him."

"Beneficial? How?"

"If we put his fingers in a coning shape, then we might be able to put a spoon in his fist, so he can feed himself a little. He won't be able to grip things the way you and I can, but if his fingers are always in a gripping shape, then we can put tools in his hands so he can help himself as much as possible. It would also be easier for him to push a motorized wheelchair with his whole hand, rather than try with a finger."

Glenn helped his wife sit down before she fell over, and then he collapsed into a chair next to her. Becky watched her exhausted parents, who looked crumpled and broken, leaning against the wall for support. She watched her brother's face as the therapist described what his future would bring. He did not appear to be overwhelmed, afraid, or worried about any of it. He just looked . . . determined.

CHAPTER SIX

"Good things come to those who wait. Better things come to those who don't give up. And the best things come to those who believe."

- Author Unknown

Bryan stared at his right hand, shifting back and forth slightly as the bed swayed his body side to side. He willed it to move, but with no success. He concentrated with all his might to have just one finger twitch, but to no avail. Christine told him it would take some intensive physical therapy to even discover if hand movement would be possible again. Bryan tried to tell her he was ready. He wanted to start physical therapy as soon as possible. Christine chuckled at his eagerness and told him to wait patiently. She would help him stretch his muscles, but the big stuff had to wait. First he needed to recover from his bed sores and get out of traction. Bryan tried to convince her that he could handle it, but Christine only smiled at him and left the room.

He continued to lay in bed, feeling bored. His family had finally left, after much convincing on his part that he would be fine. He could tell how exhausted his parents and Becky were, and he didn't mind them leaving to shower and clean up either. The room started to smell a little musty. They promised to return in a few hours. Bryan knew his mom wouldn't rest, even though she needed to. They were going to stop and pick up his little sisters on their way home. He knew as soon as she did, especially little Jenny would demand attention and his mom would oblige.

The thought of Jenny made Bryan smile. He hadn't seen her in over a week. He couldn't wait to see her blonde head poke through his door and fill the room with her sweet giggle. It would be a welcome change to all the tears that had been shed in his room. Bryan looked around at the bare, white walls and wondered if he could get Glenda and Jenny to draw some pictures for him to spruce things up a bit. Instead of signing a cast, he could have them fill the whole room with color. The thought brought a smile to his face. He knew it would be awhile still before his family came back, but he glanced over at the door just in case. He watched it for signs of movement but saw none. He tried closing his eyes. His body could probably use some more rest, but sleep wouldn't come. He was too excited for their arrival. He looked to the door and waited.

Jana glanced at her baby blue phone for the hundredth time. When was Bryan going to call? She knew he was supposed to get home two days ago, but when he didn't call all day yesterday, she assumed the trip had gone late. Or maybe he was sunburned and tired and needed some time to recover. She understood that. But this didn't make any sense! The afternoon was wearing on and he hadn't called or stopped by. Jana heard a rumble outside and flew to her window. She pushed the white, lacy curtains aside, but saw nothing. Bryan's motorcycle was louder than that anyway.

She tried flipping on the TV, but didn't really pay attention to the show playing in front of her. She had taken the entire day off work, and she knew Bryan had fibbed to his boss about the exact day he was returning so they could spend the whole day together. Jana jumped up and flipped the TV off again, muting the background noise. This was stupid. Why was she waiting for him anyway? Jana decided to go to his house and find out what was going on herself. She slipped on her shoes, grabbed her keys, and was about to reach for the doorknob when her doorbell rang. Jana jumped back in surprise. She reached for the handle again and opened the door.

Becky and Glenda stood on her front porch. Glenda's eyes looked red and puffy. Becky appeared to be sunburned, with wet hair dripping down her back. She knew Bryan's sisters really well, having spent a lot of time with his family, but it was strange to have them in her house without Bryan around.

"Hey, Jana, can we come in?"

"Sure." Jana stepped back from the open door. "Sorry, I just wasn't expecting you guys. I was actually about to come over and see you. How was the trip? Where's Bryan?"

Glenda sat on the couch, her face buried in her hands, her shoulders shaking.

"Glenda?"

Becky cleared her throat and finally spoke. "Bryan was in an accident."

Jana jumped from her chair, clutching the keys so tightly they dug into her palm. "Where is he? I need to see him."

Becky got up and tried to guide Jana back to her chair. "He's at the hospital."

"Which one?"

"University of Utah."

"What happened? Is he okay?"

"He broke his neck."

Jana gasped. She clutched her stomach, suddenly feeling nauseous.

"He's still alive, he's talking and everything and he's still, well, Bryan. But he is paralyzed. The doctor said he will definitely never walk again. He might be able to get back some use of his arms, but for right now, he can't move anything."

"When can I see him?"

"That's why we're here. We're heading back up to the hospital so Brenda, Glenda, and Jenny can see him. We wondered if you want to come, too?"

Jana flew out of her chair so fast, it moved back several inches. She had the front door open before Becky or Glenda could even get off the couch. "What are you guys waiting for? Let's go!" The girls quickly got to their feet and jumped in the car before Jana could drive away without them.

Bryan heard voices in the hallway before he saw anyone, but he knew it was his family. He smiled and waited anxiously for them to appear. Glenn pushed the door open first and held it while he ushered the girls in. Brenda and Glenda approached his bed cautiously.

"Hey, guys," Bryan said. "I missed you." He moved his eyes back to the doorway as it opened again and Jana walked in. His smile widened even more. Jana rushed to the bed and reached over the side to hold his unmoving hand.

"Hey, stranger," she smiled at him.

"Sorry I didn't call sooner, I've been a little . . . tied up."

Jana grinned. He was still her Bryan. "I was just afraid you had found a new girl to replace me while you were gone."

"Not possible." Bryan smiled at her.

Jana took a step back and let Jenny come through. The small seven-year-old remained huddled by the door, cowering behind Carol Jean. She didn't like the look of that steel thing going through Bryan's head.

"Hey, sweet girl," Bryan whispered. "Don't I get a hug?"

Jenny inched toward the bed and peered over the edge. Glenn lifted her up to see better, and she wiggled free from his grasp. She climbed up the bed and curled up on top of Bryan, her head resting on his chest.

"I'm not sure . . ." Carol Jean reached up to pull Jenny down, but Bryan stopped her.

"She's fine, Mom," he smiled. Jenny snuggled into her brother until the gentle rocking lulled her to sleep. He continued to talk with his family until Glenn looked at his watch and said they needed to go.

"We are going over to visit your grandpa tonight," he said.

"Does he know yet?" Bryan asked.

Glenn shook his head.

"Be gentle," Bryan whispered.

Glenn nodded, and then he reached down to carefully scoop up a still-sleeping Jenny. She transferred her head to Glenn's shoulder but remained asleep.

"If it's okay with you guys, I think I'll stay here a little longer," Jana spoke up. "I can get one of my parents to come pick me up later."

Carol Jean gave her a hug. "That would be wonderful. Thank you," she said. She turned to Bryan. "I'll be back in the morning."

"You don't have to be here early, Mom. I'll probably be asleep and I know you really need to catch up on sleep, too."

Carol Jean waved off his protests. "I'll see you in the morning," she said.

Bryan rolled his eyes. He said goodbye as his parents guided his sisters from the room and down the hall. He could hear their voices getting fainter and fainter as they walked away.

"So how are you feeling?" Jana asked, moving closer to his bedside now that they were alone.

"I've got a bit of a headache," Bryan smiled mischievously.

Jana laughed. "No kidding."

Bryan's voice grew more serious. "So I was afraid you might not want to be with me still, since the accident."

"Of course I would. You haven't changed, and I fell in love with you, not your legs or your arms."

Bryan smiled. Jana tried to bend down to kiss him, but she misjudged the speed of the rocking bed and got knocked in the chest with it. They both broke into laughter.

Grandpa Carroll woke in his armchair to the soft whirring of his lawn mower starting. He grinned and stretched before carefully rising to his feet. It had been a few weeks since he'd seen Bryan, who was busy with work and then the trip. Grandpa Carroll walked over to the refrigerator and pulled out a pitcher of lemonade. Taking two glasses from the cupboard beside his fridge, he set them on the counter and poured two large cups. He opened his front door and stepped out into the bright sunlight. His other grandson, Richard, was walking up and down the lawn carefully, making a nice, even pattern in the grass. Grandpa Carroll froze. Richard turned and saw him standing there, lemonade in hand. He smiled and waved. Grandpa Carroll moved across the green lawn toward him.

"What are you doing, Richard?"

"Just mowing your lawn, Grandpa."

"But . . . well, Bryan normally does that."

Richard just shook his head. "I know, Grandpa, but uh, Donna asked me to come."

Grandpa stared at him blankly. "Where's Bryan? I know he's home from his trip. Why hasn't he come to see me?"

Richard glanced around, avoiding eye contact. "I'm not sure, Grandpa."

Grandpa Carroll's eyebrows turned down as he scowled.

"Would you like me to finish?" Richard asked.

"Yes, yes, I'm sorry." Grandpa Carroll shook his head and seemed to see Richard for the first time. "Thank you, Richard, it was very kind of you to come." Grandpa Carroll held up the lemonade, placing it in Richard's open hand.

"Thank you." Richard placed the cold glass to his lips and drank until the cup was drained. He handed the empty glass back to Grandpa Carroll, who nodded and walked back inside.

Glenn and Carol Jean held hands tightly as they walked up the three small steps to Donna's house. They both took a deep breath before Glenn reached up and knocked. Donna opened the door slowly until she saw who it was.

"He's in the living room, watching TV." She spoke quietly.

Glenn led Carol Jean past her and they stopped in the open doorway.

"Are you sure you're ready for this?" Carol Jean asked.

"It will only be harder the longer we wait," he whispered back. "Hey, Pop!" He spoke animatedly as they entered the room.

"Back from the river adventure, huh? So where's Bryan? He hasn't been to see me yet."

Glenn and Carol Jean exchanged a look. "Listen, Dad, there was an accident on our trip."

Grandpa Carroll sat up and turned the TV off. "What do you mean?"

"Bryan was cliff diving with some friends and he broke his neck."

Grandpa Carroll shook his head. "No, no, Bryan is an excellent diver."

"I know Dad, but it was just an accident. He's still alive, but he is paralyzed from the neck down."

Grandpa Carroll continued to shake his head fervently as he tried to process the fateful words. He got up slowly from his chair and walked out of the room.

"Dad, where are you going?"

Donna pushed the curtains aside and looked out into the yard. She sighed and looked at her watch, and then checked on him again. He was still out there. She opened the back door and yelled out, "Dad, Glenn and Carol Jean need to go. Do you want to say goodbye?" Grandpa Carroll didn't respond. He hadn't responded to anything since they told him about the accident. He just got to his feet and walked outside. Now, an hour later, he was still walking the same circle around and around the camper parked in the yard. The grass that used to be green and lush now had a distinct ring around it from Grandpa's steady footfall as he paced.

"Not my Bryan, not my Bryan," he mumbled. His feet continued to tear up the grass as he stepped, leaving only dirt behind. "Please, God, not my Bryan."

CHAPTER SEVEN

"Acceptance doesn't mean resignation. It means understanding that something is what it is and there's got to be a way through it."

- Michael J. Fox

Glenn reached out next to him but felt nothing. He opened his eyes, but couldn't see anything in the darkness. It was the middle of the night but he couldn't feel or see Carol Jean anywhere. He rolled out of bed and walked quietly down the hall. He saw no lights on to indicate where she had gone. Jenny's door was slightly ajar, so he reached out and gently pushed it open a little further to peer inside. There lay Carol Jean, cradling their sleeping seven-year-old in her arms.

"What are you doing?" Glenn whispered.

Carol Jean looked up, her face pallid, her eyes red and swollen. She seemed to cling to Jenny's sleeping form as she stared at nothing in particular.

"Carol Jean?"

She still didn't respond. She continued to stare into the darkness, numb with grief. Glenn moved forward and tried to lift Jenny from her, but Carol Jean pulled away.

"I can't let my baby go," she finally whispered.

"She's asleep. Do you want me to put her back in bed for you?"

Carol Jean didn't seem to hear him, or she chose not to respond. "How am I supposed to keep my babies safe?"

Glenn finally seemed to understand. This wasn't about Jenny.

"Why Bryan, my only son? I was even there. I could have stopped him."

"No, you couldn't have done anything. Even if you had told Bryan what was going to happen to him, he would have jumped anyway, just to see for himself. That's how he's always been." Glenn knelt on the floor beside Carol Jean, placing a hand on her leg.

"But how do I keep my babies safe from things like this?" Carol Jean buried her face in Jenny's neck. "How do I keep this from happening again? How am I going to take care of him?" Carol Jean seemed to be asking herself these questions as she held Jenny and rocked her.

Glenn took her hand and tried to pull her to standing. "You need some sleep. Please, put Jenny back in bed and get some rest."

"I'll never sleep again." Even as she spoke the words, Carol Jean obliged. She carefully laid Jenny back on her bed and tucked the covers around her. She kissed her forehead, lingering for a moment, fearful of what might happen if she left.

"Jenny will be fine," Glenn assured her as he guided Carol Jean back to their room.

They climbed into bed and continued to lay awake, staring at the ceiling.

"All right, I'm going to wrap your fingers around this cone now, and then I'll tighten the straps around your wrists," the nurse explained.

"Thanks, Margie," Bryan said quietly.

It had been a couple of weeks since Bryan's accident. Everything seemed to be going smoothly and the doctor felt he was recovered enough for the cone splints now. His sores had healed, and he was finally out of that stupid rocking bed.

The blue foam cone, as Margie called it, reminded Bryan of the spongy handles on exercise equipment. Margie carefully wrapped each of Bryan's fingers around it, spacing them evenly. She tightened the Velcro straps across his hand and around his wrist to keep the splint in place. It looked like the type of brace someone would wear to heal a sprained wrist, only this one had a handle for the patient to clutch, rather than the hand remaining straight.

Jana got up from her seat to get a better view of what Margie was doing. She placed a gentle hand on Bryan's shoulder and leaned in.

"How long does he need to wear those?" she asked.

"A few weeks."

"And then he'll never be able to straighten his fingers again?"

"He will still have the ability to straighten them, if someone pulls them out, but they will return to the curled shape on their own after this."

She continued to watch curiously as Margie put his other hand in a similar splint. Jana had been by Bryan's side every single day for the last couple of weeks. Bryan was grateful his accident happened during the summer. With the steady stream of visitors, it made the long days in the hospital far more enjoyable. He wasn't sure what he was going to do once school started up again and everyone returned to their busy schedules.

"All set," Margie said. "Can I get you anything else?"

"I'm good, thank you."

As soon as the door closed behind her, Jana climbed on top of Bryan's bed, snuggling into him with her head resting under his chin.

"Oh, I almost forgot!" she said. Jana sat up and reached for something. "I brought you a present."

Bryan smiled as she pulled a long, rolled up poster out from under his bed. She unrolled it and held up a large blue poster with the cutest puppy he'd ever seen. At the top in black, curly letters it read: *A hug would make my day*. Jana lowered the poster, beaming at Bryan.

He laughed. "That's great!"

"I knew you'd love it," she said, climbing down from the bed. Jana reached into her purse and pulled out some tape. She hung the poster on his wall, directly opposite the bed so he could see it right in front of him. "Now when I'm not here, you can still think of me." Jana sat back against Bryan's bed, examining the poster from his point of view. When she was satisfied with how it looked, she sat down beside Bryan again and kissed him passionately. Bryan was caught off guard for a moment, but it didn't take long for him to recover and respond.

Grandpa Carroll came into the room a few minutes later, carrying a magazine under his arm. When he saw the two of them kissing, he cleared his throat loudly.

"Oh, did I miss them putting the splints on?"

"They just finished," Jana said, jumping up.

Grandpa Carroll looked disappointed.

"What did you bring, Grandpa?" Bryan asked, trying to pull the focus away from Jana's red face.

Grandpa's eyes lit up. He lifted the magazine out from under his arm, holding it up for Bryan to see. "The newest issue of *Car Craft*. I thought you might like it if I read to you."

Bryan's smile broadened. Jana took the car talk as her cue to leave. "Well, I better get to work," she said, bending down to kiss Bryan. "Do you need a ride home, Grandpa?"

"Oh no, I took the bus here and Donna is picking me up later. Thank you, dear."

She smiled sweetly and slipped out the door.

Grandpa sat down in the chair Jana had just occupied and cracked the magazine open. It made a satisfying crinkling sound as he folded the cover back, cleared his throat, and began to read.

"Morning, Bryan!" The chipper blonde nurse entered his room and opened the blinds to let in some sunlight. Bryan squinted at the light change. "You ready for some stretches?" she asked.

"Yeah, let's do it."

Margie straightened his legs carefully, pulling down on his foot and then pushing it up again to stretch Bryan's muscles. When she was done moving his legs around, she went on with his arms. She pulled his left arm straight and then, as he was doing the up and down motions with her, suddenly Bryan's hand jerked out of hers and hung in the air on its own.

"Muscle spasm?" Margie asked.

Bryan's mouth opened wide, his eyes growing wider to match. "No," he said, shaking his head slowly. "I did that. I wanted to lift up by myself, and I concentrated really hard on my hand and it just lifted up on its own."

Margie stood silent for a moment, her mouth hanging open like a hungry fish. She clapped her hands while jumping up and down. "You did that?" she shrieked. "Do you feel anything?"

Bryan lifted his limp arm so that it barely raised above the bed. It fell back down again with a soft thud. "I don't feel anything, no. Just a little pressure here and there, but I couldn't tell you how soft the sheets on the bed are."

"I've got to tell Christine," she said, dashing from the room. She was back minutes later, the grinning therapist by her side.

"Fantastic!" Christine exclaimed. "This is exactly what we've been hoping for."

"So will I get full mobility back?" Bryan asked, more out of curiosity than hope.

"No, probably not. Based on where your break was located, it's very unlikely you will ever feel anything again. And the amount of things you can do with your hand will be limited. However," she added, "it never hurts to try." She winked at Bryan.

After they left him alone, Bryan stared down at his left hand. He concentrated all of his thoughts on lifting it again. This time he began shaking from exertion before the hand even budged. He was able to roll it back and forth very slowly on the bed, but he must have worn himself out from lifting earlier. *Oh well,* he thought to himself. *I'll get it tomorrow.*

>♦< >♦< >♦<

"Are you ready for this?" Dr. Jensen asked, smiling. Bryan gave him an incredulous look and the doctor chuckled.

"I know, I know," he said, putting his hands up in defense.

Several people snickered at the doctor's attempt to lighten the mood. Everyone had gathered around Bryan's bed for this momentous occasion. Jenny even carried a big Mylar balloon with her that said *congratulations* in neon green. After six long weeks of being in traction and not even being able to turn his head, the doctor was finally loosening the screws and removing the traction bar.

"So still no surgery?" Glenn asked.

"No," the doctor said as he and Christine prepared for the removal. "We did another set of X-rays and everything seems to be healing up nicely without it." Dr. Jensen looked to Christine and once she nodded her ready, he began.

Carol Jean made Jana and Grandpa Carroll sit behind her (not that they fought her) as she sat close by Bryan's side and held tightly to his curled fingers. Bryan squeezed his eyes shut as the doctor started unscrewing the large metal screws from his skull. The grinding sound made Carol Jean's stomach churn, but she held strong and remained unflinching by his side.

Once the device was off, Bryan felt a huge release of pressure. Dr. Jensen slipped a foam collar around his neck for added support. Bryan stretched his jaw wide and with encouragement from Christine, tried moving his head to one side. The reaction was not what he had expected. He immediately felt a wave of nausea wash over him. He started to have tunnel vision and feared he was going to pass out.

"It's okay, just take it slow," the therapist coached him.

Bryan kept his eyes shut and lay still. He gradually sucked in a breath and then let the air flow out again, concentrating on his breathing instead of the pounding headache that threatened to overtake him. After several more long, deep breaths, he swallowed the lump that had risen in his throat and opened his eyes again slowly. The room seemed ridiculously bright. As he looked around at the nine faces staring into his own, he forced himself to smile.

"Whew! That's worse than getting high," he joked.

"Oh, Bryan," his mom said. The other adults laughed. Glenda and Jenny soon joined in, though they weren't sure why.

"How are you feeling?" the doctor asked. He shined a light in Bryan's eyes and felt around his neck and face carefully.

"Like I've been hit by a truck," he answered, closing his eyes again to prevent the room from spinning.

"Well, that's to be expected when you haven't had any neck movement in several weeks. Despite the dizziness, does it feel good to stretch your neck muscles?"

Bryan had to really concentrate on looking past the dizzy feelings he was experiencing to feel the stiffness in his neck as he tried to turn his head. His muscles burned with lack of use. He wished he could reach his hands up to soothe the aching pain and rub some of the tight knots out. As if reading his mind, or perhaps from watching him struggle, Jana stepped forward and began rubbing his neck and tops of his shoulders very gently and cautiously.

"You seem to be doing pretty well," Christine nodded.

Bryan wasn't sure if she was joking or not, but he didn't see a smile on her face.

"It's not going to be a quick or an easy transition. You haven't passed out yet, which is a really good sign. Just continue taking slow, deep breaths and we'll hopefully be able to move you down to your new room in the next few weeks."

The quiet chatter in the room died down. "A new room? So he'll be ready for rehab in just a few of weeks?" Glenn asked.

"Yeah, he'll be ready to leave the ICU just as soon as we've got him used to sitting up and settled into a wheelchair," Christine answered, smiling. "Then he'll start physical therapy shortly after, depending on how he's doing."

Jenny clapped. "Does that mean he can come home?" she asked, bouncing up and down.

"Oh, sweetie, not yet," Carol Jean soothed. "Bryan will be leaving the ICU, not the hospital, in a couple of weeks."

Jenny looked confused and disappointed.

"How much longer will he be in the hospital?" Carol Jean asked, turning to the doctor.

"It's too hard to say. It depends on how he's healing. Once he's moved into a regular room he can start rehabilitation and physical therapy, but that can be a slow process, especially with spinal injuries. He'll probably be here for at least four to six more months."

Carol Jean's face fell. She knew he'd be in the hospital for a long time, but six more months seemed like an eternity.

"Wait," Bryan spoke up, "so you aren't going to be my therapist anymore?"

Christine smiled. "I'll miss you, too." She patted Bryan's hand. "I'll stop in and check on you from time to time to see how you're progressing, but no, sadly, I am an ICU occupational therapist. I have to stay here and pass you on to my rehabilitation colleagues. You're in good hands though, I promise."

Christine didn't waste any time. She allowed Bryan the night to rest, but bright and early the next morning she was standing by his bedside, smiling.

"Our goal is to get you sitting up today," Christine said. "I know this might not seem like much, but after lying down for over a month and being in traction for most of that time, sitting up is really going to be a feat. Are you ready to try?"

Bryan nodded. "What do I need to do?"

"Try and keep your head up."

That sounded simple enough. A four-week-old baby can hold up his head. The blonde nurse who had been there for his first arm movement stood on the other side of the bed. She and Christine each took one of his legs and wrapped them tightly with ace bandages.

"What's that for?" Bryan asked.

"We're trying to force the blood out of your legs and into your head, so you don't pass out."

Once they were done wrapping him, Margie helped Christine roll Bryan from his bed onto the table they wheeled in.

"I'm going to count to three and we'll start cranking the table up a little at a time."

"You tell us if we're going too fast," Margie added.

Christine continued, "Then Margie here will help me put on this brace to support you in the sitting position." She held up a rather intense-looking contraption that consisted of two pieces: a plastic shell backing piece that went from his waist to the top of his head and a metal breastplate which strapped to the front and came up under the chin to support his neck.

"It's called a turtle shell brace," she explained. "You'll have to wear this whenever you are sitting up in bed or going to be in a wheelchair." Christine showed him a thick black band. "And this is your abdominal binder. It's used to help keep the blood from pooling in your abdomen so you don't faint when sitting up."

Bryan's eyes widened as she described all the things he had to wear just to sit up. "Okay," Bryan said. "Let's do this."

"One, two, three!"

Bryan felt pressure on his biceps as the two of them held his arms steady and Margie turned the crank. She continued to move him upwards slowly, about half an inch at a time. Once he was almost completely sitting up straight, a severe headache slammed him immediately, and he had to squeeze his eyes shut. When he opened them again just seconds later, he could see blackness creeping in from the corners of his eyes. Bryan's head rolled back and he passed out.

"All right, lay him back down," Christine ordered. "That was pretty typical. When he wakes up we'll try again." Margie cranked the table back down until Bryan was lying flat once more.

Bryan's head swam. He felt tired and dizzy and nauseous all at the same time. Sweat broke out all over his forehead and dripped down his neck and face. The room felt alarmingly hot. He peeked one eye open to find his therapist and nurse leaning over him.

"How did that feel?" Christine asked.

"Great," Bryan mumbled, opening his other eye. "Can we do it again?"

"As soon as you're ready," Margie responded. "Don't push it."

Bryan took several slow, deep breaths. "Let's try again," he said, despite his pounding headache.

"All right." They both got back in position and waited for the count. "One, two, three."

Bryan felt the same pressure and head rush once he was sitting up, but this time he felt more prepared for it. When the blackness threatened to overtake him again, Bryan closed his eyes and breathed slowly in and out. He focused on his breaths and soon was able to open his eyes again. The brace had been placed around him for support.

"You did it." Christine gave him a genuine smile. "How is your head? Are you feeling dizzy?"

"Yes, but not as bad as the first time," Bryan said. His body began to tremble and the sweat continued to pour down his face. They allowed him to stay sitting up for about twenty minutes before Christine declared they had pushed him enough for one day. Bryan wanted to argue and tell them he could do more, but he felt so exhausted. The thought of laying back down and napping was far too appealing.

With their arms around him for support, Margie and Christine slowly moved his body back onto his bed again.

"Well, Bryan, you did great for your first day," she enthused. "I'll be back to practice some more tomorrow."

"Thank you," Bryan whispered, closing his eyes.

"We'll see you tomorrow," Christine said.

This time Bryan didn't respond. He was already asleep.

Glenn sat in his cubicle at work, his fingers poised at the computer, yet he wasn't typing anything. He stared right beside his computer at the family picture they took at Bryan's graduation, just weeks before the accident. He looked at his son's bright, hopeful smile. He couldn't understand why this had to happen to them. He was angry, confused, and sad all at the same time.

"You all right, Glenn?" one of his coworkers asked.

Glenn didn't notice the man until he asked again. "What? Oh yeah, sorry," he said. "I'm fabulous, marvelous, and wonderful." Forcing a smile, he glanced back at his family picture and jumped to his feet. "I'm taking an early lunch," he said. "I gotta go." He brushed past the startled coworker and left the building. He didn't have a plan, and he wasn't really thinking. He just got in his car and drove. Soon he found himself in the hospital parking lot, so he decided to go in.

Glenn sat beside Grandpa Carroll while Christine stood behind Bryan, helping him turn his neck from side to side.

"It's good to see you sitting up," Glenn said.

Bryan was focusing too hard to respond. Christine had been to his room every day, helping him become comfortable with sitting up and moving his head around again. Bryan was amazed at how much energy and concentration it took to do something as simple as sit up in bed. It truly felt like he was an infant, starting from scratch to learn how to control his body on his own.

As Christine moved on to muscle strength, she placed a thin, white tube in Bryan's curled fingers. He raised his arms until they were perpendicular to his body. Bryan held it there for a full minute, Bryan's best time to date, until his arms shook and his hands became sweaty.

"Excellent," Christine praised. "You're coming along very quickly, Bryan. I suspect we'll have you cruising around here in a wheelchair in no time."

Bryan looked at Grandpa Carroll and they shared a smile. He glanced at the two canes Grandpa used to help him walk and said, "You can get a chair next, and then we'll race down the hall."

Grandpa chuckled. "You're on."

"All right." Christine removed Bryan's turtle shell brace and helped lower him back down on the bed. She then carefully stretched his arms, legs, and neck.

"I'll see you tomorrow, Bryan. I think you're almost ready to sit in a wheelchair, and then you'll be ready to move down to rehab."

Bryan smiled. "Really?"

"Oh, yes, you're improving rather quickly. It's about time we see if we can get any use out of those," she said, nudging Bryan's arms.

"I'm ready," Bryan said.

"I know you are," the therapist replied. "You definitely are."

As Bryan and Grandpa continued to visit, Glenn walked over to where Christine washed her hands.

"How is he doing?" Glenn whispered.

Christine turned to face him and smiled. "He is doing amazingly well!" she said. "Most patients with breaks lesser than Bryan go through the five stages of grief. They are in denial about what has happened to them, unable to cope with the reality of never being able to walk again. And in Bryan's case, never be able to fully use his hands either. Once the reality finally does sink in, it's quickly followed by anger. The patient then goes through a stage of bargaining, followed closely by depression. Correct me if I'm wrong, but Bryan doesn't seem to have experienced any of these. He's skipped straight over the first four steps and gone straight to acceptance. He's just ready to face his new life straight on."

Glenn nodded. He was all too familiar with the grief and anger she described.

>♦< >♦< >♦<

"So what do you think of this bad boy?" Christine asked the following morning.

Bryan glanced away from the TV to see Christine pushing a large, black wheelchair through the open door to his room.

"Is that for me?"

"All yours!"

"Wow," Bryan whispered. He was too shocked and excited to think of anything smart-alecky to say. After two long months of being confined to a bed, Bryan had finally done well enough to earn himself a ride.

Bryan stared at the chair, his eyes glowing with excitement. "I can't believe I finally get to be out of this bed!" he exclaimed.

"You earned it," Christine responded. "I've never seen someone work so hard."

Bryan spent most of the day convincing nurses to push him around the hospital so he could see something other than his TV screen, and actually explore.

The following morning after breakfast, Christine entered Bryan's room with another man and woman he didn't recognize. They both looked stern and foreboding.

"What, am I in trouble?" Bryan whispered.

Christine looked at them and then back at Bryan. "Why, you scared?" she smiled. "No, this is Dr. Estrada, and this is

Mary Knight. She's a resident who will be assisting him. Dr. Estrada is the head of rehab. They're here to evaluate you for physically therapy and rehabilitation."

Bryan perked up at those words. His stomach jumped and his heartbeat quickened. Finally! The day he had been waiting for was here. He wished he could sit up to hear what the physical therapists were saying. Since that wasn't an option, he strained his ears and tried to catch a word or two. It sounded like the doctor was explaining to Mary how to help him sit up. Nothing too exciting or mysterious.

"All right, Bryan, are you ready to begin?"

"Boy, am I!"

The doctor tried to smile, but on his severe face it looked more like a grimace.

Christine parked the chair up against Bryan's bed and pulled his sheets down. "Oh, good," she said. "It looks like the nurse already put the belly band on for you this morning." She stepped back and watched as the other two performed their evaluation.

Mary moved to the opposite side of the bed. Together, she and Dr. Estrada lifted him into a sitting position, just like Christine had done the previous day. She strapped him back into the giant turtle shell brace and transferred Bryan into his new wheelchair.

"How does that feel?" Dr. Estrada asked.

"I don't know. Why don't you tell me?" Bryan said with a smirk.

"Bryan here is a bit of a smart aleck, if you couldn't tell," Christine piped in.

"Yes, I gathered that," Dr. Estrada responded. "Poor choice of words on my part."

Doesn't this guy crack a smile for anything? Bryan wondered. "I knew what you meant," Bryan said. "Everything seems to be normal. I don't feel too dizzy or anything."

"Good. Okay then, first can you show me what you are able to do already?"

Bryan raised his arms above the bed and then lowered them again. He had gotten much smoother at performing that skill, almost completely jerk free. He had also been practicing a lot since there wasn't much else he could do while lying in bed. He watched TV and he raised and lowered his arms. That was about it.

"If you put a spoon in my hand, I can usually get it to my face, too."

Dr. Estrada picked up a spoon from his breakfast tray and placed the handle in Bryan's curled fingers. Very slowly and very carefully, Bryan raised the tip of the spoon until it touched his lips. The spoon tilted slightly as it raised higher and higher. If there had been any food on the spoon, it most likely would have fallen off.

"Can you feed yourself soup?" the doctor asked.

Bryan chuckled. "Not even close. I'm pretty good with pudding or peanut butter though, you know, things like that." Bryan let the spoon drop back onto his lap as he lowered his left arm again.

"Are you left handed?"

"No," Bryan said, "That's just my stronger arm. I don't have enough control over the right one to get a spoon that high."

"It looks like you have adequate movement. We just need to concentrate on building strength. Is that right?"

"Yeah," Bryan said. "If I could get to the point of transferring myself from the bed to my own chair, that would be awesome."

"Well, that would be our ultimate goal. Hopefully we can get you there. The first step is muscle strength. If your hand shakes from the weight of a spoon, imagine how much harder it would be to lift your entire body off the bed."

Bryan nodded. "Just tell me what I need to do."

"Practice, practice, and more practice," the doctor said while he continued to jot notes on his clipboard.

Bryan was starting to feel like a circus monkey as the doctor asked him to complete one task after another. Dr. Estrada took thorough notes after each one. Once he and Mary were satisfied, they bid him farewell and Bryan was finally able to rest once again.

"Does this mean I'm moving soon?" Bryan asked once they were both out of earshot.

"The rehabilitation physical therapists always come up and evaluate patients who are getting ready to transfer downstairs. That way they know where you need to start in physical therapy. So, yeah, with them being up here, I'd guess you're getting moved in the next day or two."

CHAPTER EIGHT

"The only way to get through life is to laugh your way through it. You either have to laugh or cry. I prefer to laugh. Crying gives me a headache."

\- Marjorie Pay Hinckley

Nedra scanned over the monitors and double-checked that she'd written down the numbers correctly. She clicked her pen twice before moving on to the next patient. She walked between the four beds, confirming each of her patients had satisfactory vitals as part of her morning rounds.

Another nurse, clad in her white uniform, entered the room behind her.

"Where have you been?" Nedra asked without turning.

"I was helping the new patient get settled."

Nedra whipped around. "We have a new patient?"

"Yeah, didn't you see the form come in? Well, obviously not if we're having this discussion."

"Which room?" Nedra asked.

"Two thirteen," the other nurse replied, lifting several bottles on the medicine cart until she found the one she had been looking for. She measured out two large, white pills and placed them in a small paper cup. "Spinal injury from six weeks ago. He's a C4-C5 quad."

Nedra nodded as she measured out two pills herself and administered them to the next patient. "I'll go in and introduce myself as soon as I'm done here."

>♦< >♦< >♦<

Nedra stood in the open doorway of Room 213, studying the new patient. Born and raised in California, she could only assume she was staring at a fellow Californian. Everything from his shaggy, sandy-blonde hair to his tanned skin screamed surfer boy. She hadn't meant to stare, but his good looks caught her off guard. Now she realized she had been staring too long, but thankfully he hadn't seemed to notice.

"You gonna come in, or you helping hold up that door frame?"

Or not. Nedra straightened up and brushed off her shirt before approaching his bed and that playboy smile. "So what are you in for?" she asked, leaning against the metal frame of his bed.

"I was cliff diving. It was the best swan dive of my entire life! Unfortunately, I didn't have the best landing." Bryan made a loud popping sound with his mouth. "Then a short six weeks later and I am here. So, what do we need to do to get this party started?"

"Just a minute, superman, you may be out of traction now, but that doesn't mean you can dive straight into physical therapy."

"Why not?"

"Because your body experienced something very traumatic. We need to ease it back into small things first if we want it to cooperate."

Bryan sighed dramatically. "When do I get to start physical therapy then?"

"I'll take you down to the rehab room tomorrow and they will probably start you with some simple stretches. The therapists will look over your evaluation from upstairs and decide how much you can do."

"Stretching? That's it? Come on, I need a real challenge. Why don't I run a mile for you?" he asked with a wink.

"If you can run a mile, then you certainly don't belong on my floor. You're free to leave," she said, holding her hand up to the door.

"Well, I'm pretty comfortable here. Maybe I'll stick around for just a little while longer."

Nedra smirked. "I thought you might. Well, I need to finish up my rounds now. Why don't you rest for awhile and I'll be back to check on you later. Your roommates should be back from physical therapy soon."

Bryan smiled and told her goodbye. She seemed like the kind of nurse he could have some fun with. He'd just have to test out his theory and see how she handled it.

As Nedra passed through the door, three guys came rolling into the room.

"Speak of the devils," Nedra said. "Good luck, Bryan!" With a wave she was gone.

"Hey, hey! Looks like we've got a new roommate. I'm Danny. We'll be sleeping next to each other," he said, followed by a chuckle. Danny appeared to be quadriplegic as well. He was in a motorized wheelchair, his arms and legs thin and limp.

A nurse accompanied them and lifted Danny, placing him in the bed beside Bryan's. "Anyone need anything?" she asked.

"Deep tissue massage."

"A sponge bath."

"Mouth-to-mouth."

The guys all laughed, Bryan joining them. The nurse just rolled her eyes and walked out of their room.

"So whaddya in for, pardner?"

Bryan looked at the boy who spoke. They appeared to be around the same age. Everything about him looked and sounded cowboy, from the slight twang when he spoke to the black cowboy hat on his head. The strange thing was that this other kid was lying on his stomach on a gurney, driving it around with his hands. As he wheeled past, settling on the opposite side of the room, Bryan noticed he only had one leg.

"I was in a cliff diving accident," Bryan said. "I'm Bryan, by the way."

"Nice to meetcha, Bryan. I'm J.D.," he said.

Bryan stared back at him for a moment, not sure what to say next. This was his first encounter with other people who were like him.

J.D. chuckled. "It's all right, you kin ask."

"What's your story?" Bryan asked.

"For my leg or this fancy new ride?" J.D. smiled, patting the wheel below his gurney.

"Both."

"Well, when I was sixteen I got dared to play chicken with one o' them trains." He paused. "The train won."

Bryan cringed, but J.D. continued to smile wickedly in return.

"Then two years later I done got in a car accident and BAM, broke my neck and lost the use of my other leg."

"Why are you on your stomach?" Bryan asked.

"I'm gittin' there. Just hold your horses. So I started gittin' a bad pressure sore on my tuckus. That's when they brought me back in for some rehab and I gotta stay on my stomach so the sore can heal. Thankfully still got my arms though." He waved them around to show off. "Unlike Danny over there," he said, pointing to Bryan's neighbor.

"Yeah, you big showoff!" Danny smiled. "Mine was actually a diving story too, but a little different from yours," he said, looking at Bryan. "I was at this great party with some friends and we had way too much to drink. My buddy pulled out a joint and we passed it around for awhile. Well, then one of them had the brilliant idea that we should all go swimming. Someone remembered a pool was opening up not too far away so we all went down there and jumped the fence. I tore off my clothes and climbed up onto the diving board so I could be the first one in. I dove straight in. It wasn't until I broke my neck smashing into the concrete that I realized the pool was empty. They hadn't filled it yet."

"Oh!" Bryan gasped, squeezing his eyes shut against the mental image. "Are you a quad, too?" he asked.

"Yeah, I'm a C4 complete," he said. "You?"

"C4-C5," Bryan stated. "What about you?" Bryan asked, looking over at the fourth guy who lay in the bed opposite his on the other side of the room. He hadn't spoken up yet.

"I'm Art," he said. "I'm a quad, too. I've regained a lot of functionality with my arms since I got here. I can transfer myself and everything, but I've also been here the longest," he added, nodding at the other two.

"And what happened, if you don't mind my asking?"

"Naw, I don't mind. We're all in the same boat. I was playing football in Montana," he said. "One bad tackle and snap."

Bryan looked around at the other three guys as they started talking again. It felt strange after the last couple months of feeling so isolated to suddenly be surrounded by guys who were just like him. It was strange, but it was comforting.

>♦< >♦< >♦<

Nedra slowly walked down the hospital hallway, ready to check on her patients one last time before handing them off to the next nurse. As she neared Bryan's room, she was almost run over by a student nurse racing out.

"I need a doctor! Where's the doctor?"

Nedra jumped into action. "What's wrong?" she asked as she ran for the crash cart.

"He moved! His leg moved! He can walk! It's a miracle!"

Nedra stopped immediately and peered at the excited student nurse as he bounced up and down. She gently took him by the arm and guided him back into the room.

"Bryan, stop teasing the student nurses!" she said, waving a finger at him.

Bryan was laughing too hard to respond. The student nurse looked between the two of them and his shoulders slumped in defeat. "I'm sorry, I'm sorry." Bryan could barely get the words out as he continued to laugh.

Nedra lowered her eyes at him and glared. Bryan stopped laughing and attempted to hold a serious face. Nedra looked at the student nurse and explained. "With this sort of injury, the muscles will still occasionally spasm. It doesn't mean they're working again, it just makes his legs or arms twitch. Bryan here thinks it's funny to make you student nurses run into the hall searching for a doctor because he's 'suddenly healed.'" She shook her head and watched as the student nurse sheepishly excused himself from the room. She turned on Bryan. "Why do you keep doing that?"

"I can't move my legs, I can barely move my arms, and I've been in this hospital for over six weeks now. You'd be bored, too. I have to do something to keep myself entertained!"

Nedra thought about it for a moment and then rolled her eyes. "Carry on," she said, waving her hand at him.

Bryan's grin widened and he laughed softly to himself again. He watched as Nedra went around the room and tucked in each of her other three patients, kissing them good night. She stopped at Bryan's bed last and gently tucked his blankets around him before bidding him goodnight.

"Don't I get a kiss?" he asked.

"Only my good patients get kisses," she teased. She threw her long, brown hair over her shoulder and strutted from the room.

The following morning, Nedra was getting Bryan ready for the day when a young Hispanic man showed up, pushing a wheelchair.

"Hi there, Bryan, I'm Ricardo. Dr. Estrada asked me to come pick you up. Would you like to go for a ride down to our rehab room?"

"Yes!"

"I'll leave you to it then," Nedra said, removing Bryan's breakfast tray and folding up his small table.

"Throw your arms around my neck and we'll get you there."

Bryan put his arms around the orderly, like a big hug. With Nedra's assistance, the two of them hoisted Bryan out of bed and into his new seat. Ricardo secured the thick, black buckle around his waist so he couldn't slide out of the chair and positioned his arms on the arm rests. Ricardo got behind Bryan and began pushing him toward the elevators. Once inside, Bryan watched as Ricardo pressed the number one with his thumb, and then he took a step back while they both waited for the lift to roar to life.

"Are you a physical therapist?" Bryan asked.

"No, no," Ricardo chuckled. "I'm just your delivery driver. We'll turn right in here," Ricardo said, holding open the large, glass door with his foot and maneuvering Bryan through it.

Bryan rolled into the wide, open room. His roommates were all in there, working on endurance and muscle strength, along with some other patients he hadn't met yet. His friends each said hello and then continued with what they were doing.

Ricardo pushed Bryan over to the physical therapist, who took over. He walked Bryan around the room, allowing him to explore his new surroundings. On one side of the room were two long, low platforms about twenty-four inches high and ten feet deep. As Bryan rolled past, he realized the platforms were the same height as his wheelchair seat. Both boards were covered in exercise mats. Just past the platforms, he saw two sets of handrails that were used to help patients walk again. Bryan saw lots of free weights, medicine balls, and several unfamiliar exercise machines. Some ropes hung down from the ceiling, with a black brace hanging from them. They went around the room a couple of times, the doctor explaining each piece of equipment as they went.

When they passed by some weights the second time, Bryan asked if he could try them out. Dr. Estrada placed a one pound ankle weight around his left wrist and asked him to try and lift it.

Bryan took several deep breaths before attempting to lift the weight. Bryan grunted and then lifted his arm as hard and high as he could. It barely raised above his lap before his arm crashed down again with a thud. "Again," Bryan said with determination. He got his arm ready, took a deep breath, and then raised his arm again. The doctor counted to five this time.

"Again!"

With each new turn, Bryan held the weight up for two additional seconds until Dr. Estrada told him it was time for a break.

"I can't stop now. I'm improving!"

"Give your muscles a rest, Bryan. You don't want to overdo it your first day."

As his physical therapist spoke, Bryan began feeling tired and a little dizzy. The room started to spin, his feelings of nausea apparent on his face.

"Bryan, are you feeling okay?"

Bryan had to close his eyes to stop the room from whirling around him. He only managed to get one word out. "Dizzy," he whispered.

Dr. Estrada grabbed the handles on the back of his chair and carefully tipped the wheelchair backwards so Bryan was lying down. It didn't take long for the blood to flow back into his head and he was able to open his eyes again.

"I think we overdid it today," he said, frowning. "This is definitely the longest you've ever been sitting up."

Bryan smiled up at him. "What are you talking about?" he asked through labored breaths. "I feel great."

Dr. Estrada looked at Bryan and couldn't help but laugh.

"So what's going on at home?" Bryan asked, settling back into his pillows.

Glenn had driven Grandpa Carroll to the hospital for a visit. Bryan was still a little tired from his excursion to the rehab room, but he was excited to see them.

"Oh, not too much. Mostly just getting your sisters all ready for school to start back up again."

"I'm sure they're thrilled with that."

Glenn rolled his eyes. "Oh, it's an absolute joy. Becky and Brenda need new clothes, and then getting Glenda and Jenny to pick out supplies they need for classes they don't want to take. I'm also trying to make sure everyone is signed up for the extracurricular stuff they want. Jenny's soccer moves up to multiple times a week this year. And of course there's the constant whining that we aren't going camping this year." Glenn quickly covered his mouth. He hadn't meant that last part to slip out. For as long as Bryan could remember, his family took a yearly camping trip with Grandpa Carroll. When they were little, the trip had always been to Yellowstone. As they got older and after they bought their boat, the family started camping near lakes instead. They always went in August, right before the new school year started, kind of as a last hurrah to end the summer season.

"So you guys aren't going anyway?" Bryan asked.

"How can we, with you in here? It wouldn't be the same."

"But if the girls are complaining about going . . ."

"We've just never missed the trip before. It's not that they want to go without you, they just want to go. And Jenny doesn't understand why you can't leave the hospital and take a vacation with us." Glenn laughed nervously.

"You could always go without me."

"And leave you behind with no one to come visit? Absolutely not. Your mother would never allow that."

"Don't worry about it, Bryan," Grandpa jumped in. "The girls will get over it. Besides, I'm willing to bet if we went ahead and drove all the way to the lake without ya, they would be regretting it before we even had time to launch the boat. The trip just wouldn't be the same. I doubt anyone would be able to have any fun."

"All right," Bryan responded, trying not to smile.

His childhood trips to Yellowstone were some of his favorite memories. His parents and sisters always camped in the trailer together, while he and Grandpa would rest in the sleeper attached to the back of the truck, just the two of them. Grandpa had taught him how to fish in Yellowstone—the start of many other fishing expeditions. He remembered catching his first fish ever on the Yellowstone Bridge and pretending to go on bear hunts with his sisters through the woods. Once he hid behind a giant rock while they were hiking and jumped out to scare his parents when they finally caught up. Then there was the first time he got up on water skis, and the first time he learned to slalom. The memories washed over Bryan in floods. He was glad they weren't going without him. He wasn't sure he would be able to handle it if they left him behind.

CHAPTER NINE

"Success is not final, failure is not fatal: it is the courage to continue that counts."

- Winston Churchill

So it will pretty much be the same as it is now. I'll just have to visit in the evenings instead of during the day." Jana tried to smile, but Bryan could tell it was forced. She sniffled and tried to avoid eye contact with him.

"Jana, look at me." She continued to glance around the room. "Jana, why won't you look at me?"

She finally conceded and Bryan could see how red her eyes were from fighting back the tears.

"Sweetie, what's wrong?"

Jana wiped under her eyes with a fingertip. "I don't know why I'm being such a baby. I'm just . . . really going to miss you!" Jana threw herself across Bryan and wrapped her arms around him. How he missed being able to hold her back and stroke her soft hair.

"What do you mean, you're going to miss me?" he chuckled. "I'm not going anywhere. And it's just like you said, we'll still see each other practically every day." As the words fell out of his mouth, Bryan knew they weren't true. With school starting again tomorrow, a lot was going to change. Jana talked about seeing him every night, but Bryan knew between homework and activities, he'd be lucky to see her a couple times a week.

"Well, I gotta go. I have to be up early tomorrow." Jana stuck out her tongue, making a face. "I'll come see you right after school."

"I can't wait." Bryan smiled.

"Love you," she said. She bent down and kissed him good night. "Oh, hey Nedra," she said, passing the nurse as she came in. "Take good care of him for me."

"I will," Nedra responded. "Good night." She knelt down beside Bryan's bed and emptied his leg bag into a large plastic container, which she then carried carefully into the bathroom and poured down the toilet. "These are things she is going to have to learn how to do. She knows that, right?" Nedra said, holding up the now empty container.

"Yes. She is very aware that any future we have together is not going to be exactly like the one we had planned. She said she's ready to learn."

"All righty," Nedra said with a smile. "We'll put the girl to work then." She turned on the radio and began preparing Bryan for bed. "Do you mind the music?"

"Mind? Of course not! I love Kansas!" he said, referring to the song blaring through the speakers.

"Oh, me too," Nedra agreed.

Bryan closed his eyes and let the music flow through him while Nedra filled a small, plastic tub with warm water and began washing him with a sponge.

"I miss this," Bryan commented.

"Getting a sponge bath by a beautiful woman?"

Bryan laughed. "That part's nice too, but no. I meant the music. I love music! Anytime I was in the shop, or in my car, or even just hanging out at home, I always had music playing. I usually had it so loud, I could feel the bass vibrating in my teeth. My mom didn't care for it that much, but I loved to feel the music through my whole body. Now that I'm here, I can't turn the music on, and whenever a nurse does, I don't get a say in what we listen to."

"I'm sorry. That's rough," Nedra said. She pulled off his compression socks to carefully clean his feet and in between his toes. "I'm the same way. I love, love music. I promise anytime I'm in here with you, I'll make sure the radio is on. I'll even let you pick the station once in awhile. Deal?"

"Deal!" Bryan said excitedly.

Nedra finished cleaning his body and moved up to his face. "Do you want a shave tonight?"

"Yes, please," Bryan said. "But keep the mustache. I kinda like it."

"Really?" Nedra asked, crinkling her nose. "I think they're gross."

"What? No way! Burt Reynolds? Billy Dee Williams? Those dudes rock the 'stache!"

"Just because a handful of men can pull off the mustache look doesn't mean all men should try."

"Well, I want you to keep it anyway."

"All right, it's your face. But I can't guarantee I won't slip and accidentally shave there."

Bryan gave her a dirty look and they both laughed. "So what kind of music do you like?" Bryan asked.

"Styx, Kansas, Moody Blues, you know, the good stuff."

Bryan's eyes widened in surprise. "Wow," he said. "I'm impressed. You actually have really good taste."

"Don't sound so surprised! I may be ten years older than you, but it's not like I'm ancient. Now stop talking or I'll cut you."

Bryan held perfectly still while Nedra used the small tub to rinse off the razor after each stroke. "Babe" by Styx came on the radio and Nedra began to sing along quietly while she worked. She rinsed Bryan's face and patted it dry, and then held up a small mirror for him to see.

"It looks great. Thank you," he said before adding, "You have a really nice voice."

Nedra smiled. "Thank you. I love to sing!"

"You should do it more often around here. It would probably really cheer up your patients."

"Well, maybe I will. Now open." Nedra held up his toothbrush and began brushing his teeth. "There, all ready for bed." She bent down and kissed him good night. "Sweet dreams," she said as she moved on to her next patient.

Bryan closed his eyes and let the music carry his thoughts to dreamland. He wished he could fall asleep to music every night. It was so much nicer than listening to snores from other patients or the constant beeping of machines.

The next morning, Carol Jean came into Bryan's room while a nurse fed him breakfast.

"Hey, Mom, I didn't expect to see you today."

"Well, I just dropped off all your sisters at school and figured I would swing by and say hi before I need to get back to work."

"How did drop off go?"

Carol Jean reached for the bowl of cereal from the nurse and took over feeding him. "Oh, just great," she said, spooning a big, gooey blob into his mouth. "Becky is a senior, so she is so totally over this whole school thing. And of course Brenda has always hated school and can't wait to be done. Glenda didn't say two words to me all morning—she just glared. And Jenny was excited to see all her friends again from last year."

Bryan smiled. He couldn't believe how much he missed the normal, mundane, little daily parts of living at home. "Shouldn't you be at the school, preparing lunch for 3,500 screaming, starving elementary school kids?"

"The bread is rising, the stew is simmering, the cakes are frosted, and the other ladies have everything under control. Besides, I wanted to come see my son. I feel like the last couple weeks with school and work starting again, I haven't been here as much as I wanted to."

"Well, it's good to see you."

"Tell me how things are going with physical therapy?"

"Really well. Slower than I'd like, but Dr. Estrada said we're right on track."

"Honey, everything in your entire life has been slower than you'd like."

"Well, that's true. Anyway, someone will be here to get me in just a few minutes if you want to come and watch."

Carol Jean glanced down at her watch. "I can spare a few minutes."

When Bryan finished eating, she set the bowl and spoon on his tray and dabbed his mouth and chin with a napkin. As if on cue, Ricardo entered Bryan's room, pushing an empty black wheelchair.

"Have no fear, your ride is here," he said, holding his hands out in front of the chair. Good morning, Mrs. Carroll. How are you doing today?"

"I'm well, thank you," she responded. "And please, call me Carol Jean."

Ricardo grunted slightly as he hoisted Bryan into the chair. "Are you coming downstairs with us, Carol Jean?"

"Yes, I think I might."

"So how is Bryan's physical therapy going?" she asked the doctor once they arrived downstairs.

"Great! He's made a lot of progress in the last few weeks since we began. He's sitting up and keeping his head up without any problems, and he's starting to gain some muscle back in his arms."

"How are you doing that?" Carol Jean asked.

"Well, let me show you. We were going to start with arms today anyway." Dr. Estrada picked up an ankle weight, eager to demonstrate Bryan's progress. He placed it in Bryan's curled hands, tying the straps around his wrist so they wouldn't drop. He slowly assisted Bryan in moving the weights up and down. Having his fingers curled definitely helped with gripping the weights, since he couldn't actually hold them on his own.

Carol Jean smiled as she watched the progress her son was making. "Well, I better get going," she said. "Keep working hard!"

Several days later, Bryan bubbled with excitement to be going home for the first time. The nurse couldn't feed him breakfast fast enough. The moment Glenn walked into the room, Bryan announced he was done eating.

"We'll see you back here tonight. Have a fun day with your family, Bryan!" The chipper young nurse spoke enthusiastically, motioning with her hands.

"Does he need to be back by a certain time?" Glenn asked.

"Around 9:00 p.m. works well, so the night nurse can help get him ready for bed and everything, but there is no set time. After all, he is your son."

Bryan and Glenn both thanked her as Glenn grasped the black handles of the wheelchair and pushed Bryan out of his hospital room.

"Wait, Dad, let me do it," Bryan said. He placed his hands on the wheels and inched forward, all the way to the elevators.

"Bryan, that's amazing!" Glenn said excitedly.

"I've been working really hard in physical therapy to move my own chair," Bryan said.

Glenn resumed pushing once they reached the parking lot. Bryan was completely out of breath.

"Does it feel weird to be coming home for the day?" Glenn asked.

"A little," Bryan admitted. "I'm so used to nurses checking on me every hour. It will be weird to be on my own today. I think the strangest part is that I'm only visiting. It seems weird to visit my own house, and then have to return to the hospital."

"That part does feel a little strange. It's also really smart, too. It will give you a chance to glimpse what life will be like when you do finally come home, and it will give your mom and I a chance to practice caring for you."

The drive home was quiet and peaceful. Bryan watched out his window as all the familiar roads and houses flew past. Everything seemed so different now. Summer faded into fall, but life continued on as normal for most people, while he had been in the hospital for the last three months.

When Glenn pulled into the driveway, Bryan smiled at the sight of Grandpa Carroll standing on the porch. He leaned heavily on his canes, but straightened up quickly when he saw them arrive. Once Glenn parked, he removed Bryan's wheelchair from the trunk and carefully transferred Bryan from the car to the chair.

"What took you so long?" Grandpa teased.

"Hey, Dad!" Glenn waved. "He's all yours."

Bryan looked from his dad to his grandpa, who winked in response to Bryan's confused expression.

Once Glenn got both Bryan and Grandpa situated in the living room, he disappeared to work on the yard. Grandpa removed a catalog from inside his jacket and placed it on Bryan's lap. Bryan looked down and his confused expression transformed into a smile.

"What's this for?" he asked.

"Well," Grandpa began, "after you placed fifth in that troubleshooting contest at school, they sent this catalog over for a discount on tools."

"I remember," Bryan said thoughtfully.

"Then you got in that accident so we never had a chance to order any car tools yet. I figured we better do that before that discount expires."

Bryan's eyes lit up, and then he paused. "I don't really have money for tools right now, Grandpa. Besides," he said, looking at his coned hands. "We don't even know if I'll be able to use them again."

"Just in case, I'm buying." Grandpa winked.

Bryan's jaw dropped briefly. He hungrily eyed all the tools as Grandpa flipped through the pages. Grandpa dog-eared several pages until they had created quite a long wish list.

"You have $500 to spend," Grandpa said, after they began combing the pages for a second time.

Bryan's jaw dropped, but this time he didn't recover as quickly. "Are you serious? Grandpa, that's very generous of you, but that's a lot of money."

"I wouldn't offer it if I didn't have it," he stated matter-of-factly. "Now go ahead and pick out your tools."

CHAPTER TEN

"The future belongs to those who believe in the beauty of their dreams."

- Eleanor Roosevelt

"Shhh, be quiet! We don't want her hearing us."

"I got it. Let's go."

Bryan had to bite his lip to prevent from laughing as he and his roommate Danny gradually pushed Nedra's narcotics cart along the floor. They had to go slow, as her back was turned and they didn't want her to hear them. Danny had even less functionality than Bryan, so they pinned the cart between their two chairs and slowly rolled it down the hall. Bryan drove on the opposite side of the cart, keeping it steady with his outstretched arm. As soon as they made it out to the hallway, it was a race to the elevators. Danny bumped the up button and as soon as the door opened, they shoved the cart inside.

Nedra hurried out of the room, looking around desperately. As soon as she saw them at the end of the hall, she broke into a run.

"BRYAN! DANNY! YOU BRING THAT BACK TO ME RIGHT NOW!"

They both yelled in surprise. "Close! Come on, close!" Bryan screamed.

As if on command, the elevator doors creaked closed just in time and the lift went up to open on another floor for someone else in the hospital. Nedra came running up just a second too late.

"Augh! You boys are awful!" she yelled, smashing her fist into the closed elevator doors. She punched the up button, hoping her cart would still be there when the doors opened. It wasn't. Bryan and Danny rolled away as fast as possible in opposite directions so if she came after them, only one would have to die. Luckily for them, finding the narcotics was far more important. They could hear Nedra screaming and cursing at them even after the doors had closed and she was moving away.

They laughed as they rolled back to their bedroom. They were going to have to sleep with one eye open tonight.

"I feel like I haven't seen you in forever," Jana said, kissing Bryan again. "School is the pits. I thought senior year was going to be the best, but I'm so busy I feel like I never have time for anything else."

"I've really missed you, too," Bryan said. "Thankfully I still have your poster and picture up to help me think about you every day." He indicated the puppy poster she gave him when he first came to the hospital. It now hung in the window near his bed along with a large picture of Jana.

"So tell me about school. I never thought I'd say this, but I sort of miss it. Maybe it's just the quiet monotony of being here every day."

Jana laughed. "You? Miss school? Did they check for brain damage when they did your x-rays?"

"Ha, ha."

Bryan was about to say something else when Nedra walked into the room. She glanced at Bryan and scowled before walking past. She had been off the last couple days, so he hadn't seen her since the prank. Now he got very quiet, not sure of what to say.

"What's going on?" Jana asked, looking between them.

"Nothing," Bryan said, trying to sound innocent.

Jana didn't buy it. "What did you do?"

"I . . . uh . . . I may have stolen her narcotics cart a couple days ago and sent it for a ride on the elevator," he said, smiling sheepishly.

"You what? Bryan! That could have been really dangerous! What if it fell into the wrong hands?"

"Busted!" Danny whispered from the next bed.

"Shut up!" Bryan grinned. "You were there, too."

"He may have been there, but that prank has Bryan Carroll written all over it," Jana said. She glared at Bryan with her arms folded and her eyebrows raised expectantly.

"All right," Bryan sighed. "Bring her over here."

Bryan could hear Danny chuckling beside him as Jana got up and crossed the room to where Nedra was standing.

"Excuse me, Nedra?"

She turned around slowly. "Yes, Jana?"

"Could you come over here for a minute, please? Bryan has something he'd like to say to you."

Nedra sighed and approached the foot of Bryan's bed. Both women stood, arms folded, glowering down at him.

"I'm sorry we pulled that prank on you the other night," Bryan mumbled.

"You should be! Thankfully another nurse saw the cart come up and grabbed it for me before another patient found it."

"I'm really sorry. We didn't mean to get you in trouble."

"And you'll never do it again," Jana said.

"What? Aw, man!"

Nedra raised her eyebrows, her lips pursed in a firm line.

Bryan rolled his eyes and sighed. "And I'll never do it again," he said.

"Fine," Nedra said curtly before returning to her other patient.

"You can be a real stinker sometimes, you know that?" Jana said, sitting back down beside him on the bed.

"Yeah, but that's why you love me," Bryan said with an impish grin.

Jana laughed. "That I do." She leaned over and began kissing him again.

Nedra walked up several minutes later. "I just need to empty his leg bag and do a quick vitals check, and then you can get back to . . . that," Nedra said with a wave of her hand.

Jana stood up, blushing. "Sorry," she said.

"Hey, Nedra," Danny spoke up. "I'm really very sorry for that horrible prank we played on you the other night. We thought it would just be goofy and fun, but I realize now the ramifications of my actions and how dangerous it really could have been. I'm so sorry and I hope you will forgive me."

Nedra smiled and bent over to give Danny a hug. "Thank you, Danny," she said, sniffling. "You just made my night so much better."

"Now that was a sincere apology," Jana said. Then she turned to Bryan and whacked him on the chest.

"Ow! What was that for?" he asked.

"Oh, you couldn't feel it anyway," she said.

"True, but you still hit me," he said, jutting out his bottom lip and pouting.

Bryan looked over at Danny, who stuck his tongue out at him. Bryan quickly turned his head to see if either of the ladies had seen that but they were, of course, looking the other way.

Jana spoke up, "So, Nedra, Bryan has been here for several months now and is doing much better with his wheelchair and his arm strength. I feel like I need to start learning how to take care of him after he's home. How do I go about doing that?"

"Well, as the patients become more and more comfortable with getting around, we start taking them out so they can become adjusted to normal life again. He's going to need to learn how to maneuver around people in a crowded restaurant and things like that. And yes, you're going to need practice with feeding him and dressing him and those everyday things."

Jana looked at her, surprised. "So I can take him out of the hospital for a night?"

"Yeah." Nedra nodded. "I think Bryan is about ready for a break from this place. It would be wise to take a nurse with you, too, so she can show you the ropes and teach you what to do. It can be overwhelming the first time on your own."

"That would be amazing!" Jana said, clapping her hands excitedly. "Could you go next week?"

"Me?" Nedra asked. She started to shake her head. "Oh, I don't know. Can you find another nurse to go?"

"Please! I haven't really gotten to know any of the other nurses as well as you. Come on, it'll be fun!"

Nedra sighed, looking down at Bryan. "Oh, all right."

"Yay!" Jana jumped up and hugged her. Nedra stood stiffly for a moment and then awkwardly patted Jana on the back.

"I have Thursday night off," she said. "Does that work for you?"

"Yes! I will be here." Jana nodded enthusiastically. "Where should we go?"

"The mountains!" Bryan spoke up. "Please, I haven't been outside in my beautiful Utah mountains in so long." He almost sounded desperate.

"Okay." Nedra smiled. "I know a spot up American Fork canyon called Cascade Springs. It's beautiful up there, especially this time of year with all the fall leaves. And the hiking trail is nice and wide, and wheelchair accessible," she added.

"Sounds perfect." Bryan grinned. He couldn't wait to go.

"It's a date then!" Jana said, her smile just as wide as Bryan's. "I'll see you soon," she added, kissing him goodbye.

Oh, goodie, a date, Nedra thought. *That won't be awkward at all with me as your third wheel.*

Nedra began preparing her patients for bed shortly after Jana left. J.D. and Art could both do a lot for themselves, but Danny and Bryan needed more help. Sometimes it felt like she was the cute, older babysitter trying to persuade a group of rowdy brothers to settle down and get to bed before their parents came home. J.D. cruised around the room, challenging the other guys to wheelchair battles. He stopped very quickly when he bashed into Nedra's ankles and she gave him the death glare.

"Sorry, Nedra!" He backed up very quickly and settled down for bed.

Nedra reached for the stereo and turned on some music. A loud, upbeat Kiss song was playing. Bryan grinned. "Oh, man, I love this song!" he said. Nedra quickly changed the station until she found some much quieter Kenny Rogers. Bryan made a face.

"Will you change this, please?" he asked, grimacing.

"No way. You boys need something to calm you down." Nedra closed her eyes and started to sing along.

"You're making me wish that accident had killed me," Bryan said. He squeezed his eyes shut as though he were in pain. Nedra turned the music up louder.

"Oh please, make it stop! What happened to our deal?"

"Hmmm," Nedra said, standing over him and smiling wickedly. "I think that deal was broken when you took my narcotics cart for a joyride."

Bryan pretended to be in anguish. "All right, uncle, uncle! You win. I'll never steal your cart again. Just please, make it stop!"

Nedra switched the music off and Bryan breathed out a sigh of relief. "Thank goodness," he mumbled.

Nedra smiled at him. "You big baby."

Bryan laughed.

Once all four of them were tucked in bed, Nedra went around the room and kissed them each goodnight on the forehead. When she came to Bryan she paused.

"Truce?" she asked.

"Truce," he agreed.

She bent down to kiss his forehead and Bryan moved his head up quickly so that she kissed him square on the lips. He kissed her back. Nedra's cheeks flushed and she pulled away quickly, her eyes wide with shock. She looked around to make sure the other guys hadn't noticed. Thankfully no one saw.

"Uh-goodnight," she stammered. She tried to leave the room, realized she was facing the wrong direction, then quickly turned and stumbled out the door.

"Goodnight." Bryan smiled happily. His lips still tingled from their kiss, lingering in a way Jana's never had before.

"Aw, man, y'all aren't gonna believe this," J.D. said, pulling away from the window. "Prince Charmin' is out there tryin' to woo that cute secretary."

Art and Danny wheeled over to the window and looked out. "Oh, dude, it's that cute blonde one!"

"The guy doesn't stand a chance."

"What does he think he's doing? I thought he had a girlfriend."

"He wants to keep his options open, I guess," said J.D. with a smile.

"Player," Art mumbled, grinning.

Bryan looked up from his lunch out on the hospital terrace and saw his roommates watching. He waggled his eyebrows at them and then looked back at his date. She was a really cute girl, with short blonde hair and a bright smile. She worked the main reception desk downstairs. All the guys had their eye on her, but it was Bryan who had enough guts to ask if she wanted to have lunch with him. She held his sandwich up for him to take another bite. He chewed carefully and realized, cute as she was, he couldn't help but wish Nedra were the one feeding him instead. When he noticed his audience was still watching, he stuck out his tongue at them. They laughed and finally moved away from the window.

When Bryan rolled back into his room thirty minutes later, the other guys hooted and cheered. Bryan smiled at them in return.

"So . . . what's the story there?" Art asked.

"Tryin' to get a little somethin', somethin' while the Mrs. is away, huh?" laughed J.D., pointing to Jana's picture.

"Oh, come on," Danny piped in. "Give the guy a break."

"Thank you," Bryan said.

"It's not like he stands a chance with her anyway!"

Bryan gave Danny a dirty look while the other two hooted with laughter.

"All right, all right, tell us how this came about."

"I just wanted to test the waters, ya know? See if I still had a chance with women, even with a broken neck."

"But what about Jana?"

"Well, Jana cared about me before I broke my neck, so that doesn't really count. I just wanted to see if I could get a woman's interest like this."

"So she was an experiment?"

"Exactly."

"Sooo, did you try and make a move? You know, in the name of science."

"I don't have to tell you guys anything," Bryan answered smugly. "I'll just let you sit and wallow in your jealousy."

Bryan rolled back out of the room. The laughter followed him all the way down the hall. "That means he got shot down!" he heard one of them yell.

CHAPTER ELEVEN

"What matters is how you choose to live from this moment forward. Your past doesn't define you, your decisions do."

-Jaime Heiner

Is that true?" Nedra asked, looking at the puppy poster Jana had given him. It said, 'A hug would make my day.'

"Absolutely," Bryan responded.

Nedra held her arms out and Bryan threw his own arms around her neck. She hugged him tightly before using the hold to transfer him to his chair.

"That was sneaky," Bryan laughed.

"You better believe it," Nedra joked. "So, you ready to go?"

"Yes!" Bryan could hardly contain his excitement. "I wonder where Jana is."

"I'm sure she'll be here soon. Let's get you loaded into the car and then we'll be ready for her when she arrives."

The black phone beside Bryan's bed started ringing. Nedra picked it up and stretched the cord as far as it would go to place the receiver in Bryan's hand.

"Hello? Oh, hey Jana, you running late?"

Nedra watched as Bryan's happy smile faded and his eyes drooped.

"No, I understand. I hope you feel better. Bye."

"Not coming, huh?"

Bryan shook his head. "She's not feeling well. She needs to stay home and rest." He looked defeated.

"Well, we can still go if you want."

Bryan perked up. "Really?"

"Yeah, why not? I already have the night off. I'm ready to go, and you're ready to go . . ." She trailed off.

"Yes! Let's go!"

"All right." Nedra clapped her hands, grabbed the handles behind Bryan's manual chair, and pushed him down the hall toward the elevators.

Once they reached the parking lot, Nedra pushed Bryan a little faster to the car to avoid the bitter breeze. Nedra unlocked her Mazda sedan and turned the key until the engine rumbled. She reached over and turned the heat knob all the way up, and then climbed back out to lift Bryan into the passenger seat. Reaching across him, she buckled his seatbelt and made sure he was secure. She folded up his wheelchair and carefully lifted it into the trunk. She climbed back inside and looked to Bryan as she buckled her own seatbelt.

"You ready?" she asked.

"Let's do this."

She smiled and pulled out of the parking lot.

"So tell me about your family," she said after they had been driving for a few minutes. "Your grandpa seems to come by almost as much as your parents. Are you two really close?"

"Very close. My dad is the youngest of four kids. His next oldest sibling is ten years his senior. So I'm his youngest grandson by quite a stretch. We're very similar in a lot of ways and we have a lot in common. My grandpa was a huge part of my life growing up. He took me fishing where I caught my first fish, he offered a sanctuary whenever I needed a break from my parents or my sisters, and he even saved my life once."

"He what? What happened?"

"Well, maybe not saved my life, but at the time it felt like it. When I was younger, my sister Becky and I used to deliver the Penny Savers. Most of the time, we would just split up the route. She would do half and I would go the opposite direction and do the other half. My sister Brenda would help Becky a lot of the time and every once in awhile my grandpa would drive me around my route. One day, he was driving me and I went up to the porch. As I was hanging the paper on their door handle, this huge dog came around the side of the house. He lunged at me and started biting me, grabbing ahold of one of my legs. I was screaming for help when my grandpa got out of the car, pulled out his cane and started beating the dog off me with it. The dog yelped and ran off."

"Wow. Scary! So are you afraid of dogs?"

"Oh, no, not at all. I love dogs. I'm not much of a cat person, though."

"Really? I have seven."

"You have seven cats?"

"Yes."

"Why?"

"I just love animals! I live alone and I have the means to take care of them, so I figured why not give as many a home as I can?"

"That's nice." Bryan paused. "What about your family?" he asked. "Are you close to any of your grandparents?"

"No. My grandparents all died when I was very young. The only memory I have of my grandma is every Christmas when we would dress up really nice and eat a fancy dinner on her finest china. I used to love that tradition. I hope to do it with my own family some day."

"And you're from California?"

"Born and raised!"

"So what brought you to Utah, then?"

"Well, I decided to get out on my own for college. I graduated from Brigham Young University and then right after graduation, the University of Utah was hiring, so I just stayed and I've been here ever since." She shrugged. "You planning on college?" she asked.

"You know, I've never really thought about it. I've always wanted to be a mechanic and work with cars, so college was never in the plans for me. I guess now, given the circumstances, it might be something to consider." Bryan got quiet as he contemplated the new options that now lay before him. "So how many siblings do you have?" he asked.

"Just one older brother," Nedra answered. "Daddy's name is Arden, so my brother is Arden junior, but we've always just called him Randy. That's how they got my name too. Nedra is Arden spelled backwards."

"Huh." Bryan had to think about it for a moment, trying to put the letters backwards in his mind. "That's clever."

"I think so. So are you named after anyone?"

"Bryan? No, my parents just liked it. My middle name is Louis, same as my dad's middle name."

"My middle name is Jane, same as my mother's name. So I'm named after both my parents."

"I like that. When I have a son, his middle name will be Mayo."

"Mayo?"

"That's my grandpa's name."

"It's an interesting name. How do you spell it?"

"M-A-Y-O."

"So just like the . . ."

"Yup, just like the condiment. He's actually named after a county in Ireland. His parents, my great-grandparents, were immigrants from Ireland."

"Oh, very cool. Carroll does sound like a pretty Irish name."

"Yeah, I think it actually used to be O'Carroll back in the day."

Nedra glanced at him and smiled before looking back to the road.

"What?" Bryan asked.

"That's just one of the things I love most about you," she said, cocking her head to glance at him again.

"What?" he asked again.

"You didn't say *if* I have a son, you said *when*. Everything with you is when, not if. You have no doubts about your future. Sometimes I wonder if you even remember that you're paralyzed."

Bryan grinned. "It crosses my mind now and then."

"I think that's part of the reason why you're doing so well," Nedra added. "Your positive outlook and can-do attitude really seem to be what's propelling your recovery."

"What else am I supposed to do? Lay in bed and wallow in self-pity?" he asked, crinkling his nose. "That sounds boring. And like a waste of time."

"You'd be surprised how many do, though. And trust me, their recovery time is a lot slower than yours."

They talked easily the whole drive. Before they knew it, an hour had passed and Nedra was pulling into the parking lot. The park didn't appear to be too busy, so she quickly found a parking spot on the front row, closest to the trails.

After parking, she unloaded Bryan and then pushed him up to the rough, wooden sign with arrows pointing to the different trails.

"Wow, it's chilly out here," Bryan said.

"I guess this is your first time really getting outside since the accident, isn't it? Well, since your limbs don't move much anymore, your blood doesn't circulate like it used to," she explained, throwing a heavy blanket over him. "Let me know if you get too cold and we'll leave. This is just one more thing you're going to have to get used to."

Bryan was cold, but he was far too excited to be out to turn back now. Nedra chose the simplest path and began pushing Bryan forward. The pathways were a combination of wide, wooden planks and concrete. They would be talking as Nedra pushed him along on the smooth concrete, then Bryan's voice would suddenly start vibrating whenever they passed over the bumpy wood.

He loved the cool, crisp mountain air. He had been breathing nothing but sterile hospital air mixed with chemicals for months now. He had almost forgotten how clean fresh air could be. They couldn't have picked a better time to come. The leaves were just starting to change for fall. Surrounded by all the different shades of red, orange, and yellow, Bryan felt as though he were staring at a huge painting. They came to a quaint bridge on the path, which went right over the top of a beautiful, blue spring. Nedra pushed him over the bridge, where they stopped in the middle to look down. Several moss covered rocks popped up all over in the spring, with a yellow plant top waving just above the water. The colors reflected beautifully in the white, foamy water as it ran beneath their feet.

Bryan took another deep breath, this time his throat stinging from the bitter air. The temperature dropped quickly with the setting sun. Bryan fought within himself for several minutes before his goosebumps and shallow breath won out.

"We better go," he finally managed to get out.

By the time they made it back to the car, Bryan was shivering. Nedra threw another cover over him and cranked the heat in her Mazda. "Do you want to drive around a little more?" she asked.

"Yes!" Bryan responded enthusiastically.

Nedra pulled the car into drive and they traveled along a narrow loop, enjoying the stunning mountains, trees, and springs surrounding them. As it started to get later, and despite Bryan's protests, Nedra finally turned the car around and started for home.

"It's probably too late for me to shave you once we get back. I guess you'll have to be scruffy for a couple days," Nedra said.

Bryan made a face, but he knew she was right. The others were probably already asleep. "O-kay," he said slowly.

"What? You'll wear a mustache, but you don't like a little scruff?

"It's way too itchy, and I can't scratch it. Far too irritating."

"Oh, I'm sorry, I didn't really think about it being itchy. I guess that makes sense."

"I'm sure a lot of it has to do with how I was raised, too. My mom was very staunch about me being clean shaven and having short hair. That's one of the things we used to fight over all the time. I like my hair a little shaggy, but she wanted it very short."

"Really? I like your hair shaggy," Nedra said, glancing over at him.

"Well, thanks. I guess my mom will get her way when I move home again. I'm sure she'll cut it first thing."

"When we get married, you can keep your hair as long as you'd like," Nedra assured him.

Realizing what she said, Nedra's face turned beet red. She didn't dare look at Bryan, who had suddenly become very quiet. She bit her lip and stared straight ahead, unblinking, until her eyes became so dry she could hardly see.

Bryan's thoughts were going all over the place as he tried to figure out what had inspired her to say such a thing. Was she joking? Did she really like him? Did she want to marry him? He didn't know how to respond, so he didn't. The longer they sat in silence, the more awkward the drive became. Nedra reached forward and turned the radio up, hoping the music would fill the awkward silence. "Babe" by Styx started playing. Nedra wanted to sing along, but she couldn't convince her mouth to open. When they finally arrived back at the hospital, Nedra wouldn't look Bryan in the eyes. She reached across his body to unbuckle his seat belt, but continued to avoid any eye contact. She slid her arms underneath him and prepared to lift when Bryan broke the silence.

"Nedra," he finally whispered. "Look at me."

"I can't," she shook her head. "I'm too embarrassed."

"Did you mean what you said?" he asked.

Nedra's cheeks flushed again, but she finally looked him straight in the face and nodded slowly.

He smiled back at her and whispered, "I love you, too."

CHAPTER TWELVE

"Our challenges don't define us. Our actions do."

- Michael J. Fox,

The Michael J. Fox Foundation

Bryan couldn't stop grinning the next day as he stretched and lifted during physical therapy. Normally he grunted and groaned while he tried to lift the large medical ball off his lap and then set it down again. But this morning, even with the additional weight Dr. Estrada assigned him, Bryan was all smiles.

"What's up?" Art asked after watching him for several minutes.

"What do you mean?" Bryan asked coyly.

"Don't play dumb. You know exactly what I'm asking."

"Nedra kissed me last night."

"Dang, boy, you really are a player!"

"No, I'm not just playin'. I'm in love with her, and I think she loves me, too."

Art's mouth opened in surprise, but no words came out for a moment. "Seriously?"

"Yes, seriously! We talked a lot last night and I really could picture a future with her."

Art shook his head. "Well, I'm happy for you then. But wait, what about your girlfriend?"

"I really do love Jana. She's been here for me since the accident. She's been my rock and is a huge part of why I haven't just given up, but I feel like we've grown apart these last couple months. Sometimes I think she's staying with me now out of duty and not because she wants to. I don't know, I can't really explain it. I think she'll be relieved, at least a little bit."

"You really think so?"

"I don't know. Maybe I'm just being hopeful."

"Well, my advice would be to break up with her sooner rather than later, if that's what you're going to do."

"I know. But how do you break up with your best friend?"

"I dunno, man. Good luck!" Art wheeled away to work on some of his own exercises.

When Bryan went back to his room, Nedra was there, changing J.D.'s bandages. Bryan grinned sheepishly.

"Hey," he said.

"Hi, Bryan," she responded. "How was physical therapy?"

"Great!"

"That's good."

They smiled at each other, neither sure what to say next.

"Look, y'all, my butt is hangin' out here for all the world to see. Think you could save your chattin' for later?"

"Yeah, you better get your butt good and bandaged so I can kick it later when we have our wheelchair races."

"You're dreamin'. I'm gonna cream ya!"

"You boys better put your race plans aside. You've got a performer coming to put on a show for you tonight."

"What kind of performer?" Bryan asked.

"I think it's a magician," Nedra said. Turning to J.D., she added, "There you are, J.D. You're modest again, not that that's ever stopped you before."

"Thank you, ma'am," he said, tipping his cowboy hat. He rolled his gurney through the room, pausing next to Bryan. "So what's with you and Nedra? Y'all experimentin' too?" he whispered.

It took Bryan a second to realize what he meant. "No, no, it's not like that," he said.

"You sure? 'Cause I ain't never seen the two of you act so polite and awkward before."

"I really like her," Bryan admitted.

J.D. thought this was the most amusing thing he'd ever heard. He started laughing loudly while Bryan told him to shut up.

"Oh, boy, you better make up your mind or all these pretty ladies ain't gonna stick around for ya." J.D. rolled away quickly, laughing as he left the room. "I'll meet ya downstairs," he said, waving.

"Yeah, bye." Bryan was frustrated with the reaction he was getting from the other guys. "Do you ever get to go home?" Bryan asked as he watched Nedra cleaning up around J.D.'s bed. "It seems like you're always here."

"Well, being the assistant head nurse, I end up covering a lot of shifts. I don't mind, though. I like my job. Why do you ask? You getting sick of me?" She smiled playfully.

"Not at all." Bryan returned the smile.

Nedra threw away the extra wrappings and garbage and then walked slowly towards Bryan, pausing right in front of him. Bryan wished more than anything that he could reach out and pull her into him. She seemed to read his mind and stepped closer.

"Do you want to come to the show with me?" Bryan asked.

Nedra bent down and kissed him lightly on the lips. "This is one of those rare moments when I'm actually getting off and about to go home." Bryan looked disappointed. "I could stop by for a minute before I leave," she said.

"Thanks. I'll save you a seat." Bryan followed his roommates out the door.

Nedra smiled to herself as she finished cleaning up. She then hurried downstairs to join the others.

Bryan grinned when Nedra entered the room. She briskly walked passed the other patients and settled into a chair beside Bryan. Nedra rested her hand on top of his as the magician got up and began performing for them. She pulled his fingers straight and weaved her hand with his. When the other guys saw them holding hands, they didn't laugh this time. They all kept glancing at Bryan and Nedra, who were unknowingly stealing the show.

Nedra and Bryan went out whenever she had a night off. They went to movies, out to dinner, and sometimes just drove around and talked. Jana became busier with school and since Bryan didn't want to break up with her over the phone, she still didn't know.

On Halloween morning, the air was cool and crisp, and a light layer of frost painted the ground outside. Bryan looked out his window and shivered.

"I guess we won't be going outside much anymore," he said to no one in particular.

He heard a cheerful laugh outside his door and Carol Jean entered the room. Bryan immediately threw his covers over his head and pretended to go back to sleep. "Just kill me now," he mumbled.

Carol Jean wore neon green leggings and a huge, round, bright orange pumpkin costume around her middle. She carried a jack-o-lantern bowl filled with candy and skipped from bed to bed, tipping her brown, stem hat at each of the patients and offering them a treat.

"Oh Bry-an!" she sang. "Trick or treat!"

Bryan continued to pretend he wasn't there even though the huge lump on his bed was a dead giveaway.

"Go away." He tried to shoo her with his left arm while keeping the rest of his body covered by blankets. "I don't know you, crazy lady. Please leave me alone."

"Oh, you big party pooper!" she said, shaking her head. She held the bowl out for Danny. "Would you like a treat, Danny?"

"Yes, please! Thank you, Mrs. Carroll. Can I have a Reese's?"

Carol Jean opened the chocolate for Danny and put it in his mouth. She skipped over to J.D.'s bed. "How about you? Would you like a Halloween treat?"

"Why, I'd love some. Thank you, ma'am!"

Art eagerly waited for his turn. When Carol Jean brought him the bowl, he asked for some M&M's. She happily poured a bunch onto his outstretched tongue.

"These are my favorite," he happily said through a full mouth.

"Any of you boys want to come with me? I'm going to the other rooms on this floor too."

"I'll escort you, ma'am," J.D. said, wheeling forward. "Just lead the way."

"Last chance," Carol Jean said, looking at Bryan.

"Oh, all right, I'd love a Snickers," he said begrudgingly.

"Well, don't sound too excited about it," Carol Jean said as she opened his wrapper. "Goodness gracious, you'd think I was trying to give you a shot or something instead of chocolate." She popped the candy bar in his mouth and rolled her eyes.

"Do you have to dress like that?"

"It's Halloween! You're the one who looks ridiculous."

Bryan had to smile at that. His mom soon left the room to spread more chocolate and cheer among the other patients.

"Your mom is a hoot!" Nedra entered his room a short time later carrying a candy bar from Carol Jean.

"Yeah . . ." Bryan sighed.

"Oh, come on, she's helping to brighten this place up."

"By wearing a crazy costume and embarrassing me."

"You really are a party pooper."

Bryan tossed his arms around Nedra's neck and she helped him into his wheelchair for the day. "Come to the PT room with me. I wanna show you something."

"I'm not done with my rounds." Nedra held up her clipboard.

"Oh, come on, it will just take a sec."

"I really should get this done first," she said.

"Now who's being the party pooper?" he teased, his eyes challenging her.

"Fine." Nedra set her clipboard down and followed Bryan as he zipped through the hallway. His arms were getting stronger and faster at pushing his wheelchair every day.

Bryan sped up to one of the long, firm beds and Nedra helped him transfer out of his chair again. Bryan settled himself in the center of the bed and carefully positioned his arms on either side of his body.

"Watch this," he said. With tightened lips and a furrowed brow, Bryan concentrated all his effort on lifting himself off the bed. His arms shook slightly, but slowly, his bottom raised off the bed an inch, and then two inches. Bryan's arms shook harder and he dropped back down with a grunt.

Nedra stood back, her eyes wide and bright. "Wow! Nice work!" she said, rushing forward to hug him. "You'll be transferring yourself from bed to chair in no time!"

Bryan smiled, but it took all the energy he had. "I've been working really hard the last week to show you that. My arms are definitely getting stronger."

"That's incredible. There'll be no stopping you now! I better finish up my shift. Do you want me to help you back in your chair?"

"No, I think I'll work some more for awhile," he breathed heavily.

"Just don't overdo it," Nedra said.

Bryan smiled innocently. "Who, me?"

That night Bryan lay in bed watching Halloween movies on TV. He felt a little lonely. Halloween was a huge deal in his family, as Carol Jean demonstrated earlier that day. He laughed at the memory of her prancing around in bright green and orange. Every Halloween, for as long as he could remember, he and his sisters would go trick-or-treating together. As they got older, they would go with their friends or to parties. No matter what plans they had, at 9:00 p.m. that night, everyone came back to the Carroll's house for homemade spudnuts and hot apple cider. Bryan glanced up at the small round clock that hung by the door. He squinted to see the hands in the dark. It was 8:30. He was thirty minutes away from missing the big party. The thing he loved most about their tradition was everyone was invited. His friends always came along, in full costume, and never complained about having to hang out with his family. Carol Jean was a hostess through and through. She loved nothing more than having a horde of people at her house enjoying each other's company.

Around 9:30, Bryan heard a knock at his door. He had started to doze and needed to blink a few times to see clearly. A cute little witch in a black cloak dashed through the room and climbed onto Bryan's bed. Grandpa Carroll followed closely behind her, carrying a plate of spudnuts. At least Bryan hoped they were spudnuts. From the tantalizing smell, he couldn't imagine they were anything else. He quickly perked up.

Jenny pulled down her hat and cackled at Bryan, her green fingers wiggling in his face in an effort to look threatening.

"Oh, no! Save me, Grandpa, from the scary witch!"

Jenny giggled and pulled off her hat. "No, Bryan, it's just me!"

"Jenny, is that you? Wow, your costume really fooled me. Now give me a hug--I've missed you, kiddo!"

Jenny wrapped her small hands around Bryan and squeezed. "I miss you, too! When are you coming home?"

"The doctor thinks I might be home in time for Christmas."

"Really?" Jenny sat up. "Yay!"

"Here, Jenny, why don't you feed your brother one of these spudnuts while they're still warm? Your dad will be back to pick us up in just a little bit."

Bryan's mouth watered. "They're still warm?"

"Yup. Your mom gave us a fresh batch here and demanded I put them next to the heater in the car so you could have a warm one."

Bryan opened his mouth wide and Jenny shoved almost the entire spudnut inside.

"Whoa! Whoa! Just hold it out so your brother can take bites."

"Whoops."

Bryan's eyes widened as he tried to chew the mass. It was still delicious, but he couldn't respond to Grandpa around so much chewing. Once he finally had the entire thing eaten, he smiled at them both. "Thanks for visiting! And thank you for bringing the spudnuts. I was missing them tonight."

"We figured you might be." Grandpa smiled. "I tried to come on my own, but this little lady wouldn't have it."

Jenny smiled proudly, and then reached for another spudnut for herself.

"Haven't you had enough?" Grandpa asked. "I thought these ones were for Bryan and his friends."

Jenny giggled again and pushed the rest of hers into her mouth. "All gone," she said, displaying her empty hands. Grandpa chuckled and shook his head as he turned to Danny. "Would you like one?" Grandpa stood carefully, with support from his canes, and gestured toward the plate.

"What's a spudnut?" Danny asked, sucking in a deep breath of the sugary sweet aroma.

"They're homemade doughnuts, basically," Bryan answered. "My mom uses potato flour instead of regular flour.

"Yeah, I'd love one!"

"Jenny, would you go feed one to Danny, please?" Bryan coaxed his little sister. She jumped from his lap and grabbed one from the plate Grandpa offered.

"Remember, let him take bites," he added. Jenny nodded. She walked slowly toward Danny, looking back at Bryan.

"It's okay, he won't bite."

Jenny glanced up at Danny, who smiled at her. As she held the spudnut toward his mouth, Danny growled softly. Jenny jumped back and, seeing the wide smile on Danny's face, she giggled and offered him a bite.

"Wow, this is incredible," Danny said, licking his lips clean. "Do we really have to save some for the other two knuckleheads?" He looked across the room at their empty beds.

"Where are they?" Grandpa asked.

"A resident took them out tonight. Thought they'd be back by now."

"That just means more for us," Danny said, eyeing the plate eagerly.

Jenny followed Danny's eyes to the plate and began feeding him a second spudnut.

"So how are you? Anything new to report?"

Bryan smiled. "Do you remember Nedra?"

Grandpa raised his eyebrows. "Isn't she one of your nurses?"

"Yeah." Bryan's eyes lit up at the mention of her, which Grandpa noticed.

"What about Jana?" he whispered, looking to make sure Jenny wasn't listening. She was busy talking to Danny.

"I don't know. Things started to feel a little forced with Jana and me. Right about the same time Nedra started showing interest."

"So you two are what, dating?"

"I'm in love with her, Grandpa."

"What are you talking about?" Jenny asked, climbing back onto Bryan's bed.

"Do you remember my nurse, Nedra?" Bryan asked her.

Jenny thought for a moment, tapping her chin with her index finger. "Oh, yeah, is she the old one?"

"She's not old!"

Grandpa looked at Bryan, his eyes wide with question.

"She's ten years older than me," Bryan muttered.

Grandpa whistled. "So that means she's only ten years younger than your mom?"

"I guess. But it's not like that matters. I grew up a lot that day on the beach."

"It's true," Grandpa said, nodding. "You did."

Bryan pursed his lips. "Other than you thinking she's old, what else do you think of Nedra?" he asked again.

Jenny shrugged. "She's nice. She told me she has lots of cats. Can we go see her cats? I can't have a cat. Can I go play with hers?"

Bryan smiled. "I'll ask."

Jenny turned and looked at the plate of quickly disappearing spudnuts. "Are you going to finish those?" she asked.

CHAPTER THIRTEEN

"The foolish man seeks happiness in the distance; the wise grows it under his feet."

-James Oppenheim

"You know what I realized today?" Nedra asked. "You haven't played any practical jokes on me in awhile." She nuzzled her head under Bryan's chin and waited for his response. They were back at her house after going out to dinner. She helped situate Bryan on the large beanbag chair, and then positioned herself in front of him so Bryan could wrap his arms around her. It was getting late, but they were comfortable cuddling and neither had the motivation to leave yet.

"I'm afraid if I did, you'd break up with me," Bryan said.

"Oh, are we going steady?" Nedra prodded him with her finger. "'Cause last time I checked, you still haven't broken up with your current girlfriend."

Bryan flushed red. "I know, I know! I just don't have the heart to do it!" he said.

"What are you waiting for—our golden anniversary? 'Cause I'm pretty sure the longer you wait, it's not going to get any easier."

Bryan sighed. "I know. She just hasn't really been around a whole lot lately. And I really don't want to lose her friendship. I care a lot about Jana. My family cares a lot about

Jana. I'm pretty sure my mom told her once that if we ever broke up, she was adopting Jana and getting rid of me!"

"Look, I know this is hard for you, and I know she means a lot to you, but you aren't doing her any favors by waiting either." Nedra rubbed the back of his hand with her thumb as she spoke in a soothing voice. She turned her body to face him and leaned in for a kiss when the phone in her kitchen rang loudly. Nedra jumped, causing her and Bryan's foreheads to collide. "Sorry!" she said, getting up and rubbing her aching head with her hand.

"It's okay," Bryan said, blinking slowly. "Is it the hospital, wondering what you've done with me?" he joked. He quieted quickly when he saw the look on Nedra's face. "Ned? Is everything okay?" he whispered.

Nedra put up her hand to shush him. Her eyes grew wide; her skin blanched. Her hand flew to cover her mouth as she choked back a sob. She whispered her goodbye and walked toward the chair. She sat back down but continued to stare straight ahead at the blank wall.

"Nedra, are you okay?" he asked, wrapping his arms around her slowly.

"My dad died," she whispered.

Bryan tightened his grip. "Oh, Nedra, I'm so sorry!"

Nedra sat stiffly, unable to fully process the startling news. Bryan continued to sit quietly and hold her. He didn't say a word; he just held her and waited until she was ready. Several minutes passed and neither spoke. Nedra slowly started to lean into him until she completely melted into his chest. Bryan held her so tightly his muscles ached, but still, he didn't let her go. Nedra finally laid her head on Bryan and began sobbing into his chest. Once she allowed the tears to come, they continued in steady streams. Through her tears and ragged breathing, Nedra shared all her memories of her father, both good and bad. Bryan couldn't make out all the words she told him, but he continued to listen quietly and he never loosened his grip.

The longer Nedra talked, the more Bryan realized he never wanted to stop listening and he never wanted to let her go. His face flushed, his ears burned, and the hair on the back of his neck stood up. A huge lump formed in his throat as somewhere deep inside him. He needed to make Nedra his forever. He licked his suddenly dry and chapped lips, waiting quietly for a break in the conversation. Nedra grew quiet and her crying softened. Bryan cleared his throat and whispered, "Will you marry me?"

Nedra whipped around so fast, her ponytail slapped him across the face. "Are you kidding me right now? My dad just died!" Nedra began crying again. Her head ached from the emotional overload. She bent forward, her elbows resting on her knees, her head in her hands as she tried to fight back the confusion she was feeling.

"Nedra, I love you. I love how you genuinely care so much for everyone around you. I love how feisty you are and that you're not afraid to speak your mind. I love how passionate you are about life and the things you believe in. I want to be with you forever. To discover what life has to offer together, side by side. Nedra, will you please marry me?"

Nedra sat up slowly and turned back to face Bryan. Her eyes were red and swollen, her mascara leaving trails of black lines down her face. Her nose dripped, which she quickly wiped away with the back of her hand. She continued to sniffle as she looked at Bryan, studying his eyes with her own. He stared back, his expression sincere and pleading.

"Okay," she whispered.

Bryan's eyebrows raised, his eyes lighting up. "Okay? Really?"

"Yes." Nedra smiled, which lit up her whole face. To Bryan, in that moment, she was the most beautiful woman in the entire world.

"I'm going to miss you," Nedra said, nuzzling Bryan's nose and kissing him lightly on the lips.

"I'll miss you, too. When do you get back?"

"Well, the funeral is tomorrow. I think my flight is the next day. I've gotta double check with Randy. He arranged for me to come home." Nedra's throat tightened as she choked down her emotions. "Thank goodness for my generous brother and his wife. I never would have been able to afford this on my own."

Bryan put his arms around her and hugged her. "Go enjoy a couple days with your family," he whispered. "I'll be waiting right here for you when you get back."

Nedra nodded and started to pull away, but Bryan held on.

"So when do you want to get married?" he asked.

"Bryan Carroll, are you trying to stall? I've got a flight to catch, ya know."

Bryan grinned. "Maybe."

Nedra chuckled softly. Well, let's see, it's November now, so December, January, February," she began counting months off on her fingers. "Probably summer sometime. Don't you think? Like June or July. That would give you enough time to get home and start getting adjusted to life outside the hospital. And that would give us enough time to plan everything. We can talk about this more when I return. I really gotta get going."

Bryan pulled her in closer and kissed her passionately.

"Oh, I, uh . . ." Glenn walked in the room and upon seeing the two of them kissing, he stumbled over his words, unsure how to respond.

Nedra pulled away quickly, flushing pink. "I love you," she whispered. She turned sideways and squeezed past Glenn through the doorway. "Bye." She waved over his head and exited hastily.

"So is there something you need to tell me?" Glenn asked, approaching Bryan's bed.

"I'm not sure what you mean?" Bryan asked.

Glenn swiped his hand through the air. "Never mind. So how are you doing today?" he tried to change the subject.

"Pretty good. I feel like I'm ready to get out of here. Thanksgiving went well at home, I thought. I just want to go home and stay there. No more hospital food, and people prodding me all the time, and the boredom. I'm ready to get out of this room and do something other than stare at a TV all day."

Glenn nodded, patting Bryan on the arm. "Soon enough," he said. "Just keep with the physical therapy and I'm sure they'll let you come home soon." Glenn held up the white paper sack he was carrying. "Would you like a sandwich for lunch?" he asked.

"Thanks, Dad."

Glenn reached into his bag and pulled out two sandwiches. He placed one in Bryan's curled fingers and Bryan was able to bring his hand to his mouth and take bites. When their lunches were gone, Glenn got to his feet again. "Well, I gotta get back to work. I'll see you soon."

"Bye, Dad."

"Bye."

Glenn walked from the room, pausing in the doorway to look back at Bryan. He wasn't sure what he had walked in on, or what it meant.

That evening when Glenn got home from work, he pulled Carol Jean into their bedroom and closed the door.

"What's the matter, Glenn? I've got a roast in the oven," she said, pointing to the door.

"I just...I'm not sure," he said, looking at Carol Jean and scratching his head. "I just have a hunch about Bryan and one of his nurses."

"What?" Carol Jean stared at Glenn, all thoughts of dinner suddenly gone from her mind. "Which one?"

"Nedra. Do you know her? She's got the really long, brown hair."

"I think I can picture her. Can't say I know much about her. Why do you think there's something going on between them?"

"I walked in on them kissing this afternoon."

"What?" Carol Jean's face reddened. "That woman is ten years his senior! What on earth is she thinking, going after my son like that? And my son who is taken, too! He's still with Jana, isn't he?" Carol Jean grabbed her sweater off the back of the door and reached for the handle. "I'm going down there right now to put a stop to this."

Glenn softly reached for her hand and tugged her back. "I don't think that's a good idea."

"And why not?" Carol Jean huffed, putting her hands on her hips.

"Because they're adults. If we tell them they can't date, that will just make them want to even more. If we tell them they can't get married, they'll just run off and elope."

"Marriage? He's only eighteen! And he just broke his neck a few months ago!"

"I know," Glenn spoke softly, patting Carol Jean's hand. "But I just have a hunch. I saw the way they were looking at each other."

Carol Jean tore off her sweater and threw it on the ground. "Fine, but if they do get engaged, I can tell you now I'm certainly going to have something to say about it!" She stomped from the room in a huff.

>♦< >♦< >♦<

"What do you mean, you're engaged?" Carol Jean didn't mean to shriek so loudly, but Bryan's announcement had completely caught her off guard. She put a hand to her head and sat down in the nearest plastic chair.

"This is good news, Mom. Just smile and say congratulations," Bryan tried to joke.

Carol Jean still couldn't wrap her mind around the big announcement. "So you're engaged to your nurse . . . Nedra?"

"Yes, Mom, we're thinking about a wedding this summer sometime."

"But she . . . bathes you and everything, doesn't she? That seems so inappropriate. She won't even be able to wear white at the wedding. Oh dear." She shook her head.

"It's not like we're both naked, Mom." Bryan rolled his eyes. "We've kissed, of course, but nothing else."

"And what about Jana? I never realized you two had broken up! When did that happen?"

"Well . . ." Bryan trailed off as he stared out the window.

"You haven't even broken up with her? Bryan Louis Carroll! What are you thinking?"

"I'm thinking I found an amazing woman who I love with all my heart. I'm thinking I found a completely unselfish partner who not only loves me in return, but is willing to take care of me for the rest of my life."

Carol Jean closed her eyes and took a deep breath. "I'm sorry," she said, clenching her teeth. "You just completely caught me off guard. I didn't even realize the two of you were dating, let alone getting close to marriage. This is going to take some getting used to."

"Honestly, Mom, it came as a shock to me, too. One day she was just my nurse and the next day she was suddenly so much more. I can't really explain it."

"Why didn't you even tell us you were dating?"

"It all happened so fast, and I know you and Dad are still struggling with the accident and everything. I was just afraid of how you might take it."

"It's a lot of change to deal with, Bryan."

"I know, Mom. I'm the one dealing with it, too."

Carol Jean blew out a large breath of air. "Have you told your father yet?"

"No, I was going to next time he comes to visit."

Carol Jean nodded, massaging her forehead. "In the summertime, you said?"

"Yes, probably. We haven't picked a real date yet, but we'll do that after I'm released from the hospital."

"Does she have a ring yet?"

"No, not yet. Once I'm back home, we'll take care of that."

"So it's not official yet. Things could still not work out?"

"No, Mom," Bryan said, irritated. "It's official, and we're not changing our minds. Nedra isn't super picky about a lot of the details, but we are getting married this summer in California."

"California?"

"Yes, in Oakland. Nedra's family all lives in California. Of course we're getting married there."

Carol Jean paced around the room, holding her hands behind her back. "I guess I'll start planning a reception then. But you can't give me a date yet?"

"No, Mom, I can't." Bryan was trying his hardest to keep his cool but the longer his mom stayed, the more frustrated he became. "I do have some other news, if you'd like to hear it. I thought I was giving you the best news first."

Carol Jean looked at him with tired eyes. "What is it?" she asked.

"The doctor set my release date for next week. I'm coming home December twelfth."

CHAPTER FOURTEEN

"Strength does not come from physical capacity. It comes from an indomitable will."

- Gandhi

Nedra pushed Bryan up to the storefront and they both peered inside. She pulled the glass door open and, while holding it in place with her foot, Bryan pushed himself inside. They couldn't see anyone in sight, neither customers nor workers, but they continued and began perusing the waterbeds.

"It's kinda weird, shopping for a bed for us," he said.

Nedra smiled. "I know. It will be weird sleeping in a waterbed after being on a mattress for so many years."

"Yeah, for me, too," Bryan said. "But the doctor thinks it will be the best thing for me."

"Absolutely." Nedra nodded. "It will be so much harder for you to get bedsores with the constant movement a waterbed offers and . . ." she trailed off. Bryan was watching her, smiling ear to ear. "You already know all this," she said.

"Yeah," Bryan admitted.

"So I don't need to explain it to you."

"No, but it's okay."

Nedra laughed. "Sorry, I'm just so used to explaining everything out to my patients and their families. It's a bad habit, I guess."

"Not at all," Bryan said. "So, where do we begin?"

"I guess we just look and see what we like the best," she shrugged.

As they began walking through the store, it didn't take long for them to realize each waterbed was displayed up on a stand, a couple feet above the floor.

"Well, this should be interesting," Nedra said. She backed Bryan's chair up to the nearest platform, and then popped a wheelie to pull him up to get a closer look. They considered a few different options, glancing at each other for confirmation. Neither seemed particularly interested until they came to a large, king size bed with an intricate swirling design around the edge, carved into the wood.

"Wow, this one is beautiful," Nedra said, running a hand along the smooth wood. "Want to try it out?"

"Why not?"

After popping Bryan up onto the stand, Nedra bent in front of him so Bryan could wrap his arms around her neck. She scooped her hand under his thighs and carefully lifted him from the chair. She plopped him on the edge of the bed and pushed him a little further in. She went around to the other side and climbed in. They both moved up and down with the waves as the bed settled back down.

"Seems comfortable," Nedra said.

"Yup," Bryan stated.

"And plenty big enough."

"Uh-huh."

Nedra scooted back over to the edge and hoisted herself back out. She turned around and playfully pushed on the bed, causing Bryan to bounce up and down again. She laughed at his surprised expression, and then went around to the other side to pull him out. She lifted Bryan carefully, cradling him in her arms and placed him back in his wheelchair. Tipping the chair forward, she tried to slide him back over the edge of the stand.

"You better go backwards," Bryan said, "so you don't trip."

"No, I'm fine."

"You need to go backwards, Ned."

"No, I've got this," she insisted.

Nedra's foot slipped and she lost her grip on the wheelchair. Bryan slid off the edge, spilling out of his chair, and landed SPLAT in the middle of the store. He lay sprawled out on the floor, laughing hysterically. It was incredible how the almost empty store suddenly felt very crowded. People from all over the place appeared, asking a red-faced Nedra if she needed any help.

"No, I'm fine," she said. "It's okay, I got it." She bent down and lifted Bryan carefully off the floor. "I think it's time to go," she said amidst the stares and whispers. Bryan only laughed harder.

After spending six months lying in a bed and being bored in a hospital, Bryan was finally getting released to go home! He woke up with a huge grin on his face and waited patiently for his dad to come and pick him up so he could leave for good. It was Nedra's day off, but she promised to come by the house later. As another nurse helped him dress and eat breakfast, all he could think about was getting home.

"Let me be naked and hungry," he joked with the nurse. "Just get me outta here!"

She smiled patiently and continued helping him prepare for his departure. Once Bryan was dressed and fed, she helped him into his chair. The moment his body hit the cushion, he sped off toward the physical therapy room to say goodbye. It felt strange, wheeling down this hallway for the last time. Once he got inside the room, he said goodbye to Dr. Estrada and the other therapists. He rode around, bidding farewell to everyone he had met on his journey. When he made it back to his room, Glenn was standing in the doorway, talking to Christine.

"I think someone is excited to get out of here," she said, smiling.

"Hi!" Bryan said excitedly.

"It's good to see you moving around and doing so well." Christine pointed to Bryan's chair with her chin.

Bryan beamed. "I'm getting married, too!"

"That's what your dad was just telling me," Christine said. "Congratulations! You've got a great future ahead of you. Good luck with everything." Christine shook hands with Glenn and patted Bryan on the shoulder. "I sincerely hope I won't be seeing you around," she added, smiling.

"No offense, but me neither."

"Take care, Bryan."

"I will, Christine. Thanks."

"You ready to go?" Glenn turned to Bryan.

"Yes!"

"See ya 'round." J.D. waved. "If ya ever wanna race, just give me a call."

"I will." Bryan laughed.

"Don't get into too much trouble without me," Danny added, smiling.

"You either," Bryan replied. "And no more drinking and diving."

Danny looked down at his immobile body. "I think I'm pretty cured from that."

"Anyone heard from Art lately?"

"Sounds like he's back in Montana and doing really well," Danny said.

"That's awesome."

Glenn turned his chair around so Bryan could call a final goodbye to his friends. With one last glance around, Glenn pushed him onto the elevator and they watched the doors close for the last time.

As Bryan rolled through his front door, it was like being in the house again for the first time. Everything seemed so strange now that he sat at a different height. He noticed things he never had before, like that end table sticking out a little far. He would have to be careful when going past so he didn't catch a wheel. He noticed the space between the coffee table and the couch was too narrow for a wheelchair.

Jenny ran and jumped onto his lap. "Faster, faster!" she yelled as Bryan zoomed them around the house.

"That's enough, little daredevil," Glenn said, scooping Jenny off Bryan's lap. Glenn carried Bryan down the stairs to his room in the basement. So much had changed in Bryan over the last six months, it almost felt like being in a stranger's room. The waterbed he and Nedra ordered had arrived, leaving no space for anything else in the small area. The rest of his furniture was gone, probably packed away in storage somewhere. Glenn walked over to the bed and set him down.

"I'll be right back. Let me go grab your chair."

"When am I getting my motorized chair?" Bryan asked.

"We got it yesterday, actually. I haven't had a chance to bring it inside the house yet."

"By yourself?" Bryan asked in alarm. "It's probably really heavy, Dad."

"No, Duane is coming over to give me a hand. You'll have to reserve your motorized chair for upstairs and driving around the neighborhood. There's no way we'll be able to get it downstairs."

Bryan lay in bed looking around at the car posters on his walls. His room seemed so quiet. He had grown accustomed to sleeping with a lot of background noise, and he didn't even realize it until now. He wondered what tonight would be like, without the beeping machines, Danny's snoring, or a TV playing.

A few minutes later, Bryan heard grunting and scuffling upstairs.

"Turn this way."

"Wait, try it like this."

After a loud thud, Glenn appeared in the doorway wiping his brow.

"There, we're all set!" He reached down to grab Bryan.

"Wait, Dad, it's a lot easier to have me put my arms around your neck before you pick me up."

Glenn obeyed and then carried Bryan into the family room to place him in his manual wheelchair. "Your new electric one is upstairs and all set up," he said.

"Thanks, Dad."

Just then, Duane walked down the stairs.

"Hey, Bryan! Long time, no see!" Duane said. He reached out to shake Bryan's hand. Bryan lifted his arm, showing his coned fingers and Duane quickly dropped his hand to his side. "Oh, uh, sorry!" he stammered.

"Don't worry about it," Bryan said. "No big deal."

"I've really been wanting to talk to you, Bryan," Duane said, shifting from one foot to the other. "I am really sorry for what happened to you."

"It wasn't your fault," Bryan said.

"But I feel responsible."

Bryan was confused. "What? Why?"

"I'm the one who told you about the cliffs in the first place. I got you boys excited about it, and then I brought you to them myself."

Glenn waved off his apology. "Duane, please," he piped up. "This was not your fault at all."

"It's really not!" Bryan added. "I probably should have checked how deep the water was before jumping. But you know what wondering 'what if' does? It keeps you trapped in the past. And I'd rather spend my time looking to the future. Besides, if I hadn't gotten in the accident, I never would have met my beautiful fiancée."

"You're engaged?" Duane asked, his mouth gaping open. "Wow. Congratulations. I didn't realize . . ." he trailed off.

"We haven't told a lot of people yet," Glenn said uneasily.

"She's coming over tonight if you want to meet her," Bryan said.

"She's coming tonight?" Glenn asked.

"Yeah, she has to teach you and Mom a few things. Plus she's going to help get me to bed."

Duane glanced between father and son. "Naw, I better get going. But thank you. I'm sure I'll get to meet her soon." While Glenn walked him out, Bryan looked around the family room. The spacious room was half carpeted and half tiled. On one side of the room along the far side of the wall sat a fireplace, a TV, his stereo, and some shelves. The couch rested in the center of the room with the back towards the tile. Bryan knew he'd be spending most of his time down here, since he obviously couldn't get up the stairs on his own. He glanced from the fifteen feet of open tile to the hallway which led to his and Becky's bedrooms. The space would be all his during the day, without roommates to share with. Fun as they were, he was looking forward to the alone time.

Glenn came back down the stairs as Bryan practiced maneuvering around the room. Figuring out the spacing between furniture was harder than he thought. Every time he tried to go a little faster, he ended up bumping into the couch.

"So Nedra is coming over tonight?"

"Yeah, that's the plan. You guys need to start getting to know each other."

"That's true." Glenn nodded. "Is she going to be here for dinner? Your mom will want to know if she needs to set an extra place."

"I'm not sure. She had some things she needed to take care of and was going to stop by when she's finished up with her errands."

Glenn looked like he wanted to say more, but he continued to nod. "Okay then. I'll be upstairs if you need anything."

Bryan spent the afternoon watching TV and practicing driving around his room and family room. He only bumped into the couch and end tables a few times before he had a pretty good grasp on the distance and could zoom past them without a collision. His sisters all came down at different times to visit with him and watch as he practiced driving.

A few hours later, when Jenny was getting her third ride, Glenn returned. "Dinner's ready," he announced.

"Woo-hoo!" Jenny jumped from Bryan's lap and bounded up the stairs.

"I guess she's hungry," Bryan chuckled.

Glenn scooped Bryan up with a groan and carried him up the stairs.

"You okay, Dad?" Bryan asked when he set him in the high-backed kitchen chair.

"Yeah," he said, wiping the sweat from his brow. "I guess I should have been working out, too, to prepare for your arrival."

"I'm sure you'll get used to it. Dinner looks great, Mom," he added while Carol Jean dished him up a plate. She smiled in return, setting the food in front of him.

After blessing the food, everyone dug in. Bryan sat back and waited for his turn. When no one offered to feed him he said, "Could I have some potatoes, please?"

Carol Jean looked over at him patiently sitting there, his plate still full. "Oh, sweetie, I'm so sorry!" she stammered. "Having you all sitting around the table again reminded me of how it used to be and for a minute there, I completely forgot." She scooped up a large helping of mashed potatoes and held the spoon up for Bryan. She fed him a few bites and then set down his spoon to take a few bites from her own plate. She got involved in the story Brenda was telling and forgot to feed Bryan again until he cleared his throat loudly.

"Oh my goodness," she said, slapping her forehead, "I'm so sorry, Bryan! I'll get better at this, I promise."

Nedra knocked on the door as they finished eating.

"Oh, hello, Nedra," Carol Jean said politely. "Would you like to come in? We're just finishing up dinner."

Jenny got up and hugged Nedra's legs.

"Finish your food please, sweetheart." Carol Jean prodded her back into her chair. "Aren't you girls going to say hello?" she asked, looking at her older daughters.

Becky, Brenda, and Glenda, who were all friends with Jana, mumbled their greetings. Nedra kissed Bryan lightly and pulled up a chair next to him. "Oh, I'll do this," she said to Carol Jean, sliding his plate closer to herself. She knew just the right amount of food to scoop up and fed Bryan with proficiency and speed.

When he was finished eating, Nedra picked him up with ease and carried him back downstairs, following Bryan's instructions of where to go. They snuggled on the couch together, watching a movie, until Glenn and Carol Jean came down. Carol Jean flipped the light on, stinging their eyes.

"Oh, Mom, some warning would have been nice," he grumbled.

"Funny, that's what I was thinking," she muttered.

"What?"

"Nothing."

Glenn nudged her. "Can you walk us through some of the things we need to know?" he asked.

"Sure." Nedra jumped up.

She proceeded to teach them how to empty Bryan's leg bag. She went through all of his medications again and when he should take them. She showed them the best way to pick up Bryan and how to transfer him to his bed or a couch. As much as they practiced and tried to help Bryan the way Nedra was explaining, they simply didn't have as much experience. Nedra was fast and proficient. Carol Jean grew frustrated and walked upstairs without uttering a word of explanation.

"I better go check on your mom," Glenn said.

Nedra placed a hand on his arm and gently stopped him. "Can I go?" Glenn looked at her skeptically. "Please?"

"All right." He motioned up the stairs and invited Nedra to pass him. "I'll stay down here and keep Bryan company."

"Thanks." Nedra walked up the stairs and passed the girls, who were watching a movie in the living room.

"Have you guys seen your mom?"

Becky waved her on. "She's probably in her room."

"Thanks." Nedra walked down the narrow hallway. She was completely unfamiliar with this part of the house. As she walked past each door, she peered inside, but so far, there was no Carol Jean in sight. When she heard movement coming from the last room at the end of the hall, she tapped the closed, white door with her knuckles. "Carol Jean? May I come in?"

Nedra put her ear up to the door, but she didn't hear anything. Maybe she imagined the noises. She was just about to walk away when she heard a sniff and Carol Jean's soft voice saying, "Come in." Nedra pushed the door open slowly to reveal a red-eyed Carol Jean sitting on a large, king sized bed. Nedra walked across the room and sat down beside her.

"I know you don't like me."

Carol Jean was startled by her boldness. "It's not that," she stammered.

"Your family was already practically planning a wedding for Bryan and Jana. I must have come as a great shock to you."

Carol Jean nodded and wiped her nose with the crumpled tissue she held in her fist. "There is just so much that has changed in the last six months. It's a lot to take."

"I understand that," Nedra said. "But I really do love your son."

"How can you understand it, though?" Carol Jean asked quietly. "Bryan is my first baby. He was a difficult child, but we made it past that stage and I got to watch him grow and mature. Then I had to watch him suffer on that beach for eighteen hours. I was afraid we were going to lose him. All I could do was bring him water and pray that he was going to be all right. I felt so completely helpless. I had always been able to take care of my children, but this time it was out of my control. There was absolutely nothing I could do. I watched helplessly as the doctors put him on ice and told us they couldn't do anything until his swelling went down. I have four other children to care for, so I couldn't be at the hospital all the time. Every time I was away, I felt guilty that strangers were taking care of my son instead of me."

"But that's our job. It's what we like to do," Nedra interrupted.

Carol Jean shook her head and continued. "I didn't say it made any sense. I just want you to know how I feel. I have felt completely helpless for the last six months. The only thing I could do was visit Bryan in the hospital and bring him treats occasionally. I couldn't stop the accident from happening, I couldn't get him help sooner, and there was nothing I could do to help him in his recovery. I was counting down the days until my only son would return home to me and I could finally do something for him. I was fully prepared to feed, clothe, and care for Bryan for the rest of his life, if need be. And then suddenly, only weeks before he was coming home, I find out he is engaged to a woman who is practically a stranger to us. Someone who is going to take my place as his caregiver and again, I have to just sit back and watch helplessly."

"I'm trying to teach you what to do." Nedra shrugged.

"I know, and I do see that. But especially tonight, it became very clear to me that my son doesn't really need me anymore. In just a few months, he'll be married and my job as his mother will be done. It's just a lot sooner than I expected, and I'm afraid I'm not coping with it very well." Carol Jean dabbed her eyes with the tissue again. "It makes things difficult, too, when you're significantly older than he is. I always thought when Bryan married, it would be a girl, someone I could welcome into the family as another daughter. But you are only ten years younger than me. You're a grown woman. I don't know how to be a mother to someone who isn't that far off from my own age."

"I don't think Bryan is done with you." Nedra put her arm around Carol Jean's shoulder. "I still go to my mom all the time for help and advice. And honestly, this came as a shock to me, too. I usually see my patients as little brothers, not love interests. I've had the privilege of watching how much Bryan has grown these last six months. He is so much stronger and more mature than any of the other patients I've had who are like him. I know you had to watch him suffer on the beach that day, and I'm truly sorry you had to go through that. But that day on the beach is when Bryan went from a boy to a man. If I had met your son as the pre-accident eighteen-year-old, I probably would have still viewed him as a boy, too. There's no way I would be in love with that Bryan. I'm in love with Bryan now, the one who decided, while laying in the hot sand, that he wasn't going to give up on life. He wasn't going to feel sorry for himself, and he never has. He wasn't going to waste his time with questions of why and what if. He chose to remain as normal as possible and continue to live his life to the fullest. That's the Bryan I love. That's the Bryan I want to build a family with and have as my partner for eternity."

"How did it go?" Bryan asked when Nedra returned to the basement almost an hour later. He bit his lip in anticipation, looking to Nedra for any signs of how she was feeling, but she gave away nothing.

She finally smiled at him and said, "Well, I don't think everything is resolved yet, but I do think we at least understand each other now."

Bryan nodded. "And was there any screaming or fighting involved in this understanding?"

Nedra laughed. "I guess you'll never know," she said with a wink.

CHAPTER FIFTEEN

"Happiness does not depend on what happens outside of you but on what happens inside of you; it is measured by the spirit with which you meet the problems of life."

- Harold B. Lee

lenn pulled toward the front doors of the Salt Lake International Airport and crawled along the curb, one car in a long line of holiday travelers.

"What airline again?" he asked.

"American," Nedra said from the backseat.

Glenn followed the signs and moved along slowly with the traffic. "It's crazy out here!"

"It's always like this right before Christmas. Thank you so much for the ride," she added. "It really beats paying those huge parking fees."

"It's not a problem. Do you need us to pick you up, too?"

"That would be great, yeah. Bryan has my itinerary."

"All right, have a safe trip," he said, finally landing a spot by the entrance.

Glenn opened his door and climbed out while Nedra leaned over the front console and gave Bryan a kiss. "Bye, I love you!"

"I love you, too! I'll see you in a week."

"Please take care of everything while I'm gone," she said.

"I will. I promise," he smiled.

She kissed him once more before climbing out of the car. Glenn stood on the sidewalk holding her suitcase, which he had retrieved from the trunk.

"Merry Christmas," he said, handing over the large bag.

"Merry Christmas!" She smiled and gave him a small hug. Turning, she waved to Bryan before disappearing through the glass doors.

Christmas morning was always a big deal at Bryan's house. He awoke to the smell of homemade cinnamon rolls wafting down the stairs. Jenny came running into his room and jumped onto his bed.

"It's Christmas! It's Christmas! Let's open presents!" she yelled, bouncing and waving with the bed by his feet. She climbed off the waterbed and disappeared back up the stairs as quickly as she had come.

Glenn walked into Bryan's room, shaking his head and laughing at his youngest. "Oh, to have her energy again," he chuckled.

"Morning, Pop! How are you?" Bryan greeted him.

"I'm fabulous, marvelous, and wonderful!" he exclaimed with a cheerful smile.

"I should've known." Bryan smiled back.

"Now let's get you upstairs before there isn't anything left to open," he said, bending down and scooping Bryan up. Glenn had gotten used to carrying Bryan now. He could actually get him up the stairs without grunting and groaning.

He set Bryan on their long, blue couch next to Brenda, who was curled up with a blanket, and ran in the next room to grab his camera. As Bryan looked around the room at his sisters, he realized this would be their last Christmas all together. By this time next year, he would be married. Becky had a serious boyfriend, and Brenda would be a senior in high school; he couldn't believe how fast his family was changing. Becky sat in the armchair across the room, looking half asleep. Glenda crawled around under the tree, picking up the best-looking presents and shaking them.

"You better not break any of mine," Brenda warned.

Glenda ignored her and kept up the search. Jenny sat on her feet, bouncing on her knees. "Let's go! Let's go!" she cried.

"All right, we're coming." Carol Jean and Glenn came into the room and sat on the loveseat beside the tree.

"Who do you think wants to go first?" Glenn asked, looking around the room. "Should we go oldest to youngest?"

"Nooooooo!" Jenny wailed.

"Oh, stop teasing," Carol Jean said. "Go ahead and open one of yours, sweetie," she said to Jenny.

After taking turns from youngest to oldest several more times, the floor was covered in torn wrapping paper. Bryan looked at the small pile beside him that Brenda had helped open. He got some new shirts, several ties, a couple of records, and some treats. He realized most of what he got was food or clothes, and it made him chuckle. This was how Christmases were probably going to be from now on.

Once the paper was all picked up, they enjoyed cinnamon rolls and juice for breakfast. Bryan had only been home for about two weeks, but he was already starting to put on a few pounds. He could tell because his mom had struggled to button up his pants the last two mornings. He didn't feel an ounce of regret, though. After eating hospital food for six months, he had a lot of catching up to do with his mom's cooking. After his third cinnamon roll, Glenn carried him back downstairs and got him dressed for the day.

"Jana is going to be here soon," Glenn said.

"Yeah, I know," Bryan frowned.

"Are you ready for this?"

"As ready as I'll ever be," Bryan said.

"It's not too late to change your mind."

"Dad, please."

"Okay," Glenn said, surrendering. He helped Bryan into his wheelchair and Bryan drove around the room until he heard the doorbell ring a short time later.

Bryan's stomach dropped. He definitely should have stayed away from that third roll. Now it was threatening to make a reappearance. He could hear Jana's happy chatter as she walked down the stairs. He wanted to run. His throat became very dry when he saw her standing on the last step. She paused for a moment and then rushed toward him.

"Oh, I've missed you so much! I can't believe it's been almost a month," she said, throwing her arms around his neck.

Bryan watched over her shoulders as Glenn turned and walked back up the steps, shaking his head.

"I'm sorry I couldn't ever make it over," Jana said, sitting on the couch beside Bryan so they were at the same eye level.

"I understand," Bryan said quietly. "You were really sick and then between school and work and trying to catch up, it made complete sense. You were really good at calling, though."

Jana smiled. "I didn't want you to feel like I had completely abandoned you. Well, here," Jana pulled a present out of her coat pocket. "Merry Christmas."

Bryan could feel his heart thumping out of his chest. He couldn't believe Jana hadn't mentioned how loud it was yet. He raised his arm and placed it on top of the beautifully wrapped gift that lay in her open hands.

"Jana," his voice squeaked slightly. "Jana, before we open gifts or anything, I really need to talk to you."

"O-kay," she said slowly. "What's going on?"

"I want you to know first of all, how much your friendship means to me. Truly. Your love is what has gotten me through the hardest trial of my entire life. Your face kept me going when I thought I might die. Your love is what propelled me to push forward and never look back. I will always love you for that."

"I'll always love you, too," she said, lifting her right hand and placing it on top of his. "Bryan, what's going on?"

Bryan cleared his throat. "Well, uh, you remember my nurse Nedra?"

"Of course."

"She and I ended up spending a lot of time together both in and out of the hospital, especially while you were away. And, well, we fell in love and we're getting married."

Jana's jaw dropped. She quickly pulled her hand off of his and looked down. "Are you serious?" When she looked up again, there were tears in her eyes.

"I really, really never wanted to hurt you Jana. You have meant so much to me."

Jana shook her head slowly and got to her feet, legs trembling. "You're getting *married*?"

"Yes," Bryan whispered.

"And you couldn't have bothered to tell me this before now?" Jana's voice got louder with each word.

"I wanted to talk to you in person. I wanted you to understand how much your love and support has meant to me."

"Well, obviously it didn't mean enough, did it?" Jana walked away from Bryan, her shoulders trembling. She turned around when she reached the bottom step and looked down at the present that was still in her hand. She threw it on the ground by Bryan's feet. "Merry Christmas." She spat out the words.

Glenda immediately rushed to Jana's side when she reached the top of the stairs. She hugged her tightly while Jana's crying grew louder. Carol Jean and Brenda came over, and they all embraced. They guided Jana to a chair in the kitchen and sat around the table beside her. Carol Jean made her a cup of cocoa and they listened and cried with her as Jana spilled her emotions.

Bryan sat in the basement in the dark, listening to Jana sob above him. He felt completely miserable. She had truly become a part of his family. After going on trips together and spending holidays together, Bryan's family all viewed her as another sister. He only hoped they could someday love Nedra and welcome her into the family, too.

When Glenn and Bryan picked Nedra up from the airport a week later, the wounds were still fresh. Thankfully, seeing Nedra's face again reminded Bryan why he had gone through all that. After tossing her suitcase into the trunk, she climbed in the backseat. Her smile was giddy as she squeezed Bryan's shoulders from behind, giving him the best hug she could with a seat between them.

"How was your Christmas?" he asked.

"It was nice. Very quiet. A little strange with just Mom and me, but nice."

Bryan laughed as he thought of his sisters on Christmas morning. "My Christmas was definitely not quiet."

"I hope we're able to have a big family," she said. "Christmas was always just Randy and me, so I've never known anything else. A loud Christmas sounds nice."

Glenn cleared his throat from the front seat. "Can you, uh—can you have kids?" he asked Bryan.

"We know it won't be easy, but we're planning on trying," Bryan said.

When they got to Nedra's house, Glenn got out of the car and pulled her suitcase and Bryan's wheelchair from the trunk. He opened Bryan's door, unbuckled him, and bent down low to lift him from the passenger seat. Glenn pushed Bryan's wheelchair toward the front door and was about to leave when he looked at Nedra standing there with a wheelchair and her large suitcase.

"Let me help you," he offered.

Nedra's initial instinct was to refuse, but after looking between Bryan and her suitcase, she realized there really was no easy way to do it. "That would be great, thanks."

Glenn ran back to the car and removed his keys and then followed Nedra and Bryan inside, carrying her heavy bag behind them. He watched as Nedra bumped Bryan up one step at a time of her split level home.

"Do you need a hand?" he asked apprehensively.

"Oh no, we do this all the time," she said. "I'll bring him back tonight around ten," Nedra added once they reached her living room. "I have work in the morning, so we won't be out too late."

Glenn nodded and leaned her suitcase against the wall, just inside her door. "See you tonight, Bryan," he called up the stairs.

Nedra walked back down and closed the front door behind him. No sooner had she done so when two of her cats greeted her. She stroked their fur gently, and then hefted her bag up the stairs and dropped it off down the hall in her bedroom. She quickly made a sweep through the house, checking on all her babies.

"They all seem to be happy and healthy," she declared, looking around. "Boy, it sure feels weird to be back. A week away felt like such a long time."

Bryan sighed. "Tell me about it! My sisters, except Jenny of course, are mad at me for breaking up with Jana on Christmas. They've barely even looked at me all week."

"You did it on Christmas?" Nedra looked at him, disapproving.

"Oh, no, not you, too. It's the only time I could do it! She was already coming over that day, and I wasn't going to pretend we were still together for the entire holiday, just to break up with her the day after. That seemed just as mean."

"You're right. It was not going to be an easy task, no matter what day it happened." Nedra bent down and kissed him on the cheek. "I'm proud of you, though. I know that wasn't easy to lose a friend who has meant so much to you."

"I just hope she can forgive me someday and we can be friends again."

"I hope so, too," Nedra said. She pushed Bryan over to her large, comfy beanbag chair and transferred him onto it. He sank down just enough. She curled up beside him and he held her for awhile.

"Where are we going to live once we're married?" Bryan asked, breaking the silence.

"I'm not sure," Nedra said, looking around her small house. "This place is definitely not wheelchair accessible. And we're certainly not moving in with your parents." They looked at each other and laughed loudly.

"No way!" Bryan added. He couldn't even imagine the problems that would create.

They sat in silence for several minutes, each trying to come up with some viable options.

"It's too bad we can't live in married student housing up on campus at the U," Nedra said.

"Wait, why can't we?"

"Because you have to be a student at the university to qualify."

"So it sounds like I need to become a student then," Bryan said.

Nedra thought about it. "Do you want to go to college?" she asked.

"You know, my dad always told me not to settle for being a mechanic. He's been encouraging me to go to college and be an engineer for years. I never really paid much attention to his advice. I was always going to be a mechanic, so college wasn't a part of my plan. Since I can't be a mechanic anymore, why not? What else am I going to do with my life? I've got to find something to do to keep my mind working or I'll go crazy. How else will I earn money for our family, anyway, with all those kids you want?" He smiled at Nedra.

She looked at him and saw that his mind was set. Bryan was going to college. "Okay," she said. "Are you going to study engineering?"

"Yeah, I think I will. When I was a kid, I used to fix kids' toys from all over the neighborhood. I was pretty good at it, too. I've always been fascinated with how things work. Maybe that's part of the reason I was so drawn to cars. I loved how I could pop the hood and discover what made them run."

Nedra watched Bryan closely. "Well, if it wasn't so late already, I'd suggest a car drive up to the U and pick you up an application. Given the circumstances and that the sky is already dark, why don't I grab one after work tomorrow? I can bring it by tomorrow night."

"Sounds great!"

"Speaking of which, how did your parents do with getting you ready for bed every night?"

"Oh my word," Bryan rolled his head around. "They can be so frustrating! And so slow, too."

"Well, I do have a bit more practice," Nedra said slowly.

"I am just so glad you're back to help me from now on. No more going out of town unless you take me with you!"

"Well, next time I go to California, this July, you will be coming with me."

"I can't wait to meet your mom. She sounds like a character," Bryan said.

"Oh, she is."

"How did she take the news of our engagement?" he asked. Nedra had been waiting to tell her mom until she could tell her in person.

"She's very happy for us. She's assured me she wants to pay for the reception in California." Nedra paused, and her tone seemed to shift.

"What's wrong, Ned?"

"My mom also brought up a really good point. But I don't want it to come across the wrong way."

"What's that?"

Nedra took a deep breath. "Well, Daddy never would have approved of you. Not you, as a person," she stammered, "but because you're 'handicap,'" she said, making quote marks in the air. "He wouldn't have allowed us to marry, knowing that I am going to have to take care of you for the rest of your life. Daddy was very protective and prejudiced that way."

Bryan considered her words.

"Everything seems to have happened in just the right order, with just the right timing," she said.

Bryan smiled and reached for Nedra, who fell into his embrace. "I'm so glad I met you when I did, then," he whispered.

"Me, too," Nedra said, nuzzling his neck. "Me, too."

CHAPTER SIXTEEN

"It does not matter how slowly you go so long as you do not stop."

- Confucius

Bryan and Nedra were snuggling in her house once again, enjoying a nice, romantic Valentine's Day, along with Jenny. Nedra was still trying to win over Glenn and Carol Jean, so she and Bryan offered to take his youngest sister for the night so the two of them could have a date night alone. Jenny was having the time of her life, throwing yarn balls, dangling string, and snuggling with all of Nedra's cats.

"So because of your disability, the government is going to completely pay for college?"

"Yup!" Bryan said, a smug grin on his face. "I knew I made that dive for a reason," he joked.

"That's incredible!"

"I know! Now when I start school next month, I won't be stressed out about how much it's costing us, since I have a feeling I will be there longer than four years."

"Oh, yeah? Did you decide to become a doctor?" Nedra teased.

"Yeah, can't you picture me performing surgery? 'All right nurse, please place the scalpel in my curled fingers'," he said, holding up his shaking arm to demonstrate. They both laughed.

"I'm hungry," Jenny announced.

"What should we get for dinner?" Nedra asked. "Pizza or Chinese?"

"Oh, pizza, pizza!" Jenny clapped her hands.

"You got it." Nedra stood up to grab her phone book. After finding the right number she asked, "What kind do you like?"

"Cheese!"

"And?"

"Cheese!"

Nedra laughed. "One big, cheesy pizza coming right up." She dialed and put the phone to her ear, holding the receiver away from her mouth. "Do you think many people order pizza for Valentine's?" she asked, looking at Bryan. She moved the receiver back to her mouth when someone answered. "I guess so," she said after placing their order. "They said it'll be about an hour. Possibly two if we wanted delivery."

Bryan's jaw dropped. "Wow, a lot of lonely people out there tonight."

"Yeah, either that or people who are just trying to avoid crowds. I opted to pick it up. Think you two will be okay here without me for a few minutes?"

Bryan looked at his little sister, who had gone back to scratching one of the cats behind her ear. "I think we'll manage."

After stuffing themselves with cheese pizza and watching *American Bandstand,* it was getting late and time to get Jenny home. When they pulled into the driveway, another car was already parked there.

"Who's that?" Nedra asked.

"That looks like Brett's car," Bryan said.

"Becky's boyfriend?"

"Yeah."

"I wonder what they're doing here. It seems early for them to be ending their Valentine's date."

"I dunno," Bryan said.

"Uh-oh, we lost her," Nedra said, glancing in the backseat.

"Is she asleep?" Bryan asked.

"Yeah." Nedra smiled at Jenny, who lay curled up on the backseat, her long blonde hair serving as her pillow. Nedra climbed out of the car and got Bryan's wheelchair out of the trunk and ready. Once Bryan was seated, she lifted Jenny gingerly from the back seat, and lay her sleeping form across her brother's lap. She walked ahead to open the door as he drove inside.

The kitchen lights were on and they could hear loud, cheerful voices coming from that direction. Jenny sat up, rubbing her eyes as they entered the room. Carol Jean and Glenn were back from their date and accompanied by Brenda, Glenda, Becky, and Brett. They each held a cup in their hands, an open bottle of Martinelli's on the table. Becky ran over to her big brother, flashing her left hand in his face.

"I'm engaged!" she exclaimed excitedly. "Brett proposed tonight!"

"Wow, congratulations!" Bryan said.

Nedra stood by the refrigerator, emotionless and unmoving. "When?" she asked.

"Tonight!" Becky said, happily skipping over to show off her new ring.

"No, I mean when are you getting married?"

"We were just looking over the calendar and thinking about a wedding in June."

"No," Nedra said.

"What?" Becky looked at her quizzically.

"No, Bryan and I were engaged first, so we have to get married first. He's also the oldest. You can't get married before us."

"It's not my fault you planned such a long engagement!" Becky huffed, her excitement replaced by annoyance. She looked down, spinning her ring between her thumb and index finger.

"Nedra!" Carol Jean exclaimed. Everyone had stopped talking, all eyes were now focused on her and Bryan.

"We'll just have to move up our wedding then," she announced. "We're getting married next month." With that said, Nedra walked from the room, pushing a silent Bryan in front of her.

The date of March fifth was chosen, leaving no wiggle room for planning. Nedra immediately got to work, booking flights, securing their housing at the university, and giving any feedback that was required for her receptions. Nedra's mom and some good friends from her neighborhood handled the California reception, while Carol Jean planned one for Utah. Nedra didn't want to ruffle any more feathers, so she gave Carol Jean full control over the details of their reception. She was busy trying to get work off and making travel arrangements, so she didn't really mind handing over the parties.

A few weeks before the wedding, Bryan was home alone, like most afternoons. His dad got him dressed and into his chair for the day before leaving for work. When everyone left for school or work, he spent the afternoon building muscle strength, practicing with his chair, and watching TV. Bryan was having a particularly rough morning. His left arm, which had always been his strongest, was suddenly giving him problems. He could barely push hard enough to get his chair to move. He'd break, have to rest, and then try pushing the wheels once again. This resulted in him having bursts of movement instead of continually pushing around the room.

Bryan tried to navigate his way around the couch, a feat he previously accomplished at least a hundred times. He was moving along much slower than normal. Bryan paused, took a deep breath, and pushed forward as hard as he could. The sudden burst of speed caused his left wheel to catch on the corner of the couch. Bryan completely lost control as his chair went up onto one wheel and tipped over. He slammed his head into the floor as the chair came crashing down. His head spun as he lay on his side, unable to move. His legs were still buckled to the chair, so his head was lower than the rest of his body. It didn't take long for Bryan's head to start pounding. He closed his eyes to prevent himself from fainting. He lay like that for over four hours, completely helpless.

When Carol Jean got home from work to feed Bryan lunch, the house felt eerily quiet. She could usually hear Bryan pushing his wheelchair around for exercise, or the TV would be on. The hairs on the back of her neck stood up and she raced down the basement stairs. She gasped when she saw Bryan on his side, his face purple and sweaty.

She quickly unbuckled his lap belt, allowing the rest of his body to fall to the ground. Bryan gasped and looked at his mom.

"Thanks," he whispered. "So what's for lunch?"

Carol Jean shook her head. Pulling as hard as she could with both arms, she lifted his chair upright again. She grunted and groaned as she slid her arms under his body and hefted him back into a sitting position. "So what happened?" she asked, securing his buckle across his lap again.

"I'm not sure, really," Bryan said, looking down at his left hand. "Something is going on with my arm. My left side has always been the strongest, but for some reason today my right is stronger and I can barely get my left to move."

"How did you tip?" Carol Jean asked, examining Bryan and checking for any injuries. He seemed to be fine.

"Oh, my wheel nicked the edge of the couch and—timber!"

Carol Jean didn't find his jokes amusing. "How long were you like that?" she asked.

"A few hours, I guess."

"A few hours? Oh, Bryan! Maybe we should call the doctor to make sure everything is okay."

"I'm fine, Mom," Bryan soothed. "Just a little dizzy from the head rush. I am hungry, though. Can we eat?"

Carol Jean made them each a sandwich, but she continued to watch Bryan closely while they ate.

"I'm fine, Mom!" he said again.

When they were finished eating, Carol Jean stood up and turned on the TV for Bryan. "I know you say you're fine, but please don't try and move around again until we get home. Just relax and watch some TV for awhile, okay?"

Bryan conceded, even though he knew his mom was overreacting. Carol Jean moved slowly toward the stairs, looking back several times at Bryan to make sure he hadn't budged. "I'm fine, Mom! Get back to work, before you're late!"

Carol Jean looked skeptical.

"I swear, Mom, I won't move a muscle until you get home this afternoon. Scout's honor."

Finally satisfied, Carol Jean walked the rest of the way up the stairs and left the house.

That night, when Nedra came over, Bryan explained again to her what happened.

"Your left arm wasn't working at all?" she asked.

"It still worked a little bit," he said, "but I feel like I'm back to when I first had movement again. I can barely push my chair forward, whereas a few days ago, I was zooming circles around this room."

"Hmmm, that's really weird," Nedra said. "We better call the doctor tomorrow and make an appointment. It's probably something we should have looked at before we leave for California."

"Yeah, I guess you're right," Bryan sighed.

Four days before the wedding, Bryan found himself back at the University of Utah hospital. He was gradually losing function in his left arm, making it harder and harder to get around.

Dr. Barney performed an Electromyography (EMG) and a Nerve Conduction Study to see if they could determine the cause of his sudden problems.

"When I compared the results from the EMG and Nerve Conduction Study with those we did a few months ago, it's very obvious you have suffered a significant loss in nerve conduction. You need to meet with the neurologist as soon as possible."

"A neurologist? When?" Nedra asked.

"You need to call as soon as possible, or Bryan could continue to lose function."

"Tomorrow we will be on a plane heading to California to get married," Nedra said.

"Can it wait?" Bryan asked.

"It's ultimately up to the two of you, but this needs to be taken care of soon. If not tomorrow, then as soon as you get back."

"We'll be back March eighth," Bryan said.

The doctor nodded. "That should be just fine."

"Wait!" Nedra said, interrupting his departure. "Then we have our Utah reception. You can't be in the hospital during our reception."

Bryan looked at Nedra and then back to the doctor. "Do you think we can push it back another week?"

Dr. Barney sighed. "Just do what you can. You may not be able to get in right when you get back anyway. Just call and make the appointment first."

Bryan and Nedra looked at each other and nodded.

"Great," Dr. Barney said. "Take care of yourself, and if you have any other problems or questions, don't hesitate to call. In the meantime, please be careful."

"Thank you, doctor," they both said.

Nedra pushed Bryan out the door. "We better get home and get packed," she added. "Our flight leaves pretty early tomorrow."

"I thought we didn't leave until 10:30 a.m."

"Yeah," Nedra said with a smile. "Like I said, early."

CHAPTER SEVENTEEN

"A good life is when you assume nothing, do more, need less, smile often, dream big, laugh a lot, and realize how blessed you are."

- Author Unknown

Jane Hall sat in the airport, her short legs crossed at the ankles. She flipped through the book that lay open on her lap, but wasn't absorbing anything she read. She continued to glance at her watch every few minutes, watching time pass slowly. When the announcement was made that the flight from Salt Lake City was landing, Jane got to her feet and walked over to the large windows covering the wall. She looked out at the runway and watched as the huge, black wheels touched down on the tarmac. They squealed as the plane slowly approached the huge, bright windows.

Once the long, white jet bridge connected, Jane turned away from the windows and moved toward their gate. She shifted from one foot to the other as she anxiously watched the flight attendants pull open the heavy door. When passengers began making their way down the tunnel, Jane looked for signs of a wheelchair. After what felt like hundreds of people walking through the door in floods, Jane saw the silver tip of a wheelchair roll through.

The man sitting in the wheelchair was tall and slender, with sandy blond hair. His legs were thin from disuse. His long arms lay stretched out on the black armrests, his fingers curled under his hands. Pushing the chair with a large blue carry-on strapped over her shoulder was a short, curvy young woman with long brown hair. Jane's smile spread across her face at the sight of them, and she rushed forward.

"Mom!" Nedra rushed past the wheelchair and met her mother in an embrace. It wasn't long ago that she had been home for her father's funeral, but as she returned to her mother's arms, it felt like forever.

"Hello, Bryan!" Jane reached for Bryan's hand and held it between both of hers. "It's about time we met!" She greeted him with a warm smile.

"It's nice to meet you, Jane." He returned the smile.

"Now you listen to me," she said, looking straight into Bryan's eyes, her tone firm and serious. "Don't you let my daughter run this marriage. I know how bossy she can be. Marriage is a partnership, whether both partners can move on their own or not."

Bryan chuckled. "You got it."

"Gee, thanks, Mom." Nedra feigned annoyance.

Jane turned to her daughter. "I mean it," she said, staring her down.

"Yes, Mom, I know. Can we get going now, please?"

"All right," Jane turned in the direction of the luggage carousels and led the way.

Once Nedra had gathered their things, the three of them moved swiftly through the airport and out into the parking lot. Jane took over wheelchair duty while Nedra walked behind them, a large bag in each hand.

"So when does your family arrive? Do they need to be picked up from the airport?" Jane asked.

"No," Bryan responded. "They are all driving, along with my best man. I think they're coming tomorrow."

"Don't you have some young sisters? That's a long drive for little ones."

"Jenny is the youngest and she's seven, so not too small. Plus my family enjoys road trips. I'm sure they'll be fine."

Once they all got settled into the car, Jane turned her focus to Nedra. "We need to stop by Nyla's house first thing so she can take your measurements and get started on the dress."

Nedra nodded her head.

"Remind me who Nyla is?" Bryan asked.

"She's my best friend Marsha's sister. You'll get to meet them both today. Right now, it sounds like."

"And she has enough time to make your wedding dress? I don't know much about sewing, but the wedding is in two days."

"Nyla is a sewing wiz. She assured me she could have it done in no time," Nedra said.

"Wow. Okay then."

When they pulled up to the brown brick rambler, Nedra was still getting Bryan out of the car and into his wheelchair when Marsha came dashing out of the house.

"Nedra!" she squealed.

Nedra was so startled and excited that she almost dropped Bryan.

"Whoa! Me first, then go hug your friend."

"Sorry, Bry!" Nedra carefully removed the neck brace he still wore in the car. After she buckled him into his chair, she dashed for Marsha and the two friends embraced.

Bryan chuckled as he watched them, holding onto each other and bouncing in the driveway.

"Should we go inside?" he asked.

"So this is Bryan?" Marsha asked, looking at Nedra.

"This is him," Nedra said, beaming.

"He's cute!"

"I know, he is, isn't he?"

"Still sitting here," Bryan said.

Marsha laughed and bent down to give Bryan a hug. His right arm wrapped around her with relative ease, but his left felt heavy and uncooperative.

"We didn't really forget about you," Marsha said, straightening up. "So how was your flight?"

"Good." Nedra nodded. "It's only an hour from takeoff until landing, so not too bad. We spent more time trying to get through security, checking his wheelchair at the gate, and then waiting for our stuff at baggage claim than we did actually flying through the air."

Marsha nodded. "Yeah, I bet."

Bryan noticed another woman standing on the front porch watching them all. She finally cleared her throat loudly.

"You guys coming in or what?"

"Yes! We're coming, we're coming." Nedra grabbed the wheelchair and pushed Bryan to the door. "Sorry, Nyla," she said, giving her a quick hug. "I appreciate this more than you could ever know!"

"Oh, I know," Nyla said with a smile. "So you told me fairly simple on the phone, right?"

"Absolutely. I'm not really picky. I just want long sleeves and white. The rest I'll leave up to your creative genius."

"Wow, I wish all my customers were as easy as you."

Nedra shrugged. "I'm just excited to be his wife. I care more about the marriage than the wedding."

Jane nodded her approval. She spoke up for the first time since arriving at their home. "That's the way to have a marriage that will last."

Nyla and Marsha both agreed.

"Is your family just so excited for your wedding?" Marsha asked Bryan while Nyla led Nedra into another room for measurements. Jane hunkered down on the couch and quickly fell asleep.

Bryan chuckled. "I'm not sure excited is the right word to describe how most of them are feeling."

Marsha looked puzzled. "What do you mean?"

"Well, I'm only nineteen and Nedra is twenty-nine to start. Then I went from a brand new high school graduate, to paralyzed, to being engaged to a woman they barely know in just a matter of months. It's just a lot to process."

"I guess I can see that. They couldn't ask for a better daughter-in-law in my book."

Bryan smiled. "I couldn't agree with you more. They are still struggling with me dumping my last girlfriend for Nedra. They weren't too thrilled about having to come all the way out to California, either."

"What's wrong with California?" Marsha asked.

"Nothing. It's just far to come, with not a lot of notice, and all my sisters are still in school. It's hard for everyone to miss school and work. At least these are the things my mom told me. I honestly wasn't thinking about their schedules when we were planning our wedding. We figured out what worked the best for the two of us, and everyone else will come if they can. Like Nedra said, we aren't big on all the wedding details. It's the marriage we're looking forward to. I don't even know what food will be at the reception. Jane basically planned everything for here, and my mom planned everything for the reception back in Utah."

"So Nedra didn't plan either of her receptions? I mean, I know Nyla and her mom planned this one, but I didn't realize she wasn't planning the one for Utah, either."

"I think she told my mom she liked the color blue, but that was about it."

"Wow, that surprises me. Nedra usually likes to be in charge."

Bryan couldn't help laughing. "That she does! She also is trying to keep the peace with my family. Plus she may like to be in charge, but she doesn't really love planning events. There's a difference."

"I guess that's true." Marsha nodded.

Nedra and Nyla came back into the room. Nedra bent down and gave Bryan a kiss on the lips. "All set," she said. "You ready to go meet my brother now?"

"Absolutely," Bryan said.

Nedra softly shook Jane awake. The three of them waved goodbye as they headed back down the driveway toward Jane's car.

"Why don't you drive to Randy's house?" Jane asked, yawning. "I'm beat."

Nedra grabbed the keys her mother offered and climbed into the driver's seat.

"What should I expect from your brother?" Bryan asked. "Is he the protective big brother type, or will he be ready to accept me into the family?"

Nedra glanced at Bryan in the rearview mirror and had to smile. He actually looked more nervous to meet her brother than he had been to meet Jane. She couldn't imagine how scared he would have been to meet her father if he were still alive. Then again, she knew exactly how that meeting would have gone. Her dad would have forbidden the marriage, telling Nedra she couldn't marry a cripple. Nedra quickly pushed the negative thoughts from her mind. She was getting married in two days. Only happy thoughts were allowed.

"You don't need to worry about Randy at all," Nedra said. "He and his wife, Cynthia, are two of the nicest people you'll ever meet. He might not have been the nicest to me when we were kids, but he's thankfully grown out of that. Randy's never really been the protective brother type. They are both economists, so they are very intellectual. Randy will sit down and talk your ear off about the economy and he'll share some amazing stories about their travels all over the world, but he's definitely not the type to sit you down and discuss your intentions."

Bryan breathed a sigh of relief. He didn't really feel especially protective of Becky or Brenda, probably because they were so close to his same age, but when the time came, if any guy ever touched his baby sister Jenny, he'd sock them right in the face.

"We're here!" Nedra announced, pulling into the long driveway. Bryan didn't realize how late it had gotten until Nedra pulled him out of the car and he could see the sun fading behind the trees. He suddenly felt very tired from their day of traveling. And very hungry!

Jane knocked loudly on the front door while Nedra grabbed their bags from the trunk. She caught up to her mom just as the front door opened. Tears sprang to her eyes at the sight of her big brother standing in the open doorway. He was only a couple inches taller than Nedra, thin, with hair that was already turning white despite his young age. Nedra pretended to need to put the bags down for a minute to rest, so she could sniffle and cover the tears that threatened to escape her eyes. She had no idea why she suddenly felt like crying. Maybe she was just tired from all the traveling, or maybe she was feeling reminiscent from all the familiar faces today. Whatever the reason, she took a moment to compose herself.

Randy held the door open for Jane and Bryan as she pushed him through. Once they were inside, he stepped out and reached for one of Nedra's big, bulky bags.

"Let me give you a hand with that," he said.

"Thanks." Nedra wiped her nose with the back of her hand and followed Randy into the house.

Randy set down the suitcase and extended his hand toward Bryan. "Nice to meet you," he said. Bryan raised his hand as much as he could and Randy gripped it, shaking both hands up and down for them. "Make yourself at home."

"Thank you," Bryan said.

Cynthia stepped out from the kitchen, drying her hands on a small, white towel. "Food is almost ready if you're hungry," she said.

As if on cue, Bryan's stomach growled loudly and everyone laughed.

"I'll take that as a yes." Cynthia smiled as Bryan nodded.

"Can I help you with anything?" Nedra asked.

"No, it will just be about ten minutes. Arden, why don't you show them to their rooms so they can get settled."

"Right this way," Randy said, picking up Nedra's heavy bag once again and signaling them to follow. "Now you wanted separate rooms, right?"

"Yes, that's right," Nedra spoke up.

"Then this will be your room," he said, pointing at the first door they came to.

Nedra stepped into the small room. After she hoisted her large bag up onto the bed, she followed Randy and Bryan while Jane helped Cynthia finish up in the kitchen.

"And your room is just right here," Randy said, pointing to another door down the hall.

"Perfect. Thank you."

Randy nodded and left them alone to unpack.

"You're right. Your brother and sister-in-law are very, very nice."

Nedra smiled. It had been a very good day, filled with all the people she loved. If she wasn't careful, she might start tearing up all over again.

"You okay?" Bryan asked.

"Hmm? Oh, yeah, sorry." Nedra shook her head to clear it. "It's just been a very full day." She sat on the edge of Bryan's bed and reached for his hand. She was so grateful to be back in California, and so happy that Bryan was finally able to meet her family. She leaned forward and gave him a long, sweet kiss.

"Wow, what was that for?"

Nedra shrugged as Randy called them for dinner. "We're getting married. Do I need another reason?"

Bryan smiled back at her. "Nope," he said. "Absolutely not."

CHAPTER EIGHTEEN

"All our dreams can come true, if we have the courage to pursue them."

- Walt Disney

The next morning, Bryan awoke to the sounds and smells of someone cooking breakfast in the kitchen. He looked at his chair, parked next to the bed, and wished he was able to transfer himself into it. But his arms were not strong enough and his left arm was still giving him trouble. Instead, he watched out the window and waited for someone to come and get him.

Half an hour later, Nedra peeked her head in the door and found Bryan wide awake.

"Oh, you were so quiet, I thought you were still sleeping."

"Nope, just waiting," he smiled.

"You hungry?" she asked.

Bryan took a big whiff of the sausage, eggs, and pancakes. "Starving," he said.

Nedra lifted Bryan with ease and placed him in his wheelchair.

"That's very interesting to watch, you know," came Randy's voice from the doorway.

Nedra spun around. "What is?" she asked.

"Watching you, my little five foot nothing sister lift a big, heavy, what are you? Six foot one? Six foot two?" he asked, turning toward Bryan.

"I'm six feet exactly."

"Watching you lift this big six foot man out of bed as if he weighed nothing."

"It just comes with the job title," Nedra shrugged.

"So to be a nurse, do you have to take a weight lifting class as a prerequisite? Is part of the interview process to see how much you can bench?"

"Ha ha," Nedra said, rolling her eyes as she and Bryan pushed past him.

Randy chuckled. "Help yourselves to breakfast," he said. "Cynthia made plenty."

"Where is she?" Bryan asked.

"She had to stop in at work for a few hours. She'll be back this afternoon. Tell me what's on the agenda today. I'm at your disposal," he said to Nedra.

Nedra started listing off errands and tasks that needed to be performed before the wedding as she piled a plate high with food.

"Aren't you going to get any for Bryan?" Randy teased.

"This isn't all for me," Nedra replied. "We've found it's easier to just share a plate, since I'm feeding both of us anyway." She pulled out one of the wooden chairs beneath the small kitchen table. She removed the chair next to it and pushed Bryan into the empty spot. Once seated, she scooped a forkful of eggs and, pinching her nose with the other hand, fed them to Bryan. She fed herself a bite of pancake before giving Bryan another bite of eggs, trying not to gag. Randy watched in interest as she rotated back and forth, a bite for Bryan, then a bite for herself.

"If you hate eggs so much, why do you even have them on your plate?"

Nedra shrugged. "Because they're Bryan's favorite." She scooped another mouthful of soft, syrupy pancake. "Why don't you call mom and see if she needs any help with the reception?" Nedra suggested.

"Okay." Randy nodded his head and stood, lifting his phone off the receiver.

Breakfast was peaceful and quiet, but once it was over, Nedra had them dashing all over Oakland for last minute items. By the time they met up with both families for a special dinner that evening, they were exhausted.

Nedra went around the table, making introductions. "This is my mom Jane, my brother Randy, his wife Cynthia, and two of my bridesmaids. This is Marsha. I've known her family for several years now. I lived with them for awhile in college, so they are like a second family to me. And this is my good friend Carol. We grew up together. Then we have Bryan's best man, Greg, who are childhood friends as well. These are Bryan's sisters: Becky, Glenda, Brenda, and Jenny. And Bryan's mom, Carol Jean, and his dad, Glenn. Phew!" she said, sitting back down. "Did I get everybody?"

Dinner was fairly quiet, considering the large group that had gathered. Bryan's family was still recovering from their long drive and given the age differences between their families, there wasn't a whole lot in common to talk about.

"How do you think it's going?" Bryan whispered to Nedra as she fed him another bite.

She glanced at Greg and Marsha, who were laughing about something. Becky seemed to be having a good conversation with Randy and Cynthia, while Brenda listened in and occasionally nodded. Glenda and Jenny were perfecting their skills with getting a metal spoon to hang from their noses. Nedra noticed Carol Jean and Jane had their heads close together, whispering about something. When they glanced in her direction and then put their heads together again, she got nervous.

"Oh dear, I better see what they're up to," she sighed as she got to her feet.

"Who?" Bryan asked, his gaze following Nedra as she strolled around the table and landed beside their mothers.

"So what are you talking about?" Nedra asked, attempting to play it cool.

"You, actually," Jane said with her brightest smile.

"Only good things, I hope." Nedra tried to smile casually, but it looked more like she was gritting her teeth.

"We were just saying how this is going to be a very . . . different marriage," Carol Jean said.

"And that you can't run it," Jane added.

Nedra could feel her cheeks burning a little. "We had this conversation already, Mom."

"I know we did, dear, but as it turns out, your mother-in-law and I have a lot of the same concerns. You are a very take-charge kind of person and, well, frankly, kind of bossy."

Nedra's cheeks were boiling now, but she didn't want to lose her temper in front of everyone, especially when they were supposed to be celebrating. After a few deep breaths, she finally spoke.

"Bryan is a grown man." Nedra put up her hand to stop Carol Jean, who opened her mouth to protest. "He may only be nineteen, but he's not a typical nineteen. He grew up really fast in that hospital bed. He is perfectly capable of making his own decisions, and I know he wouldn't stand for a woman who wanted to just run the marriage. We work together as a team, as a partnership. We always have, and we always will. That is what marriage is all about."

Nedra returned to her seat beside Bryan and reached for his hand.

"What happened?" Bryan asked. "It looked like you were either going to cry or throw something at them."

"I wanted to do both! But I kept my cool, and hopefully they understand us now and how we view this marriage."

The next morning, clad in her beautiful, long, white gown, Nedra carefully knelt beside the soft, white altar. Bryan's chair was pushed up against the other side as close as it could get. He also wore white. With his arms resting on the altar, Bryan and Nedra held hands and stared into each other's eyes as the officiator spoke. Bryan could barely hear what the man was saying, he was so focused on the amazing woman across from him. Who else would have taken on such a difficult responsibility from the start? She viewed him as a partner and not a patient.

As Bryan stared into her luminescent green eyes, her whole soul radiated back. They were both inviting and filled with love. They glistened in the light from the chandelier above their heads. A single tear slowly trickled down her cheek. Bryan wished more than anything that he had the ability to reach up and wipe that tear away, to show her that he could be there for her physically as well as mentally. At least he could still wrap his arms around her, and he hoped that would never change.

Nedra seemed to be smirking at Bryan and that's when he realized the officiator had asked him a question.

Bryan grinned. "Sorry," he said, "I was getting lost in my bride's eyes."

"You have all of eternity for that." The old man's eyes crinkled as he spoke. "But for this part, I need you to look at me."

The guests in the small room chuckled. Bryan smiled. Looking straight into the old man's wise, soulful eyes, he said, "Okay, I'm all yours."

This resulted in another round of quiet laughter.

Bryan continued to look into the officiator's kind eyes, unblinking as he spoke. He didn't want to miss any more questions. When the time came, he said his part, his heart burning with joy as he listened to the same words being spoken to Nedra. His breath caught for a brief moment as he waited for her to also agree. She did with gusto, and Bryan and everyone else in the room snickered. When he announced the couple was married and invited to kiss, Bryan and Nedra did, again with gusto.

Nedra carefully stood, straightening out her gown, and then she and Bryan were congratulated and hugged by their close family and friends. Shortly after, they all moved outside for some pictures in the bright sunshine. It didn't take long before their cheeks were tired and sore from smiling so much.

Since the wedding took place in Oakland, there wasn't much time to spare after pictures. Everyone had to load up into their cars and then drive the hour and a half to Sacramento for the reception.

The reception that night was simple, yet elegant. Jane had paid for everything, while Nyla very generously planned the whole event. As Nedra looked around the beautifully decorated room, she knew her trust in them had not been in vain.

CHAPTER NINETEEN

"Wake up with determination.
Go to bed with satisfaction."
- Author Unknown

Bryan didn't realize how loud the reception had been until he and Nedra were in the car, on their way to the hotel. The silence in the car was almost deafening. It wasn't the awkward silence that can sometimes overthrow a first date. It was the silence of two people who were so in love, just being together was conversation enough. They were also both very tired from the wedding and the day filled with festivities.

As they got checked into their hotel, Bryan looked around the small lobby. It was kind of a dumpy looking place, but it was also the only one they could find nearby that had a waterbed. As Bryan's eyes scanned over everything from the peeling, dated wallpaper to the grimy looking carpets, he was just grateful they only had to stay here one night. Like any other newlyweds, they were both too eager to complain, so they climbed into bed quickly, despite the stained bedspread.

They slept late the next day, grateful for a morning of nothing to do and nowhere to be. Bryan couldn't believe his luck when he awoke and his eyes first rested on his lovely bride. He lay there, just staring at her peaceful, beautiful face for a moment before her jade eyes fluttered open. She smiled at him, causing a wave in the bed as she moved close enough to kiss him good morning.

Bryan moved to wrap his arms around her, but his left wouldn't budge.

"Oh, come on!"

Nedra jumped in response to his loud cry. "What's the matter?" she asked, scrambling off the bed and running around to his side.

"I'm sorry, I didn't mean to wake you. I just can't get my arm to move like it used to and it's frustrating. I wanted to hold you."

Nedra smiled. She sat back on the bed and pulled Bryan's head onto her lap. She rubbed his neck slowly and carefully, then ran her fingers through his thick, blonde hair. "Is this helping at all?"

"Yes," Bryan whispered, closing his eyes. "I just wish I knew what was going on. Why now? Why is my left arm losing strength and ability? Something is wrong."

"Well, we will go back and see the neurologist in just a couple weeks. Can I get you anything to help you feel better?" she asked.

"Just a new arm, and perhaps a new neck," Bryan teased.

"Sure, I'll get right on that," she said, softly massaging his neck some more.

Bryan smiled at Nedra. She always had a way of distracting him from any worrisome thoughts. "What time is check-in at the Homestead?" Bryan asked.

"Check-in is at 3:00 p.m., I believe. Or maybe 4:00 . . ." Nedra rolled off the bed and rifled through her purse, pulling out some crumpled papers. "Yup, 3:00," she said. Nedra shoved the confirmation papers back into the depths of her purse and turned to face the bed. She noticed for the first time how high and flat the top of the footboard was. The smooth, dark wood stood above the top of the waterbed by a couple feet, at least. Nedra grinned and began climbing on top of the footboard.

"What are you doing?" Bryan laughed.

Nedra stood up straight on the top of the footboard, and looked at Bryan mischievously. He looked at her curiously in return, not sure what she was trying to do. She turned her back to Bryan and raised her arms as if she were getting ready to take flight. Bryan's eyes widened when he finally realized her plan.

"Nedra, no!" he shouted just as she fell flat back onto the waterbed. Her height and momentum as she hit the bed caused Bryan's body to fly several feet into the air. Nedra watched him, smiling. She thought her idea would be a funny trick and make them both laugh. She forgot to take into account that Bryan couldn't reach out and catch himself. As she watched his body fly into the air, his face filled with terror, she realized her mistake. He landed safely back onto the bed, causing them both to move up and down with the waves. Silence followed.

"Sorry," Nedra whispered, afraid to look at him.

"Don't. Ever. Do. That. Again."

Bryan was excited to get to the Homestead. It was the only honeymoon they really had planned, and they could only afford one night, but they looked forward to the nicer hotel and better amenities.

After checking in, Nedra pushed Bryan's chair along the beautifully carpeted hallway all the way down to the honeymoon suite. She unlocked the door and paused in the open doorway to look around. The tall, cathedral ceilings made the room feel much bigger than it actually was. The fresh, white canopy bed was much larger than the queen they slept in last night. Bright crimson rose petals sprinkled over the top of the bed added to the romantic atmosphere. Across from the bed, a fireplace glowed, warm and inviting. Nedra eagerly pushed Bryan into the room.

"Wait a minute," she said, backing out again. Then she scooped Bryan up out of his chair, and carried him over the threshold. They both laughed as Nedra walked past the jetted tub and set Bryan onto the down comforter. She turned around to go back for his chair, pushing it the corner of the room. She also brought their bags in and set them beside the tall, ornate dresser. She knelt down to unzip her bag when Bryan shouted from behind her.

Nedra turned to see his face red and sweat pouring down his cheeks.

"This bed is boiling hot!"

Nedra ran over and lifted him from the bed. Sure enough, someone had turned the waterbed temperature up as high as it could go. Nedra moved Bryan out onto their private deck and turned down the bed.

"You okay?" she asked, twisting the lid off a water bottle she removed from the mini fridge and bringing it to his lips. He took a long drink before responding.

"Yes, but I think the waterbeds are all trying to kill me!"

A few days later, home in their own apartment, Nedra slipped into her long, white wedding dress.

"You ready to do this again?" Bryan asked from behind her.

Nedra already dressed him in his black suit. He looked sharp with his bright blue tie bringing out the blue in his eyes.

"Yes, and then I'm ready to be done so we can just focus on us for awhile, and not have to worry about everyone else."

Carol Jean had the church gym decorated with blue balloons and crepe paper. Every touch from the flower arrangements on the tables to the ribbons on the backs of the chairs was coordinated perfectly and added a state of elegance to the otherwise simple room. Carol Jean also made and decorated their wedding cake, which stood prominently on a round table in the center of the room.

"I can't believe your mom did all this," Nedra said, examining the cake more closely.

"She's pretty good, isn't she?"

"Pretty good?" Nedra asked. "Look at this!" She pointed to the fancy string work Carol Jean designed out of frosting.

As they continued to look around the room, four women entered, all dressed in black.

"Can we help you?" Nedra asked.

"Yeah, where would you like us to set up?"

"Set up?" Nedra looked around the room, confused.

"Right over here," Carol Jean said, coming into the room and pointing at a cluster of chairs.

Nedra and Bryan watched as the women retrieved their violins and began to warm up.

"A violin quartet?" Nedra mouthed. "Wow!" she whispered. "Your mom really went all out with this!"

"Well, it's not like I'm her only son and eldest child or anything," Bryan teased.

"Still," Nedra said quietly. "I'm impressed."

Guests began arriving a short time later. With the exception of a few nurses, Nedra knew almost no one. Bryan enjoyed introducing his new wife to countless family members, church friends, high school buddies, and neighbors. They couldn't believe the crowd that turned out to support them and help them to celebrate their new life together.

Toward the end of the reception, both Bryan and Nedra were getting very tired. "Sometimes I think you're lucky to be in that chair," Nedra said, hopping from one sore foot to the other.

"You can sit," Bryan offered.

Nedra sat on his lap to give her feet a break. She glanced at the long line of people who remained to be greeted. She was touched by the show of support by Bryan's parents and their friends, but she did want to get home at some point tonight.

"Home, sweet home!" Nedra said, pushing Bryan's chair over the lip and through the front door.

Bryan glanced around at the small two-bedroom apartment. The white, cinderblock walls stood bare and cold, but his eyes widened in amazement as he looked from the small kitchen to the cozy living room. It was their first home as a married couple. There could have been no windows and black streaks of mud down the walls and it still would have felt like a palace.

They unpacked boxes and set up their new home in preparation for their lives together to begin. One of the first things they did was purchase a large, brown recliner for Bryan to sit in. Bryan pushed forward with the joystick, moving slowly around the chair. His whole face broke into a smile.

"It's perfect," he said.

"Do you want to try it out?" Nedra asked.

"Sure!" Bryan's smile widened.

Nedra carefully picked him up and set him on the cushiony seat. "How does that feel?" she asked.

Bryan placed his cheek against the back of the chair and closed his eyes. "It's very soft and comfortable," he whispered. Bryan made a kissing sound with his lips so Nedra would lean closer. As her lips neared, he kissed her sweetly. "Thank you," he whispered. "I know you've given up a lot for me."

"My beanbag chair for a nice, comfortable recliner is not giving anything up," she responded.

"Your cats."

Nedra glanced around the small room, as if expecting to see one of her babies peer around a corner. She sighed. Her gaze moved to the window and the large yellow sign that was posted across the courtyard: No Pets Allowed. Nedra stared at the harsh sign begrudgingly before finally pulling her eyes back to Bryan. She saw his sweet smile looking back at her and was reassured of her decision.

"I miss them," she admitted. "But I found them good homes. Besides..." She climbed onto the arm of the large chair and snuggled into his broad chest. "You make a much better companion."

"Someday when we have a house, you can have cats again. I promise."

"But you hate cats," Nedra said, raising her head to look him in the face.

"I do, but for you, anything!"

Nedra smiled to herself and snuggled in deeper. "So are you ready for school?"

"I don't really know exactly. I'm not sure what the professors will think of me, or what they'll expect from me."

"Well, we should definitely go talk to disability services tomorrow, so you can get some aids to help in class."

Nedra hopped off his lap and gathered the pile of wood they had purchased earlier. She crouched over the floor and worked, following Bryan's instructions, to build a table a little bit wider than the recliner and just tall enough to clear the armrests. The little legs had wheels she could easily slide over Bryan's lap for homework or eating.

She stood back and admired her handiwork. "There," she said. "Now you are really ready for college."

CHAPTER TWENTY

"Everyday courage has few witnesses. But yours is no less noble because no drum beats for you and no crowds shout your name."

- Robert Lewis Stevenson

Bryan awoke far too early, from the irreverent screeching beside his bed. His eyes whipped open. He scanned around the room for the cat which was surely being strangled to death. Nedra threw one arm out from the covers and with a solid whack, the screeching was snoozed.

Bryan groaned. It was the first day of school. He never enjoyed mornings, especially when they meant school. Although college might be different, he didn't know yet. He did at least get to choose most of his classes. With eager dread welling inside, he knew sleeping was no longer an option.

"Ned," he whispered loudly. "Hey, Ned!"

Nedra started. "Wh-what?"

"I need to get up for school."

"Mm-kay."

Bryan waited a few moments. When he heard Nedra's soft snore, he rolled his eyes and tried again. "Nedra!"

She shot up like a rocket. "I'm up," she said, her eyes still closed. She yawned and stretched before finally getting out of bed.

Bryan's mind raced with questions while Nedra bathed and shaved him. He was so lost in thought that he bit her thumb as she fed him cereal from a bowl.

"Ouch!"

"Sorry!"

"Just eat the Cheerios, not me."

"Sorry, I guess I'm a little preoccupied."

"I noticed. Anything you want to talk about?"

"No. I'm just wondering what today will be like."

"Only one way to find out." She offered him an encouraging smile. "Well," she said, glancing at the clock above the stove, "this is it."

Bryan looked at the clock and then the front door. No going back now.

"You've got everything you should need in your backpack. I'll see you back here this afternoon." Nedra made sure his bag was secured to the back of his chair and then walked behind Bryan to the front door.

"Have a good day." He kissed Nedra goodbye and drove out the door. She smiled back and waved, still clad in her pajamas, before closing the door behind him. Bryan knew she was probably headed back to bed.

He drove around the side of the building to the parking lot where a red GMC van sat waiting for him. Disabled Student Services center at the University hired a man to pick up the students in wheelchairs and transport them to school. As Bryan approached, the gentleman hopped out and lowered the large, metal lift.

"Mornin'," he boomed in a cheerful voice.

Bryan carefully drove onto the lift and the man raised it slowly, shutting the doors tightly behind him. The van didn't have a raised roof, so Bryan's tall head almost brushed against the ceiling.

Once they arrived on campus and Bryan was lowered safely to the ground, he moved swiftly down the sidewalk in the direction of the engineering building. His first physics class would be a good test to see if this was really what he wanted to do with his life. As Bryan got closer to the campus, he watched everything in constant motion around him. Students buzzed in and out of buildings, moving swiftly about him as they tried to find the right building and the right classroom. Bikes and skateboards whizzed past, almost cutting him off a few times. Some students lay in the grass, talking with friends. Others walked with determination and focus, marching their feet as if in a drill line. Bryan chuckled as he watched one kid, his nose so deep in a book that he tripped over a lip in the sidewalk and almost biffed it completely.

Most of the students moved out of Bryan's way as he drove through campus. Some stared, while others stared but pretended not too. Bryan was used to having many eyes follow him wherever he went. It was human nature to be curious. He just wished people would stop pretending he wasn't there.

As he neared his first destination, Bryan charged forward, pushing the highest gear on his wheelchair so he could make it to the top of the ramp. Bryan's tires spun and he popped a wheelie, going up onto his two back tires. The momentum in which he zoomed forward, combined with the incline of the ramp, caused Bryan to tip backward. His chair came crashing down. Bryan's arm and shoulder slammed into the sharp concrete, his face skidding along the gravel.

The loud campus around him went deathly silent. Several students rushed to his aid.

"Are you okay?"

"What happened?"

"Do you need help?"

"Do we need to call someone?"

What the kids weren't expecting to hear was the laughter that broke forth from Bryan's mouth. "Well, that was stupid," he chuckled.

A couple of the students who rushed forward started to smile. No one dared join in his laughter.

"Can you help lift me back up?" Bryan asked the gathering group.

Several of the biggest guys moved forward and tried to lift the chair, not realizing how heavy it was. "We need some more help," one of them shouted. Two more guys and one girl came forward and tried to fit in around the base of Bryan's wheelchair. They counted and all lifted together, following Bryan's instructions. He bounced back into place, his head throbbing slightly from the fall.

"Do you need a push?" a petite, blonde girl asked.

"No, thank you," Bryan said. "I just need to use a lower gear next time."

The girl moved forward and held the door open for Bryan.

"Thanks," he said. "And thank you all for your help," Bryan called to the others who had lifted him before adding to no one in particular, "Shoot, I'm probably going to be late now."

Bryan moved through the building quickly and found his classroom with no time to spare. As he pulled up to a desk, the professor called the class to attention.

"Can you take notes for me?" Bryan whispered to the boy seated beside him.

The kid glanced at Bryan, looking him up and down through thick glasses which seemed to take up most of his face. "Sure," he mumbled.

Bryan took a deep breath and settled in, trying to focus on everything the professor said. *All right, college. Ready or not, here I come.*

As Bryan drove home that afternoon, his mind stung with information. He mentally checked off all the homework he had to complete before he came back to these classes, astounded at the amount expected of them. How was he supposed to get that much done in only a matter of days?

Bryan tapped on the door with his foot rest and was greeted by Nedra's expectant face. "How was it?" she asked. Almost immediately Nedra's face fell when she saw the raw scrapes on the side of his face. "What happened?"

"Oh yeah, I forgot about that." Bryan chuckled as Nedra ran for a wet rag. "I pushed the wheelchair forward too hard when I needed to get up a ramp for class. It was really dumb. I completely biffed it and my chair tipped."

Nedra gasped.

"I'm fine. Just a stupid mistake. There were plenty of people around to help. The most painful part of today was not my face. It was having to sit through my English class." He blew out a huge sigh.

Nedra finished dabbing the dirt out of Bryan's scrapes and reached for the zipper on his backpack. "Well, let's look over it. Maybe I can help you." Nedra lifted Bryan and positioned him in the large, overstuffed chair. His back sank into the soft, brown leather. Nedra reached a hand behind his chair and brought the table across his lap, and then laid his English book on it along with a sheet of plain white paper.

"What was your assignment?" Nedra asked, poising the sharp, yellow pencil just above his blank paper.

"We have to read the first five chapters of this book and then answer questions about what we read. It's basically the same thing we did in high school, but I nearly failed high school English. I didn't get it then, so I'm not sure how I'm supposed to understand it now." Bryan frowned as he spoke, his forehead crinkling as he stared at the seemingly foreign words listed under chapter one.

"Oh, these aren't too bad," Nedra said, glancing over the questions.

"For you, maybe."

"No, really, you can do this. I'll show you."

As Nedra talked him through the first question, Bryan only became more frustrated. "But that doesn't make any sense!" he argued. "There's too many metaphors. Why can't an author just mean what they say?"

"The reason why doesn't have to make sense. You just have to understand that this is what the author means!" Nedra said, the frustration rising in her own voice.

"But if I don't understand the why, how am I going to figure out the what?"

Nedra shook her head. "You're such an engineer. Most people just accept that these are the metaphors, and they stick with them."

"I'm not most people. My brain doesn't work that way. I need to understand how something works."

Nedra took the eraser and wiped away the answer she had been trying to explain, smearing grey streaks across the page. "Fine. Then you tell me exactly what to write, and I'll just be your scribe."

Bryan talked through the question out loud, explaining to Nedra exactly how he wanted it written. She began to write again, but couldn't bite her tongue when he started to give a wrong answer.

"No, that's not how you do it," Nedra said.

"That's not my answer," Bryan argued.

"But your answer is wrong."

"I thought you were just going to be my scribe. No more teaching," Bryan said through gritted teeth.

"What am I going to do? Just let you get it wrong?"

"It's my mistake to make!"

Nedra huffed and got to her feet. "Maybe we need to hire you a tutor."

"Yes," Bryan agreed. "For the sake of our marriage."

After the first few weeks of school, Bryan got into a pretty good rhythm. Nedra got him dressed, shaved, and ready for school in the morning before returning to bed for a couple more hours of sleep. She then got herself ready, cleaned the apartment, went grocery shopping, or whatever other errands needed to happen, and went to work by 3:00 p.m. Bryan spent all day on campus, driving his wheelchair from one class to the next. He arrived home in the late afternoon, shortly after Nedra left for work. She got home from work between 11:00 p.m. and midnight, put Bryan to bed, and then they would do it all again the next day. It wasn't an ideal situation for a couple of newlyweds, but Nedra's shift gave her weekends off so they could spend their time together then.

Bryan rolled into class early one morning, slid up to one of the desks, and waited patiently for more students to arrive. English had never been his strong suit, but he was actually excited for class today. His professor saw him ride in and approached his desk.

"I really enjoyed your paper, Bryan," she said softly. With a slender hand, she dropped the white sheet on his desk, face up. She gave his shoulder a slight squeeze before going back to her large desk. Bryan glanced down at the paper, his eyes rushing to see the big, red 'A' written across the top. Bryan beamed, his eyes moistening a little. He coughed to cover the emotion building up in his throat. He had never gotten an 'A' in English before.

When the classroom filled with students, the professor finished returning their assignments and then spoke from the front. "I enjoyed reading all of your papers, but one in particular was completely filled with raw emotion. You don't have to be a master of words to succeed in English, but if you can draw your audience in with emotion, then they will be able to overlook any writing flaws. So, Bryan Carroll?"

Bryan snapped his head up in attention. She smiled at him warmly. "Would you mind reading your paper aloud for the class, please?"

Bryan felt heat rising from the back of his neck as he slowly pushed his chair to the front of the classroom. He cleared his throat. The professor ran back to his desk and grabbed the paper for him. She held it up as he read aloud.

"It was on a hot June day that my life was drastically changed. I chose to make a dive this day, a dive I will never forget.

"The pond was about a mile and a half up a rocky side canyon. It was surrounded on three sides by steep cliffs. Here we chose to cliff dive. The cliffs we were diving from were about twenty-five feet high. The deepest part, about fifteen feet, was under these cliffs where the river flowed into the pond. There were several people jumping from them and soon it was my turn. I stood looking over the edge, trying to get set. The water had calmed from previous jumps and lay there glassy, enticing. It was now time for my jump. I took a deep breath and I was off into space.

"I flew through the air under perfect control and entered like a knife, slicing through the water, barely splashing. Once in the water, I allowed my muscles to relax. It was as if everything was in slow motion, yet I was still moving quickly through the water. I could see the bottom coming too fast, but it was as if it were happening to someone else and I could do nothing to stop it. My hands hit and my arms buckled. Then my head hit! It seemed like such a gentle tap, but suddenly I couldn't move a thing.

"Somehow I managed to get so I was floating with my head towards the surface. I could see the light of the surface but I could not seem to get there. I was so close to the one thing that I needed to live, but it was if it were there to tease me. I knew that by no power of my own could I reach that blessed air. A minute passed; I began to wonder how much longer I would last. I was totally helpless as I looked toward the light above, hoping that someone would come for me before it was too late. After what seemed to be a millennium, a hand appeared and pulled me to the surface. I did not know my rescuer as he brought me carefully to shore.

"He and others placed me on a piece of plywood, immobilized my head, and propped my feet on a log overhanging the water. It was about six o'clock when they sent for help, help that was over seventeen miles of rough water away. As I lay there, I began wondering how badly I was hurt and how they were going to get me out. The time grew long; night descended. I lay awake most of that time wondering what my life would be like now. Would I be paralyzed? Would I be able to have children? As the sun rose, I realized that there had been a lean-to built to shade me. By the time help arrived, eighteen hours had passed. I felt as if a weight had been lifted when I heard that the helicopter had arrived. I had been living with the fear that I would have to be rafted out over that treacherous river. Carefully they carried me down the mountain to the helicopter. The litter was supported by six men, stabilized from above by a man with a rope, and my I.V. was held by another. My mouth was parched and the wet sock they let me suck on did little to relieve my thirst. Finally, after two hours, the sun beating upon us unmercifully, we reached the helicopter. Quickly I was loaded aboard and flown to the medical aid that would mean my survival.

"After I reached the hospital at Page, Arizona, and was tested and examined, the young doctor caring for me told me that my neck was indeed broken and that I probably would be paralyzed. Thus ended the most beautiful dive of my life. I still remember that dive vividly: a high, arching swan dive, entering the water cleanly as a hot knife through butter. A perfect dive . . . that ended in tragedy."

His professor sniffed as she lowered the pages. Bryan glanced around shyly. Several girls in the class were wiping away tears while many of the other students were staring at him, their mouths hanging slightly open. Bryan quickly lowered his gaze and drove the chair back over to his desk. He could still feel several pairs of eyes burning into his back, but he tried to ignore them.

CHAPTER TWENTY-ONE

"It is difficult to say what is impossible, for the dream of yesterday is the hope of today and the reality of tomorrow."

- Robert H. Goddard

The day finally came for Bryan's appointment with the neurologist. He'd only been in school a few weeks, yet that first appointment with Dr. Barney felt like ages ago. The neurologist ordered another matrizamide myelogram, and sent Bryan downstairs to radiology.

A short time later, Bryan found himself laying on a cold, steel x-ray table as the doctor injected a special dye into his neck just below the level of injury. The table was then tipped so Bryan's feet were lifted significantly higher than his head. The radiologist stepped behind his large, lead-lined, glass booth and asked Nedra to do the same. He took a series of x-rays to see whether the dye was able to pass above the level of his injury. Once they finished, the radiologist lowered Bryan's feet and Nedra assisted him in returning Bryan to his chair.

The doctor walked into the room thirty minutes later, scratching the stubble on his chin. He held up the stack of x-rays and flipped through them several times before speaking.

"You very clearly have some blockage around your spine. However, we can't determine precisely why you are losing function. It looks like it could be scar tissue that's blocking the dye, or even possibly a cyst. Are you experiencing any sort of pain, Mr. Carroll?"

"No, I'm not," Bryan answered.

"Then here's what we're going to do. Let's hold off on surgery for now. The last thing we want to do is cause even more damage. Cutting you open to clean out the scar tissue could be very risky. I know you want answers, but unfortunately, it's just too hard to tell. If your function changes drastically, or you start experiencing any discomfort, then I want you back in here right away and we'll revisit the idea of surgery. Are you okay with that?"

Disappointed that they didn't receive any answers, Bryan and Nedra both agreed. They just hoped they wouldn't need to come back to see him for a long time, if at all.

Bryan heard a knock on his front door and looked up from his books in confusion.

"Are you expecting someone?" Dan asked.

"No," Bryan said, his eyebrows bunching together.

"Do you want me to get it?" Dan asked, already rising to his feet.

"Thanks," Bryan mumbled.

"Oh, I'm sorry, we must have the wrong apartment."

Bryan could hear the muffled voice hidden behind the door.

"I'm in here, Mom!" he called.

Dan opened the door wider to reveal Bryan's parents and Grandpa.

"Hey, what are you guys doing here?" Bryan asked. His eyes settled on Grandpa Carroll, who stood wheezing in the open doorway. "Sit down, Grandpa," Bryan encouraged. He hated to see how old Grandpa looked.

Dan quickly stepped forward, shoving the pile of open books to the floor. Grandpa smiled gratefully and sat where the books had been. His parents followed suit, squishing onto the snug sofa.

"This is Dan," Bryan introduced. "He's one of my scribes/tutors. He acts as scribe with my homework, and also tutors me in physics whenever I don't understand something." *Explaining things in such a way that don't make me want to pursue a divorce*, Bryan added, in his mind.

"It's very nice to meet you," Glenn said, rising to his feet and extending a hand.

"The same," Dan said, nodding his head as they shook. He then shook hands with Grandpa and Carol Jean. "Well, Bryan, should we pick up with this tomorrow?"

"Yes, thank you."

Dan quickly gathered his book bag and slipped out the door.

"Do you have a tutor for each class?" Carol Jean asked.

"No." Bryan shook his head. "They're more scribes than tutors. They only tutor me when I'm having difficulty understanding something. Dan helps me with physics. I think he's taken this class before because he seems to understand everything.

"What about English?" Glenn asked. "I know you always hated English in school."

"It's not too bad. I have a pretty decent teacher."

"I mean do you have a tutor to take notes for you and help with papers?"

"No, English is one of those classes where I really only need a scribe to help with the assignments. I just tell them what to say, and they type it up. Here, if one of you will put me back in my wheelchair, I can show you this new program I got. It's awesome!"

Glenn stood again and slid Bryan's table back beside his chair. He lifted Bryan gingerly and, after stumbling slightly, placed him in his wheelchair.

"Phew!" Glenn said, wiping his forehead. "I'm out of practice."

"Ouch!" Bryan flinched.

"What's the matter? Did I do something wrong?"

"No, my neck has just been really sore lately."

"Your neck?" Carol Jean asked, looking panicked.

"It's nothing, Mom, just some minor pains since my last matrizamide myelogram."

Bryan tried to change the subject quickly by leading them over to a large desk pushed against the corner of their living room. On top of it sat one of the new IBM personal computers 8088, a gooseneck microphone page turner. Bryan pulled up to the microphone, turned on the computer, and opened WordPerfect by speaking a few commands.

"When Nedra or my scribe is busy or at work, I can use this program to help type up my assignments." Bryan spoke softly, "Hotel, India, space, Mike, Yankee, space, November, Alpha, Mike, Echo, space, India, Sierra, space, Bravo, Romeo, Yankee, Alpha, November, period."

Bryan's family watched in amazement as *'Hi my name is Bryan.'* appeared on the screen. Bryan grinned in response to their shocked faces. "Pretty cool, huh?"

"It must take you forever to finish a paper, if you have to use the military alphabet." Glenn spoke in awe.

"I dunno," Bryan said. "I've gotten pretty good at it."

"Wow," Carol Jean whispered. "So how do you do your reading assignments?"

"Here, let me show you." Bryan backed up and pulled over to an interesting contraption next to the computer. The metal stand had an open book resting on it, with a small wheel attached beside it. "I got this electric page turner just over a week ago. It has a built-in sip and puff switch so to turn the page forward I just sip a little. Watch." Bryan put his mouth around the straw and sipped. The small wheel, which appeared to be sticky, moved forward and pressed against the page. Then it pulled back, lifting the top page slightly away from the rest. A metal arm then came up and turned the page.

Bryan looked at his family expectantly. They all stood, mouths gaping, behind him.

"Does it ever grab more than one page?" Grandpa asked.

"Every once in awhile it will accidentally turn five or ten pages at a time."

"What do you do then?"

"I call one of our neighbors to come over and reset it for me."

"No fancy computer program for reading?" Carol Jean asked.

"I wish!" Bryan said. "Can you imagine if I could just read my books on a computer? That would be amazing."

Carol Jean looked around their tiny apartment as if just seeing it for the first time. "Is Nedra not here?" she asked.

"No, she works from 3:00 p.m. to 11:00 p.m. on weekdays."

"So how do you get dinner?" Carol Jean asked.

"Sometimes she leaves a sandwich on the little table for me. But I usually wait until she gets home, or I can ask a neighbor to warm something up for me. Everyone is very nice around here."

"You don't eat until after 11:00 p.m. sometimes?"

"It's not a big deal, Mom. There are still a handful of snacks I can eat with just my right arm."

"Well, grab your stuff. We'll take you to dinner."

Bryan glanced at his mom with raised eyebrows.

Upon realizing what she said, Carol Jean huffed and reached for the handle. "It's just a figure of speech," she added. Bryan laughed loudly as Glenn shut and locked the door behind them.

Bryan drove around campus, whizzing by the same building for the third time. He was completely lost. Today was his first math test, but he couldn't just sit behind a desk like the other students and fill in the little grey bubbles. He had to make a special appointment with the testing center where someone could go through the test with him. That is, if he could ever find the testing center.

As Bryan started to pass the building for a fourth time, he paused. Maybe this was the right building and he just needed to go inside to look. He carefully pushed the joystick forward and revved his wheelchair to the top of the ramp. Once inside, he started to see signs and arrows pointing him to where he needed to go.

Bryan moved forward, pulling into the elevators just as someone else got out. The doors closed with a heavy snap and Bryan realized he was stuck. He tried to move forward with his chair, but no matter how close he was, his fisted hand could not push the buttons. So Bryan sat back and waited. And waited. Over an hour later, someone else finally decided to use the elevator and Bryan was relieved when the doors opened. The girl jumped back in surprise when she saw Bryan sitting there.

"Would you push number four for me, please?" Bryan hadn't spent too much time calling out for help, but his voice came out raspy regardless.

The girl didn't say anything; she simply pushed the number four and leaned back against the far wall. She kept glancing in his direction during their short ride but never got up enough courage to talk to him. As soon as the elevator doors opened again, she sped out and disappeared.

Bryan rolled along the floor, looking for room numbers. He saw a red sign on the third door he passed, announcing new testing center times.

"Finally," Bryan murmured as he drove inside. "I'm a little late," he admitted to the girl behind the counter.

She turned, adjusting her name badge, and jumped in recognition. It was the same girl from the elevator.

"I'm sorry I keep startling you," he spoke softly.

"It's not your fault." The girl waved his comment away with her hand. "How long were you stuck in that elevator?" she asked.

"Oh, probably about an hour," Bryan said.

"Really?" Her eyes grew in shock. "I'm so sorry."

Bryan tried to brush it off. "It's happened before. And it will probably happen again."

The young girl emitted a sound like a mouse squeaking as she covered her mouth. "Oh, you poor thing."

Bryan wasn't sure exactly how to respond. He didn't particularly like being pitied.

"I'm sorry," she said again after realizing she had been staring. "What can I do for you today?" All signs of her previous shyness seemed to have melted away.

"I'm here to take a math test for Professor Downy's math 101 class. My name is Bryan Carroll."

"Okay, Bryan, I see you were scheduled to be here . . . about an hour ago. Fancy that," she said, smiling brightly. "Well, don't worry about it. I'll get you in."

Bryan watched as the girl walked over to another desk and tapped the shoulder of a young man with dark, curly hair. She pointed in Bryan's direction and he watched as the young man looked back at him, nodded, and mouthed a few words. The girl bounced back a moment later.

"As soon as he's done with this test, Peter said he can fit you in."

"Thank you," Bryan said.

When Peter came to get him ten minutes later, Bryan's stomach growled loudly.

"Sorry," Bryan said. "I haven't had time for lunch yet."

"No worries. I'll try and get you through this test as quickly as we can so you can go eat."

"Thanks. So what do I need to do?"

"Well, let's come over here where it's quiet," Peter said, pointing to a long table that ran along the back of the room.

Bryan followed him closely, accidentally clipping Peter's ankle twice with the front of his wheelchair in the cramped room.

"Sorry," Bryan said. "It's a little harder to control in such small spaces."

"It's okay," Peter said, even though Bryan saw him wincing.

Peter placed the test on the table and held his pencil up, poised just above the paper. "I'm basically just your scribe," Peter explained. "You have to figure out the problems on your own and then I will fill in the answers you tell me. I can not tell you if your answers are incorrect."

"Oh, I know," Bryan said.

Peter grinned. "I just have to say that little spiel so people understand the testing center is not at fault when or if they fail."

"Do people actually expect you to take the test for them?" Bryan asked.

"You'd be surprised. All right, Bryan, tell me how to spell your name."

Peter's hand moved quickly across the page, filling in a bubble for each letter of Bryan's name, along with numbers for his birthday. With his basic information completed, Peter showed him the first math equation and Bryan began working the problem out loud. When he finished the test, his stomach growled again with anticipation.

"You better go eat that food now," Peter said. As Bryan started to roll away, Peter turned around and called him back. "Do you have someone who helps you eat?" he asked.

"My wife usually packs a lunch for me. I think I have a burrito today. I just need someone to help me warm it up and then I can go over to the disabilities center and find an aid there to feed me."

Peter tried not to let the surprise show on his face when Bryan said he had a wife. "I'm going on my lunch break right now," he said. "Do you want to come with me to the kitchen and I can heat up that burrito for you?"

"Yes, thank you," Bryan breathed.

He followed Peter down the hall and back to the elevators. This time Peter pushed the button for him so his time spent in the lift was much shorter. Bryan followed Peter down the long, white hallway into a small kitchen labeled Student Services.

"Where is that burrito?" Peter asked.

"In my backpack, hooked to the back of the chair," Bryan explained.

Peter unzipped his black bag and only had to dig for a moment before he noticed the small, cloth lunchbox. He opened the bag and dumped out a frozen burrito and a mostly melted ice pack.

Peter popped open the orange wrapper on one end and placed the burrito on a paper plate which he pulled out from one of the cupboards. After a couple of minutes, he pulled the steaming plate out of the microwave and set it on top of Bryan's left armrest.

"There you go," Peter said. "Is there anything else you need?"

"No, and thank you, Peter. Go ahead and eat your own lunch. Someone over in disability services can feed me."

"All right, well, you take care. It was nice to meet you."

"You, too," Bryan said. He pushed forward with his right arm and drove quickly to the other building so he could eat before his food got too cold. His hand felt warm beneath the plate, but Bryan didn't pay too much attention.

Once inside the building, Bryan rolled up to the front desk and was greeted by a familiar face.

"Hi, Bryan, what can we help you with today?"

"Is someone available that can feed me?"

"Sure thing. Why don't you pull right over there and I'll grab you an aid."

When the aid walked up, she smiled at Bryan and lifted the burrito to feed him. Her smile quickly turned into a scream. "Your hand!" she shrieked.

Peter accidentally set the boiling plate directly on top of Bryan's left hand and wrist. It had burned his skin so severely, large blisters were beginning to form.

"Oh my!" The kind lady behind the desk ran over when Bryan's aid shouted. "Bryan, I'm afraid you're going to have to go over to the hospital and have that looked at. You might have a second degree burn."

Bryan looked down at his hand and frowned. "Okay, but could someone please feed me first?"

CHAPTER TWENTY-TWO

"Grief is not a sign of weakness, nor a lack of faith—it is the price of love."

- Author Unknown

Nedra sat in the waiting room, flipping through a magazine, not reading a single page. She kept glancing at the clock, even though she knew his surgery had barely started. After experiencing pain in his neck for the first time since the accident, Bryan and Nedra began to worry. When the pain only increased and his function decreased, they finally called the doctor again. Here she was, six months later, staring at the clock and hoping for the best.

They're just going in to clean out scar tissue. Everything will be fine. Nedra had to repeat the words to herself over and over before she finally started believing them. An hour passed. Then two. Nedra found herself staring so hard at the surgery door that her eyes began to water from not blinking. A man dressed in green scrubs pushed the door open and walked out. Nedra's heart jumped and she began to stand, but he walked right past her to another waiting family. She sat stiffly and waited some more.

When Bryan's doctor finally emerged, Nedra searched his face for clues as to how the surgery went. He gave away nothing. When he did finally make eye contact as he approached, Nedra's stomach sank. That definitely wasn't an everything-went-well face.

"Mrs. Carroll?" Nedra looked around for Carol Jean before she realized he was talking to her.

"Yes?"

"Let's have a seat," he said, indicating two chairs.

"Look, doctor, I'm a nurse. I've given bad news more than a handful of times. I know all the techniques. Just give it to me straight."

The doctor nodded his head. "When we went in to clean out the scar tissue, we found it wasn't scar tissue at all. Those pieces surrounding the spine that showed up on the X-ray were bone fragments. When your husband broke his neck, it was an explosion fracture. What they didn't realize was that pieces of his spine broke off and wedged themselves in his spine and neck. These bone chips cutting into nerves have been what is causing his pain. The loose bone fragments are also why he is losing function in his left side. We had no choice but to fuse his spine. While we were trying to clean out the bone chips, we also severed his phrenic nerve on the left side. He no longer has the use of his lung or diaphragm on the left side."

Nedra stared at her hands while she absorbed all this new information. As soon as the doctor mentioned severing his nerve, her head snapped to attention.

"What do you mean, you severed his phrenic nerve?" The sharpness in her voice made the doctor flinch. "You're telling me my husband can no longer use half of his diaphragm now? And he lost one of his lungs? As if he didn't have enough problems to deal with already!"

"I'm very sorry, Mrs. Carroll. If we didn't remove the bone chips and fuse his spine, he would have continued to get worse."

"But you're telling me he's going to keep getting worse? He's going to lose all the mobility he gained back in his arms now? After all that work, he won't be able to move from the neck down anymore? My husband won't be able to hold me, or any of our future children?"

The doctor hesitantly nodded, his face grim. "I can't say for certain. There's a good chance his arms will not last more than a couple of years. At least he can get around on his own without the assistance of oxygen."

Nedra stared up at the bright lights of the hospital waiting room until her eyes burned. Her mind and her heart both raced with questions. The grief pulled down on her shoulders like a heavy blanket, threatening to suffocate her and their dreams for the future. She finally looked back at the doctor, blinking slowly as she tried to recover from his news.

The doctor stood slowly and Nedra followed. "Can I see him now?" she asked.

"As soon as he's awake, I'll send a nurse out to get you."

Nedra slumped back in her chair. She closed her eyes and wished for sleep, but she knew her mind would never shut down at this point. She stood again, the need to move coursing through every tense muscle in her body. Nedra circled the hospital a couple of times before ending up in front of a telephone. She had promised to call Glenn and Carol Jean as soon as surgery was over. She took a deep breath and reached for the black phone. Dialing the number from memory, she held the receiver to her ear and listened as it rang twice.

"Hello?" Carol Jean sounded anxious.

"Hi, Carol Jean, it's me."

"How did it go? Is everything okay?"

"Well . . ." Nedra had been able to keep her emotions in check while talking to the doctor, but now, with the sound of his mother's worried voice in her ear, Nedra's eyes began to pool as she spoke.

Bryan was surprised to see his mom standing in front of his door when he got home from school late one afternoon. He and Nedra had been married for over two years, but she rarely came to their tiny, little apartment.

"Hey, what are you doing here?" he asked.

As Bryan drove closer, he could see his mom had a red, blotchy face.

"What happened?" Bryan asked, panic rising in his throat.

"Grandpa Carroll," Carol Jean could barely utter his name. "He had a stroke."

Bryan's heart dropped. He felt nauseous and dizzy, as though he might be sick. "A . . . st-stroke? Where is he?"

"He's at the hospital. We thought you might want to go see him."

"Yes," Bryan said, accelerating up the sidewalk. He drove straight past his mom toward the parking lot. He knew she was behind him, but he couldn't slow down. He just needed to move forward. Now. Carol Jean had to jog to keep up with him. Bryan continued in front of her, his mind clouded over with thoughts of Grandpa.

"Bryan?" His mom's voice broke through his grief. "I know we need to take your new car, but I don't know where it is." Bryan looked at her and realized he was driving right past their blue van. He and Nedra finally saved enough money to buy a van with a raised roof and wheelchair lift, so Bryan could stay in his chair when they drove places.

"Oh, sorry." He pulled up beside the side door and directed Carol Jean on what she needed to do.

"It's fine, sweetie." Carol Jean struggled for a moment, her hands shaking. She finally got the van unlocked and lowered the lift for Bryan.

The drive to the hospital was very solemn. Neither of them knew what to say, so they chose not to speak. Bryan felt anxious as he waited for his mom to park the car, lower the lift, and get his wheelchair steadily to the ground again.

She moved in front of Bryan and led him through the bright hallways, straight back to Grandpa's room. Glenn sat in a chair beside his father's bed, his face gaunt and pale, with dark circles under his eyes. He looked significantly older to Bryan in that moment.

"Dad?" Bryan whispered.

Glenn looked up, his lips forming a tight line as he attempted to smile. "Come over here." Glenn slid his chair over and motioned for Bryan to take his place. "Grandpa will want to see you when he wakes up."

Bryan sat and looked into his grandpa's sleeping face. His cheeks seemed pale and emaciated, his skin a sickening grey color. His eyes were sunken and dark, yet he slept peacefully at the moment.

"How's he doing?" Bryan asked.

"Pretty well, considering. The doctors are hopeful he'll be able to go home in a day or two, but he's going to need pretty constant care, at least for awhile."

Carol Jean looked around the room and seemed to suddenly realize something was missing. "Where are the girls?" she asked.

"I had Donna take them home," Glenn answered. "They've had enough of hospitals and need the rest."

Carol Jean nodded her agreement.

"Is Donna up to taking care of him full time?" Bryan asked.

"I think we're all overwhelmed right now, but she's willing to do whatever needs to be done."

"I wish I could help," Bryan mumbled.

Glenn placed a hand on his shoulder and gave it a squeeze. "We know, Bryan."

Grandpa began to stir and they all quieted, watching him in anticipation.

His eyes slowly fluttered open and settled on Bryan. Grandpa tried to smile, but his face sagged, dragging his skin down on one side. Grandpa looked confused as he tried to speak but only sounds came out.

"It's okay, Grandpa, I'm here. I know what you're trying to say." Bryan tried to soothe the old man's frustrations.

Grandpa gently nodded and closed his eyes again, his breathing slow and steady.

"That wasn't long," Bryan said, frowning.

"No, he's been in and out like that all day. He utters a few syllables and then goes back to sleep. I don't know if it's the stroke, or the drugs they put him on."

"Probably both," Nedra whispered from the doorway.

Bryan's face brightened. "Hey, you're here."

"Of course I'm here. As soon as I got your message, I told them I was going on break and came straight down. How's he doing?"

"Good, we think," Carol Jean said. "They haven't told us much, except he's stable, which seems to be doctor's speak for 'not dead.'"

Nedra smiled. "If he were really serious, he would be in the ICU and not a regular room like this one."

Nedra strolled into the room and wrapped her arms around Bryan, hugging him tightly. He put his right arm around her in return and they held each other for several minutes. "How are you doing?" Her whisper tickled the hairs on his neck.

"I'm okay, now that I'm here, next to him." Nedra pulled away and looked into his glistening eyes. "Thank you for coming," he whispered back.

"Of course. He's my grandpa now, too, ya know."

Bryan forced a weak smile. "I know. You're right."

Nedra moved around so she stood behind Bryan, her small hands on his broad shoulders. They watched Grandpa's chest rise and fall as he slept peacefully, silently praying he would live.

Bryan drove through campus with a dark cloud hanging over him. Grandpa was out of the hospital now, but he was confined to a wheelchair and still struggling with his speech. Bryan didn't pay attention as he whizzed by another wheelchair going the opposite direction.

"Hey, ya cow turd, watch where yer goin'!"

Bryan stopped suddenly, causing his body to bounce, and he almost tipped out of his chair. He regained balance, using his right arm, and turned his chair around as fast as he could. Staring at him with an excited smile on his face was J.D., cowboy hat and all.

Bryan's smile equaled that of his former roommate. "J.D.! How are you?" Bryan asked as he drove closer. "I almost didn't recognize you, sitting up."

J.D. laughed loudly, causing several students to stop suddenly and turn their attention to the conversation.

"So tell me what yer up to."

"Just enjoying married life and going to school. That's all I do."

"Yeah, but the married life is pretty sweet, ain't it?" J.D. chuckled again, winking in Bryan's direction.

Bryan couldn't help but laugh along with him. J.D.'s contagious laugh was so loud and joyous, it seemed impolite not to join in.

"How's Nedra doin'?"

"She's good. And how's your wife? I'm sorry, I don't remember her name."

"Jenny. She's awesome! She's pregnant; I'm goin' to be a daddy," J.D. said, beaming.

"Wow! That's incredible!" Bryan's mouth dropped open in surprise. "So were you guys able to get pregnant on your own?" Bryan whispered, glancing around.

"It's not like it's a big secret!" J.D. exclaimed loudly. "We actually went to Dr. Harbor up at LDS hospital. Have you heard of him? He's the best OB/GYN for people like us."

"No, I've never heard of him," Bryan said. "We haven't prevented, but we haven't really been trying to get pregnant either. Babies are expensive."

"You're tellin' me! Jenny has been buyin' up all the baby stuff she can get her hands on. I dunno how we're supposed ta pay for it all!"

"Well, there are some other issues with Nedra, too. We're still not sure if we're going to be able to have kids. We want to try, though. My younger sister is actually expecting. Nedra is so mad about it," Bryan said, shaking his head.

"Mad? Why mad?" J.D. asked.

"Because we got married first, and I'm older. Do you remember my sister, Becky?"

"Oh ya, was she the hot one?" J.D. asked, laughing when Bryan made a face.

"If you mean the one just younger than me, then yes, that's Becky. Hot?" he asked, pulling a face again. "You're married!"

"Doesn't mean I can't appreciate beauty when I see it," J.D. said, shrugging. "So she went and got herself knocked up?"

Bryan ignored his crude reference. "She got married the summer after we did," Bryan said.

J.D. glanced down at his watch and glowered. "Well, I'd love ter stay and chat, but I hafta go," he grumbled. "Go see Dr. Harbor when you're ready fer a little one. He's the best."

J.D. sped away, popping wheelies every few feet to show off. Bryan chuckled as he watched him go.

That evening, his dad drove him to Donna's house for a visit with Grandpa. Bryan brought along a golf magazine he'd asked Nedra to pick up last time she went grocery shopping. Glenn helped him turn the pages, but Bryan read the words aloud to Grandpa. He hoped to repay him for all the visits when he was bored in the hospital.

Grandpa was lucid. He obviously understood everything Bryan read, but he couldn't articulate his words back. When he tried, only random syllables would come out. Grandpa's brow would furrow in frustration and anger.

"It's okay, Grandpa," Bryan soothed, but inside, his heart was breaking. He couldn't believe his hero and best friend struggled with something as seemingly simple as talking. Bryan tried to distract Grandpa by filling in his side of the conversation. He was careful not to ask any questions so Grandpa wouldn't have to try and answer. "So I ran into my buddy J.D. today. You remember him? He was one of my roommates at the hospital when I broke my neck. He was the one who rode around on that gurney on his stomach. Funny kid. Well, his wife is pregnant with their first. He said he went to a Dr. Harbor who helped them conceive. Nedra and I are thinking of going and talking to him. We knew it might be hard for me to have children, well, for obvious reasons. This doctor seems to be the best at helping couples in similar situations as us."

Grandpa just stared at Bryan as he spoke, taking in every word and occasionally nodding. Bryan could tell he understood. Grandpa's intelligent eyes never left Bryan's face, giving him a sense of knowing.

"So I think Nedra and I should go see this doctor soon. Becky is already having a baby. It's our turn next. We need to have a little boy so we can name him after you."

Bryan stopped when Grandpa started shaking his head vigorously.

"Oh, come on, Grandpa, Mayo is not that bad a name. Especially for a middle name."

Grandpa continued to shake his head.

"How else am I going to pay tribute to one of the greatest men I've ever known?"

Bryan watched as a tear escaped from Grandpa's eye and rolled down his cheek.

"I love you too, Grandpa."

Five months later, Nedra ran to the ringing phone, barely getting there in time. It was Carol Jean calling to tell them Grandpa had passed away. As soon as Bryan saw the grief written on her face, he knew what happened. He lay in bed that night, allowing the tears to run freely. Nedra wrapped her arms around Bryan and held him, his body racked with sobs. The gentle tossing of their waterbed eventually lulled him to sleep. She continued to stroke his hair, even after his eyelids closed, holding him close to her and willing the crippling grief to subside. She remembered these feelings all too well from when her own father had passed.

Bryan was asked to speak at Grandpa's funeral the following Saturday. Several of his cousins commented on how he had been Grandpa's favorite, not in a mean or jealous way, but simply stating it as though it were a clear fact. Bryan always felt embarrassed by such comments and brushed them aside.

As Bryan listened to the different speakers share stories about Grandpa's life, he couldn't help but smile. He thought back on all his great memories of playing baseball with Grandpa, going camping and fishing, playing games, and even just sitting quietly together and watching golf. His Grandpa loved life, and watching him suffer with a mouth and body that no longer worked properly for the last six months had been torturous. Bryan's tears faded into peaceful happiness as he realized how miserable Grandpa must have been, and how happy he was now to be free of those pains.

CHAPTER TWENTY-THREE

"People are always blaming circumstances for what they are. I don't believe in circumstances. The people who get ahead in this world are the people who get up and look for the circumstances they want, and if they can't find them, make them.

– George Bernard Shaw

Bryan sat in front of his computer, dictating a paper for one of his engineering classes into the small microphone. The sun had already gone down and he was getting hungry. There was a knock on the front door, followed by the handle turning. Bryan turned his chair around in time to see his sister Becky walk in, a small baby on her hip.

"Hey, Bryan, sorry I'm late. Austin decided to take a late nap. You hungry?"

"Very," Bryan said, following Becky into the small kitchen.

"What would you like for dinner tonight?"

"How about a can of chili?"

Becky smiled. "That's what I made you last week."

"Well, I like chili."

"Chili it is then. Here," she said, placing the baby on Bryan's lap. "Hang out with Uncle Bryan for a minute."

Becky crouched down beside the stove and retrieved a small bowl from the cupboard. She rummaged through drawers until she found a can opener. Once the chili was cooked in the microwave, she removed the bowl with a hot pad and carried it into the living room.

"He's getting so big," Bryan said.

"I know, they grow fast! I can't even believe he's sitting up already. Do you mind holding him while I feed you? I don't want him trying to grab the spoon, or putting his hand in the chili."

"I don't mind at all!" Bryan said, looking down into his nephew's round, little face. Bryan was grateful to have Becky and Brett living just on the other side of married student housing. It sure beat having to wait until 11:00 p.m. for dinner!

Nedra sat beside Bryan in the doctor's office, stroking the back of his hand with her fingers even though he couldn't feel it. She ran her thumb along the faint scar he'd gotten from being severely burned by a burrito only a few years ago.

A faint knock on the door announced the doctor's arrival before he entered the room. "Good afternoon! I'm Dr. Harbor," he said, extending a hand toward Nedra. She returned his greeting with a firm shake.

"I'm Nedra. This is my husband Bryan."

"So what can I do for you folks today?" His warm eyes crinkled as he looked at the couple with anticipation.

"We were told by our friend J.D. that you helped him and his wife get pregnant. Since we're in similar circumstances, we thought you might be able to help us, too." Nedra held her breath, waiting for a response.

"Ah, J.D." The doctor chuckled quietly. "Yes, he is quite a character, that one."

Bryan laughed politely. He glanced at Nedra, who remained firmly in place with bated breath, staring at the doctor.

"Well, I have dealt with a lot of couples in similar circumstances. I can see that you are not interested in chit-chat— you want answers— so I'll cut to the chase. I looked through the medical histories you provided our office, and I can see where you're concerned. Bryan can not be the father of your child without trying some pretty risky procedures. And even if you choose to forgo the risks, you aren't guaranteed his sperm will be viable. A lot of spinal injury patients do not have viable sperm, especially the longer they have been paralyzed."

Nedra nodded slowly.

"I have some good news and some bad news for you. The good news is there's a new procedure that's just recently been made available for spinal injury patients who want to have children."

Nedra sat at attention. "Really?"

The doctor raised a hand to stop her excitement. "But," he said, "and this is a big but, the procedure is extremely expensive and only available on the east coast."

Nedra sank back into the chair, feelings of hopelessness crushing down on top of her. "Oh."

"I have a colleague out there I can refer you to, but from your reaction, I'm guessing that really isn't an option in this case."

"No," Bryan said, his voice cracking. "The thing that has prevented us from coming to you sooner is money."

"All right," the doctor reached out and patted Nedra's hand. "Don't fret, my dear. We still have other options. I'm guessing since the two of you are in here, adoption is not a consideration." He stated rather than asked.

"We wouldn't completely rule it out, but I've dreamt of being pregnant and having a family of my own for so long . . ." Nedra trailed off.

Again the doctor spoke in a soothing voice. "And Bryan, how do you feel?"

"I just want to be a daddy."

The doctor looked between the two of them, their faces pallid with angst. "The other option I see working out for you two is to try a sperm donor."

Nedra twitched, her mind reeling with this new option. She hadn't really considered it before. She always assumed her husband would be the father of her children.

"We have a very stringent process here for our donors. Number one is that our records are sealed so you will never know the identity of your donor, and he will never know the identity of his donations. We have found this is the best way to deal with this type of pregnancy for everyone involved. Number two is we are very thorough on our end with the medical histories of our donors, to ensure these babies are as healthy as possible. And number three, my nurses help me match donors' looks with the fathers, so their children look as natural as possible. I see from your medical records that you are RH negative. In your case, we would probably forgo basing your donor on your husband's looks. Instead, we could easily find a sperm donor who is also RH negative, and you would most likely be pregnant in a matter of weeks."

Nedra chewed on her lower lip as she let this new information sink in. She looked at Bryan who also seemed to be lost in thought. "But then it wouldn't be Bryan's baby."

"In a manner of speaking, I suppose you're right. Bryan would not share genetics with your child, no. But he would be the parent of this baby from the moment you conceive and throughout its entire life."

"And how exactly do you find these donors?" Nedra was so used to knowing everything that doctors said to her that it was frustrating to feel out of place in her own environment.

"Well, most of our donors are either medical students or law students who come over from the university to make a little extra cash. We do a blood test and have them fill out their medical history, just as you did, so we can ensure the babies are as healthy as possible. Then you'll take some of these ovulation tests home with you." The doctor held up a stack of thin, white strips. "And then you'll call us when you're ovulating. You'll come in, lie down, we'll inject the sperm, and you're good to go. The whole thing takes less than five minutes."

Nedra nodded to show she understood, but she still wasn't sure how she felt about Bryan not fathering their children. "Well," she said, getting to her feet, "you've given us a lot to think about. We'll have to go home and talk things through, and then we'll let you know what we decide." Nedra thanked the doctor and started for the door.

"No." Bryan spoke up for the first time, startling both Nedra and Dr. Harbor. "If this is what we need to do to have a baby, then this is what we're going to do."

"You're sure?" Nedra squeaked.

"Absolutely," Bryan said. "There are a lot of things I can't do for you. We're not adding 'have a family' to that list."

Nedra laughed and cried out at the same time, her joy glistening on her cheeks. She ran over and threw her arms around Bryan, hugging him tight. She turned to the doctor and asked, "So when do we get started?"

Three months later, Nedra sat on the edge of their white, porcelain tub, holding a long, white stick in her hand. She squeezed her eyes shut, while counting slowly in her head. She knew if she stared at the test, waiting for an answer to appear, it would be torturous. Not looking was already bad enough. "Three minutes," Nedra whispered. She took a deep breath and opened her eyes. She stared at the little greyish screen. "No," she gasped. Her hand flew to her mouth, in an attempt to keep her emotions from spilling out. She threw the stick in the garbage can beside the toilet and ran from the room. She almost bumped straight into Bryan's chair.

"What's the matter, Ned? I thought I heard you yell?"

Nedra raised her chin and looked straight in her husband's concerned, blue eyes. "I'm pregnant."

Nedra stood on her tippy-toes, trying to string the orange and black decorations along the edge of their large window. The baby kicked hard and she almost lost her balance. She grabbed hold of the step ladder, catching herself before she could fall.

"Please be careful, Nedra," Bryan said, watching her with worry.

"Oh, I'm fine." She continued to decorate their apartment. It was difficult taping things around the window and on the walls, with her large belly protruding out and causing a barrier. Her short arms struggled to reach past the baby as she secured the final strip. She started to slip again, stumbling backwards as she stepped off the ladder.

"Nedra, you are going to give me a heart attack! Please stop. The baby won't care whether or not our apartment is decorated for Halloween."

"I want to start these traditions now," she said simply, continuing to work. "I bought a pumpkin to carve too, I'll show it to you later."

Bryan sighed. "I don't know if you should be wielding a knife when you're pregnant. You know how often it causes you to drop things."

Nedra walked past Bryan's large chair and pushed his engineering book closed.

"Hey!"

"You can study later," Nedra teased. "We need to get to my appointment."

Bryan glanced up at the small, round clock which hung above the television. "Oh wow, yeah, it's getting late."

Nedra had four weeks left of her pregnancy as they entered the doctor's office for her prenatal visit. The nurse checked her weight and then asked Nedra to sit while she strapped the black cuff around her bicep. Placing a stethoscope on the crease of her arm, the nurse squeezed her pressure bulb until Nedra's arm tingled. Nedra watched the nurse's forehead wrinkle in concern. She released the cuff and started the process over.

"Let's just try this one more time," she said. Her smile was tight and forced. Nedra tried to ask if something was wrong, but the nurse held up a finger to silence her. Nedra watched with dismay as the nurse's forehead crinkled again and she shook her head. She slowly removed the cuff and met Nedra's worried gaze. "Your blood pressure is way too high," she said. "Let me go grab the doctor, if you'll just step into this first room here," she said, indicating the nearest door.

When Dr. Harbor checked Nedra's blood pressure, he came to the same conclusion. "Okay," he said, "I think we need to induce you and get this baby out, for both your sakes."

"What?" Nedra hadn't meant to yell, but she wasn't ready. She wasn't ready at all.

"Head out to the reception desk and let's get your induction scheduled for the next two weeks."

When Nedra had Bryan loaded back up in their van, she placed the key in the ignition and then sat back against the seat without turning it. She stared out the windshield at the pink October sky.

"Ned?" Bryan whispered. "Is everything okay?"

Nedra turned to face him, her eyes pricked with tears. "I still had a month. I had four more weeks to get everything done. What am I going to do? My mom isn't going to be here that soon, her plane tickets aren't for another week." She placed a hand on her large belly and stared up at the car ceiling. "I just can't believe it's finally here. We're going to be parents." Nedra's breathing became short and ragged. She sat forward, clutching the steering wheel in her tight hands, trying to catch her breath.

Bryan watched Nedra's knuckles turn white, her wheezing growing more profound. "Nedra, look at me." She obliged, though she continued to gasp. "You're going to be an amazing mom! We packed the hospital bag this week, maybe your mom can change her tickets, and the baby won't know if its nursery is done or not. I promise everything is going to be just fine." Bryan stared into her eyes, willing her to believe his words.

Nedra nodded, her breath becoming steady once again. She smiled at Bryan. "Thank you." She reached out and touched his hand. "You always know how to bring me back down."

When Nedra arrived at the hospital two weeks later, they were running behind schedule. Several women who had been induced the night before had still not delivered yet. Nedra was given Pitocin, which did not work. She was given more Pitocin and an epidural. After eleven hours of unsuccessful labor, Dr. Harbor came into her room again. Nedra was exhausted and angry.

"I think it's time to start a C-section."

"It's about time!" Nedra yelled.

As they prepared her for surgery, Nedra kept asking for a mirror. The staff politely reminded her to lay down and relax so they could do their job safely.

"But I want to see it! I'm a nurse!" she complained.

Finally Dr. Harbor came over and placed a hand on Nedra's shoulder, firmly but gently pushing her back down on the operating table. "Nedra, I understand you're a nurse, but it is standard policy. We cannot allow you to watch your own surgery. If you were to go into shock or something, that would put you and the baby in danger. I know, as a nurse, you understand that."

Nedra grumbled a response and remained perfectly still while the anesthesiologist gave her another epidural. Bryan sat quietly in his chair beside her head. The doctors hung a blue screen across Nedra's chest, separating the surgery from her and Bryan's line of vision.

"I can feel that," Nedra complained, as they used the cautery to stop her bleeding.

The anesthesiologist placed a hand on her shoulder. "Are you sure?"

"Yeah, I'm pretty dang sure!"

"You're not supposed to…"

"I know."

"I can't give you anything else for the pain at this point."

"I know." Nedra gritted her teeth and strained her ears, trying to hear what the doctor was saying to his staff. She felt some tugging and a sudden whoosh of pressure being released from her insides. A tiny cry broke through the quiet of the room. Nedra wanted to sit up again, but this time the numbness of her body held her down. The doctor snipped the umbilical cord and held the gooey, pink infant above the curtain for the proud parents to see. "It's a boy."

Tears sprang to Nedra's eyes. She had wanted a boy first with all her heart. Thanks to recent technology, most of Nedra's friends were able to find out the sex of their child halfway through pregnancy. She refused to find out, fearing she would be disappointed if they told her it was a girl. She tried to turn her head to look at Bryan, but found again she was unable to move. Bryan slowly rolled up beside her, his eyes shining, as they looked at their beautiful, new son.

All too soon, the doctor whisked the baby away again to be cleaned and weighed. Nedra closed her eyes, allowing the tears to spill out past her eyelids and run down the table. She could feel more tugging as the doctor worked quickly to sew her back up. Once she had been successfully repaired, the curtain came down and the doctor smiled at her appreciatively. "You did great," he said. "He's perfect."

They transferred Nedra back onto a gurney, lifting her legs from the operating table one at a time. The nurse returned and placed the little, white bundle in Nedra's arms. "Seven pounds, fourteen ounces," she said, smiling. "The perfect size, I think. What are you going to name him?"

Nedra looked back at Bryan and he smiled. "Matthew Mayo Carroll," she announced proudly.

Over the next several weeks, Nedra felt like a walking zombie most days. She still had to wake early in the morning to get Bryan ready for school and out the door. Then she'd attempt to sleep more, crawling back into bed and closing her eyes just in time for Matt to start crying. Thankfully, her baby was a good napper, so she could get a little shuteye before Bryan returned home from school and needed help with homework.

With the help of another engineer, Bryan built a small infant seat that connected on to his wheelchair. He would drive a crying Matt around their living room and up and down the sidewalks outside their complex, lulling him to sleep. Sitting in his leather recliner at night, Bryan could wrap his right arm around his son and cuddle him to sleep while Nedra got some rest. Sometimes the family, all snuggling together, could relax and watch TV.

Once Matt learned to walk, however, it became another story. He toddled and ran all over the house, keeping his parents busy from sunrise until sundown. Matt had more energy than they knew what to do with. Bryan got up early, spending his mornings on campus, going to classes. He came home so Nedra could leave for work and spent the rest of his day chasing a toddler around the apartment.

Before Matt's third birthday, Bryan began to notice some changes occurring with his right arm. He would be driving his wheelchair on campus, and then his arm would give out. He tried to stretch the muscles by extending his arm as he waited for the strength to come back. Sometimes he could continue driving after only thirty seconds. Other times he had to wait for five or ten minutes. One night, as they were trying to calm Matt for bed, Nedra placed him on Bryan's lap. He snuggled into his dad, tired enough to go to sleep. Bryan tried wrapping his arm around him, but it simply gave out, slipping off the chair and dangling over the side. Matt crashed to the floor and began wailing for Mommy to rescue him. Nedra scooped him off the hard floor, kissing each boo-boo he pointed out.

She glanced at Bryan, her eyebrows raised. "What happened?" she mouthed over Matt's head.

Bryan looked down at his limp arm, still dangling over the side of the chair. No matter what he tried, he could not will his limb to move. Nedra's gaze followed Bryan's down to his arm. She quickly grabbed his hand and placed it on top of the armrest.

"I'll call Dr. Barney in the morning," she sighed.

"Bryan Carroll." A nurse dressed in white pants and a bright, multi-colored top called his name.

Nedra gave his hand a final squeeze before getting to her feet and pushing Bryan's wheelchair through the door the nurse held open for them. She led them back into a smaller room where she asked them basic questions and took all of Bryan's vitals before promising the doctor would be with them shortly.

"How are you doing today, Bryan?" Dr. Barney asked as he stepped into the room. He smiled, hesitantly looking over at Nedra, their confrontation still fresh in his mind. "And how are you, Mrs. Carroll?" He offered her a warm smile, hoping she would take it.

"I'm well. How are you?" Nedra answered curtly.

"Good. So what are we seeing you for today?" The doctor was thankful to turn his attention back to Bryan, but Nedra answered.

"He's losing his right hand. Bryan can't get around campus anymore without someone pushing his wheelchair, and I work. He also dropped our son. I know we thought this was a possibility; I just wasn't expecting it so soon."

"We have a fairly new machine; it's called an MRI. A lot of hospitals are starting to get them."

"I've heard of them," Nedra responded.

"Good. Well, I would recommend we do a scan with this new machine first. It will make the images so much more clear than the matrizamide myelogram did."

"Okay," Bryan sighed. "How long does it take?"

"Oh, it's not long at all. The machine is in a trailer outside the hospital. Would you like to follow me, please?" The doctor spoke with a nurse at the front desk. A short time later, she returned with an orderly, who took over pushing Bryan's chair. The two of them followed behind Nedra and Dr. Barney as they wound their way down the long, white hallways and out a side door into the bright sunlight.

The doctor guided them over to the large, green trailer. Using a trailer lift, they got Bryan and his chair inside. The room was snug without being claustrophobic. Nedra placed a hand on the huge, cream-colored machine and it beeped, causing her to jump.

"Don't touch the machine, please," Dr. Barney said, standing behind a clear, plastic screen.

"Sorry," Nedra mumbled.

Upon his instructions, she moved behind the screen with him. The nurse and orderly worked together to lift Bryan and lay him on the thin table which fed into the machine. As soon as Bryan was comfortable and secure, they stood behind the protective, clear wall and watched as Dr. Barney began pushing buttons. The tray underneath Bryan groaned to life, pulling him farther and farther into the machine until only his feet hung out. After several minutes, they pulled Bryan out of the machine and returned to his original room inside the hospital.

The doctor excused himself to review the results. Nedra followed shortly after Dr. Barney. "I'm just going to go call your mom and check in on Matt," she said.

Bryan remained in the room alone. He wasn't sure why they had done the MRI. He knew what the results would be. Nedra needed the peace of mind, to know they had checked everything thoroughly before deciding his fate. Bryan figured he was losing his right arm, just like he'd lost the left. He'd just have to find a new way of getting around. It might make school a little more difficult, but he could handle that. He knew it meant no more holding his son, though, and that was the hardest thing to lose. At least Matt was getting older, so hopefully he could still give his son rides. He'd just have to learn to hold on for himself.

Nedra came back, interrupting his thoughts. "He's napping," she said. Although her voice carried hints of relief, her forehead still creased with worry. "Has the doctor come back in yet?"

"No," Bryan said. "I can imagine it will take awhile."

Dr. Barney tapped on the door once again, announcing his presence before entering the room. He explained what they already knew. The MRI gave him a much better image of Bryan's neck, spine, and scar tissue, but he was indeed losing function on the right side and there was no way of stopping it. "I recommend you start saving for a much bigger chair that you can power by mouth. Here is a number to call for pricing and ordering," he said, handing Nedra a small, white card.

CHAPTER TWENTY-FOUR

"One who gains strength
by overcoming obstacles
possesses the only strength
which can overcome adversity."

\- Albert Schweitzer

Within a few months' time, the function for Bryan's final limb was completely gone. They had been saving as much as they could to buy him a new chair but had to take out a hefty loan to make up for the rest.

Bryan's new chair was much larger than his previous ones. With a high back, reaching all the way up to his neck, it gave him the new support he needed. The cushion under him was much thicker and softer than his previous, more basic chairs as well. The chair became a part of who Bryan was after that. He could no longer transfer to other chairs or car seats. Bryan remained in his wheelchair from the moment Nedra got him up in the morning until he went to bed at night.

For the first few days, Bryan spent a lot of time on the sidewalks outside, learning how to drive his new wheels. The motion for his chair was controlled through a long, thick straw which ran all the way from his left armrest, where the control box was located, to his mouth. Bryan would puff air into the straw to move forward. The harder and longer he puffed, the faster his chair would go. His chair had different speeds, so he didn't have to continually puff to make the chair move. He would puff hard, watching the indicator on the screen until he reached the desired speed. Then he would continue, as if on cruise control, until he sucked hard on the straw to stop. A short, quick puff of air would result in the chair turning right, and a quick suck would cause the chair to go left. Once Bryan was comfortable in his new wheels, they got rid of the old recliner. He no longer sat in it, and they needed the space in the living room so Bryan could move around.

Bryan continued to spend his days in class, working toward his engineering degree. With the help of tutors and scribes, he completed every assignment and remained caught up with his peers. Because of how time consuming even the simplest of tasks were, he could only take a couple classes at a time. After four years of college, many of the students he started with were graduating, but Bryan continued to push forward.

After a particularly tiring day at school, Bryan came home and was greeted by Nedra and Matt. Nedra gave him a quick peck on the cheek and left for work.

"Daddy, play with me?" Matt asked.

"Daddy is tired, Matt. Why don't you go play in your room?"

"No, Daddy play!"

"I can't, buddy. I have so much to do for school and it's been a very rough day."

"Tag, you're it!" Matt tapped Bryan's chair and ran for the front door, tossing it open.

"Matt, no!" Bryan yelled. He chased after Matt as fast as he could go, but Matt kept running in circles, and zig-zagging in different directions so Bryan couldn't keep up. Finally, starting to wear out, Matt ran up two flights of stairs and hid in the stairwell. "Matt, come here, please!" Bryan called. "Matt? MATT!"

Still, Matt remained in his hiding spot, unwilling to move. He giggled to himself as he listened to his father scream below.

"MATTHEW MAYO CARROLL, GET YOUR BUTT DOWN HERE RIGHT NOW!" Bryan screamed until he was red in the face. Finally, he heard the crunching of little feet on cement. Matt's thick, brown hair appeared over the railing.

"Hi, Daddy," he smiled mischievously.

"DON'T HI DADDY ME. I HAVE BEEN CALLING YOU FOR TWENTY MINUTES! GET IN THE HOUSE RIGHT NOW, MISTER!"

Matt frowned, his steps growing more tentative as he drew closer to Bryan's chair. He looked up into his dad's enraged, purple face and stuck out his tongue. Then, in a flash, Matt reached out with his tiny, chubby fingers, and flipped the switch on the bottom of Bryan's chair, turning it off. Bryan screamed after him as Matt casually walked right past, head held high, and waltzed in through their front door, closing it behind him.

Bryan remained stuck in the stairwell for over an hour until one of their neighbors found him there. Bryan quickly explained how to switch his chair back on and the neighbor opened his front door for him, which was thankfully still unlocked. Bryan drove inside, fearing the worst. Matt was happily seated on the floor, a coloring book open on his lap, a small box of crayons at his side. He looked up, watching as his dad rolled in, and then he looked back down and returned to his coloring.

>♦< >♦< >♦<

"You want another one? Really?" Bryan asked later that night.

Nedra looked at him, her eyes pleading. "I don't want Matt to be an only child," she said. "I always wanted to have four kids," she added, lifting Bryan into bed for the night.

"Four?" Bryan's eyes grew wide. "I admit, I like coming from a big family. There was always someone to play with . . . or torture," he added, smiling, "but after days like today, I'm not sure if I can handle more."

Nedra climbed into bed beside Bryan, snuggling into his shoulder. "Today was a bad day. They're not all like that, are they?"

"No," Bryan admitted. "But four?"

"Let's just take them one at a time," Nedra said.

"All right," Bryan conceded. "But if we have another one as hyper as Matt, then we're done," he teased.

Nedra laughed softly. "Deal."

The next morning after Bryan left for school, Nedra called Dr. Harbor's office. She didn't want Bryan to overhear in case he changed his mind. She told them they were ready to try again and after answering several questions, the nurse on the phone told Nedra to call again when she was ovulating, and they'd schedule her to come in.

Over the next several months, Nedra went in twice to have the procedure done. Both times resulted in a negative pregnancy test. Discouraged, she went in to see Dr. Harbor again.

"What can I do for you, Nedra?" he asked.

"Bryan and I are ready for another baby," she answered. "The last two artificial insemination procedures didn't work. I don't know what else to do. Is it on my end? Am I getting too old to conceive? Or was there something wrong with those particular donors?" Nedra paced the room as she spoke.

"Hmmm." Dr. Harbor stroked the scruff on his chin as he thought. "Here's what we're going to do. I'll have my nurse run a blood test, just to be certain that nothing is wrong on your end. I have an idea, but let's make sure everything is working properly first. I want you to go home and rest. Try not to stress. When you add stress on top of trying to conceive, our bodies tend to not work the right way. Continue to take the ovulation tests, and come back here next month when you're ovulating again. We'll try one more time, stress free, and pretend like this is no different than any other time. Does that sound all right?"

Nedra nodded slowly. "So what are we going to do that's different?"

Dr. Harbor put a finger to his lips. "Shhh. No stress, remember? I want you to be as relaxed as possible. I'll call you if there's a problem with your bloodwork. Otherwise, I'll see you next month."

The doctor strode out of the room, leaving Nedra a little confused. The nurse came in a couple minutes later and readied Nedra's arm by wrapping a tight blue band just above her elbow. She tapped the vein a few times with her index finger and looked at Nedra. "Are you ready?" she asked, holding the sharp needle point against her flesh.

"What?" Nedra looked down at her arm and up into the nurse's face for the first time.

"It's okay, sweetie, I'll be gentle," she soothed, mistaking Nedra's distraction for nerves.

Nedra's face reddened. She had probably already been a nurse for a number of years before this girl was even out of high school. And here she was, looking like an amateur.

"I'm fine," Nedra stated, her lips tight. She didn't flinch or move a muscle as the nurse withdrew several vials of blood. She thanked the young nurse the moment she was finished and hurried out the door.

The following month, after all her bloodwork was cleared, Nedra sat on the edge of the bathtub once again. She still wasn't sure what had been different. Everything from the hideous patient gown she had to wear to the injection of semen was the same as every other time before. Dr. Harbor smiled mischievously as she left his office and said he looked forward to her call in a couple weeks. Now, two weeks later, she sat stone still on the edge of the porcelain, as if any movement could change the outcome of the test resting in her hand.

"Mommy?" Matt's voice floated through the door.

"Just a minute, Matt. Mommy's going potty."

"Mommy, I come in?"

"Not yet, baby."

Matt stuck his tiny fingers through the slat under the door. "Mommy, what are you doing?"

Nedra laughed, her nerves fading as she got on her knees and grabbed at Matt's fingers. He squealed in delight, his giggle melting her heart. Did it really matter if she couldn't have more kids? She already had one sweet, incredibly active, hilarious little boy. Maybe she was only meant to have one. Opening the door carefully, Nedra peered around the corner to see Matt's huge grin staring up at her from the floor. He sat up quickly and, bending his knees, launched himself at Nedra. She caught him midair before he could collide with her head. "Whoa, buddy! You've got to give some warning before you jump on Mommy, okay?"

"'Kay." Matt turned his body around, squirming under her arms until he was comfortable. Then he pointed at the stick which remained in Nedra's hand. "What's that?" he asked, pointing to the item and crinkling his nose.

Nedra couldn't believe she had gotten so distracted, she almost forgot. Taking a deep breath, she glanced down at the stick and stared. The little blue plus sign had appeared in the window. Nedra was so surprised, she lost her balance and tipped over. Matt took this as a sign it was time to play and squealed again before getting up and jumping onto her stomach.

"Oof!" Nedra tickled him until he rolled off of her, screaming and laughing loudly.

Bryan drove into the room to investigate. "What's going on in here?" he asked, smiling.

Matt sat up, pointing a stubby finger at Nedra. "Mommy's tickling me." He hunched over to prevent his tummy from further attacks.

Nedra scooped Matt onto her lap again and whispered something in his ear. "Tell Daddy," she whispered, pointing at Bryan.

"I'm gonna be a big brother."

Bryan's face blanched as he looked in Nedra's direction. A smile slowly crept across his face. "Is that true?" he asked.

Nedra nodded, a smile splitting her face. "Yes, we're going to have another baby."

Nedra called Dr. Harbor's office as soon as they opened to share the good news. After explaining to the receptionist the reason for her call, she said, "Just a moment," and the line went blank. A moment later a man's voice came through the receiver. "Hello, Mrs. Carroll? Yes, I happened to be up here at the front desk when you called. I'm so glad everything worked out."

"Me, too," Nedra replied, "but I'm still having a hard time understanding it. What was different about this time?"

"Well," Dr. Harbor started, and Nedra could almost hear the twinkle in his eyes as he spoke. "I didn't want to say anything, because I didn't want to get your hopes up in case things didn't work out."

"In case what didn't work out?" Nedra asked.

"After giving your circumstances a great deal of thought, and after the blood test was completely normal, I went back and asked myself what was different about your first insemination compared to the other two. The only answer which came to mind was that the donors had both been different. So I went back to the original donor and voila, here we are."

"Wait, so you're saying . . .?"

"Yes. We used the same donor again. Your children will be full siblings."

CHAPTER TWENTY-FIVE

"It always seems impossible until it's done."

\- Nelson Mandela

Matt pushed away from his mom for the tenth time as she tried to cram his flailing arms into the crisp, white shirt. He slipped through her fingers again and ran toward his room, shirtless. Nedra placed a hand under her large belly as she stood.

Bryan rolled past the streaking little boy and looked at Nedra with concern. "We gotta go, honey. We're going to be late."

"I know, I know! But he wants to wear his Ninja Turtles shirt instead. I used to be much better at wrestling him into clothes before this got in the way." She indicated her pregnant belly, which now made her feel as wide as she was tall.

"Then just let him wear what he wants, 'cause we need to leave, like, ten minutes ago."

Nedra's lip pouted. "But I wanted him to look nice," she whined. She threw her arms up in the air, exasperated. "Fine." She groaned and huffed after Matt to deliver the good news.

Nedra's cheeks reddened with embarrassment as she pulled Matt by his hand past several pairs of legs until they secured their seats by Glenn and Carol Jean in the center of the bleachers. Matt climbed onto his grandma's lap and she wrapped her arms around him.

"Oh, I like your shirt," Carol Jean smiled. She glanced over at Nedra curiously. Nedra just shrugged and Carol Jean nodded her understanding.

"You didn't want to wear a tie like me, buddy?" Glenn asked. Matt made a face and his grandparents both laughed.

Nedra leaned over and shushed them all, pointing to the man who had just gotten to his feet and was walking toward the podium. "It's starting," she whispered.

"Where's Daddy?" Matt asked loudly.

Nedra shushed him again and pointed to the large wheelchair in the front row. The graduation cap blocked them from seeing Bryan's face, but his chair with the long, flowing, black cape draped around it was a dead giveaway. As the dean welcomed the graduates for the class of 1988, Matt tried waving down to Bryan. Matt grew restless as the speakers continued to talk. He climbed from one lap to another, never sitting for more than a couple minutes. When the stadium became almost unbearably warm, Nedra pulled out her program and folded it into a fan. She cooled down just as Matt saw the fan and his eyes lit up. Grabbing it from her grasp, he walked between the three of them, fanning their faces a little at a time. Even that grew dull.

"Are we done yet?" he whined, pushing his face between her knees.

"No, but pretty soon," Nedra said, pushing his head away and readjusting her skirt. "Why don't you go sit with Grandpa?"

As if on cue, the final speaker sat down and the orchestra began playing Pomp and Circumstance. Nedra tried to peer over the tall heads in front of her to steal a peek at Bryan. She watched proudly as Bryan slowly rolled forward in the procession. Her gaze was interrupted, however, by a loud banging on metal. That's when Nedra realized Matt was missing. She frantically searched up and down the aisle until she finally saw him stomping up and down the bleacher stairs. Nedra whispered a yell in his direction. "Matt, get back here! Right. Now."

Nedra was so busy trying to get Matt to come, that she didn't realize what was going on up front. When she turned around, she was startled to see that most people had gotten to their feet. She sandwiched herself between two of them and peered at the stage below.

Nedra saw Bryan heading up the ramp toward the stage. When the dean announced his name, "Bryan Louis Carroll," the applause erupted like thunder. Beginning with the first few rows, then spreading through the rest of the stadium, everyone rose to their feet.

Bryan glanced around, shocked to see the support from not only his classmates, but from complete strangers, too. He looked up into the bleachers and found his son happily banging on the stairs with his heavy shoes. When everyone around him rose, Matt stopped and looked up. Holding onto the railing, he stood on his tippy-toes and saw who they were watching. "Hey, that's my daddy!" he said, beaming ear to ear. When everyone applauded, he cheered and clapped more enthusiastically than anyone else. Bryan smiled graciously and wheeled back down the ramp on the other side.

Nedra watched in awe, her mouth agape, until slowly forming a smile. She sniffled as she clapped along with everyone else. Noticing her son had stopped, she seized the opportunity of distraction and grabbed Matt before he could find anything else to do.

After the ceremony finished, Nedra had to fight her way through the crowds to reach Bryan. When she got closer, she realized the crowd surrounded him. Many other graduates and passersby offered him friendly pats and congratulations as they went to find their family and friends. A few lingered to ask questions about his major and how he ended up in the wheelchair. Nedra used her bulging stomach to clear a path through the people as she made her way to her husband. Her hand firmly grasped Matt's wrist as she pulled him forward.

Bryan was busy answering questions, but he stopped mid-sentence when Matt jumped up on his lap.

"Hi, Daddy," he said. "Can I go for a ride?"

Those who stood closest to Bryan couldn't hide the surprise on their faces. He could only imagine what they were thinking. Not only was this wheelchair man a college graduate, but he had a family, too? Bryan smiled politely. Nedra finally sidled up beside him, her pregnancy very apparent, and their eyes grew even wider than before. Bryan just chuckled.

"Excuse me," he said, as he drove through the waves of people to an open area beside the stage where he could drive Matt around in wide circles.

Matt giggled as he kept shouting, "Faster, faster!"

Bryan happily obliged.

One week later, Nedra was finishing up her rounds at the hospital when she felt a trickle run down her leg. She hurried to the nurse's desk and explained her water had broken. Nedra called her neighbor and good friend, Shaunalee, describing the situation.

"Nedra, is everything okay?" Shaunalee asked.

"My water just broke at work," Nedra said. "I don't understand how this is happening; I'm not due for another two and a half weeks!"

"What do you need me to do?"

"I know it's earlier than we planned but can you watch Matt still, while we're in the hospital?"

"Of course," Shaunalee said.

"And can you run over there right now and help Bryan get ready? Let him know I'll be there in ten minutes to pick him up."

"You got it."

Nedra reached her front door as Shaunalee was walking out with Matt.

"Mommy!"

"Go get Daddy. I think your little sister is coming."

Matt's face brightened. "Can I play with her?"

Nedra smiled through gritted teeth. "Just go get Daddy. Please hurry."

Matt ran back inside, narrowly missing the doorframe as he whizzed around the corner. A few moments later, Bryan came speeding out after his son.

Nedra hugged Matt and thanked her friend profusely. She hurried alongside Bryan to the parking lot behind their complex to retrieve the van. Nedra could feel contractions beginning as she opened the door and pulled down on the lever, lowering the lift. It moaned as the metal slowly moved toward the ground. Bryan drove onto the ramp carefully as Nedra raised the lift once again. The lift jerked to a stop when Nedra doubled over as a particularly strong contraction hit. She grabbed onto the back of Bryan's chair, breathing slowly until the cramping passed. She shoved the joystick up again, willing the ramp to move faster. Once Bryan was in, she slammed the door shut and waddled around to the other side.

Climbing into the front seat, Nedra put the van into gear and started down the road. She had to slow down and stop several times as her contractions grew worse.

"Are you okay, Ned?" Bryan asked quietly.

Nedra nodded and lifted her foot from the brake, continuing onward. "Oh no," she said. "I forgot to refill your prescriptions."

"That doesn't matter now, let's just keep going."

"No, you're going to need your meds while we're at the hospital and we're completely out." Nedra turned and headed back toward the pharmacy. She parked the car, climbed out carefully, and pushed down on the lock before slamming it shut. She had left the keys, and Bryan, inside.

Nedra walked toward the pharmacy, her mind racing through her options. Bryan obviously couldn't unlock the doors, and she didn't have the time to wait for a locksmith. As she walked up to the counter, she doubled over as another contraction hit.

"Ma'am, are you alright?"

"I'm in labor. Please hurry."

Nedra never saw a pharmacist move so fast. They had her prescriptions filled in no time and she walked slowly back out to the van. Nedra suddenly remembered a friend had borrowed the van recently to take Bryan somewhere. She wondered if he could have left the back door unlocked. Sure enough, as she pulled on the handle, the door popped open.

Nedra heaved herself up into the back and grunted as she climbed over the backseat. She waddled past Bryan, clutching her stomach and landed in the front seat again. Bryan looked at her, concern written all over his face.

"Okay," she groaned. "Let's go."

When they reached the hospital, Nedra was grateful to see an open parking spot right up front. She parked the car and climbed out, pausing to catch her breath as she made her way around the side of the van. Nedra yanked the door open and pulled down on his lift. Right as Bryan was about to reach the ground, the sprinklers came on, showering him with cold water.

"I'm having my baby." Nedra heaved each word out with a loud puff of air. She gripped the counter with her right hand, her left clutching onto her overnight bag. Nedra was informed that her doctor was out of town and his partner would be taking over. "Of course he is," Nedra breathed.

When the doctor walked into Nedra's room he cut right to the chase. Given your history and your last delivery, I think it would be best to skip straight to a C-section."

Nedra had hoped to try for a regular delivery again, but as this point, she was relieved at the doctor's words.

"Yes, please!"

Once the beautiful, pink little girl was placed on Nedra's chest, she looked at Bryan and they shared a smile. Their family was complete.

"Do you realize what today is?" Bryan whispered, as they whisked the baby away to be weighed and cleaned. "It's June 27th."

Nedra's eyes widened. "How many years has it been?"

"Nine." Bryan watched as his brand new daughter was placed on the scale, wiped down, and then bundled. She cried and kicked the nurse the whole time, bringing a smile to

Bryan's face. *She's a fighter.* What an incredible way to commemorate the day of his accident.

Miranda Jane Carroll came into the world screaming, and never stopped. When Shaunalee and her husband, Bert, brought Matt to the hospital the next day to meet his baby sister, he was very excited to hold her for the first time. Shaunalee helped Matt sit on the small couch that leaned up against the window. She placed a pillow under his arm to help him hold Miranda up. As she lifted Miranda out of her bassinet and placed her gently in her big brother's arms, her eyes opened and she began crying. Matt's smile faded as he looked to his parents for help. Shaunalee reached for the baby and gently bounced up and down. When Miranda only yelled louder, Matt covered his ears with his hands. "I think she's broken," he said loudly.

Nedra carefully climbed out of bed and took Matt by the hand. "We'll be right back," she said, walking from the room. Nedra padded down the long, white hall in her gown and slippers. When they reached the elevators, Matt punched the button and waited excitedly for a door to open. Nedra took him down to the first floor and into the hospital gift shop.

"I want you to pick something," she said to Matt.

Matt's eyes grew wide as he looked around the small shop. After looking at several toys, he finally landed on a little spotted Dalmatian puppy. "Do I have to share this with Miranda?" he asked, his eyes filled with concern.

"No, sweetheart, this is your special puppy. I want you to remember how much we love you. A new baby takes a lot of time and attention, but I want you to hold your puppy and remember how much Daddy and I love you as we take care of your little sister."

Matt hugged the puppy close to his face as they walked back down the hall and to the elevators. When they got back in the room, Miranda lay sleeping peacefully in Shaunalee's arms. Matt looked up from his puppy at the bundle of pink blankets. "She sleeps a lot."

"Yes, buddy," Bryan said. "Babies do that."

"And she cries a lot."

Bryan sighed. "You're right about that, too."

When Matt turned his attention back to the little Dalmatian, Nedra looked to Bert and Shaunalee. "I've done nothing for the last nine months but yell at my crazy, rambunctious little boy. I'm sure that's all she heard, so that's how she thinks we communicate."

They both gave an appreciative smile right as Miranda startled awake and began screaming all over again.

CHAPTER TWENTY-SIX

"But I'm here so bruise me life,
Confuse me life
Bring on the rain, I'll do this all again
Wear me thin, so I might begin
To gain a sense of what's important"

– The Heavy and the Slow,
Andy Grammer

Bryan spent the first year after graduation looking for a job and trying to decide if he should get a master's degree. After much prayer and contemplation, he and Nedra decided they didn't want to pursue any more schooling. Since he was no longer going to be attending the University of Utah, this also meant they could no longer stay in student housing. After boxing up all of their belongings, they purchased their first home in Midvale, Utah.

Matt found himself alone in his own bedroom in the basement before he finished kindergarten. Bryan, Nedra, and Miranda took the only two bedrooms upstairs. The house could use some fixing up, but they picked it because it was a rambler, open enough for Bryan to get around. He was able to go in every room except the basement.

They had only been in the house a few weeks when Nedra bathed Bryan one night and accidentally dropped him in the shower. He slipped out of her hands and she couldn't get him up again without help. Both Matt and Miranda were too young to help, so she ran for her phone list from the church. Scanning through the names, one stood out from the rest. She remembered seeing him in church last week and he introduced himself afterward. He was a big guy. Nedra grabbed the phone and dialed quickly.

"Hello?"

"Hi, who is this?"

"Umm, you called me."

"I know, I'm sorry, I'm looking for Andy. Is that you?"

". . . Yes"

"Andy, this is Nedra Carroll. We met in church on Sunday. Listen, I dropped my husband in the shower and I can't get him back up again. I really need a hand. Is there any way you could come over?"

"I'll be right there."

Nedra paced back and forth in front of the door, jumping when it knocked a moment later. She grabbed the handle and swung it open. "Thank you so much for coming," she said. She charged through the house and into the bathroom, without pausing to make sure he was behind her. "Bryan, I've got some help," she called, announcing their entrance.

Bryan lay on the tub floor, his body bent in the position he had been dropped. Nedra's hand shook as she held it out, palm up, showing Andy how he'd fallen. "Bryan, this is Andy, Andy, this is Bryan. I'm not sure if you remember him from church."

"Let's exchange pleasantries after I've changed out of my birthday suit, if you don't mind," Bryan smirked.

Andy chuckled, immediately put at ease by Bryan's casual tone. "All right," he said, "How do we do this?"

"If you can, put one arm under his arms here," Nedra explained, leaning over the tub and pointing. "Then place your other arm under his legs here, and I'll help you lift."

"Got it." Andy stepped forward and, bending low, was able to scoop Bryan back up in his arms. He followed Nedra's directions and laid him on the bed on top of a towel. "Is there anything else I can help with?"

"No, thank you so much," Nedra said, walking him back through the house. "I really, really appreciate you coming over and helping. I'm sure I sounded crazy on the phone, but you came anyway."

"Hey, what are neighbors for?"

"Not usually this," Nedra said, opening the door for him.

Andy's smile filled his whole face. "Yeah, I guess that's true. Well, goodnight." He waved and walked back down the sidewalk.

>♦< >♦< >♦<

"Why is Dad wearing a tie today?" Matt walked into his parent's bedroom as Nedra finished straightening Bryan's tie.

"He has a job interview," Nedra said, folding his shirt collar down.

"Where is it this time?"

"A computer company called IBM," Bryan answered. "I'll be back before you get home from school."

Matt nodded.

"You ready to go?" Nedra asked. "Don't forget your backpack. And where is your sister?"

"Playing in her room."

"All right. I can drop you off at school today on my way to Dad's interview, but you gotta hurry."

Nedra scurried down the hall, scooping Miranda onto her hip. She cried and reached for her toes on the floor. "It's time for daycare, sweetie." Nedra spoke soothingly as she raced for the front door.

"We're gonna be late, Ned," Bryan said as she hurried past.

"No, we're not. Go get in the van." Nedra buckled Miranda, tied Bryan's chair down, and then climbed into the front seat. She slammed on the horn as they all waited for Matt to appear. He finally peeked his dark head around the door and sauntered toward the van, his yellow and blue backpack bobbing as he walked. Nedra honked again, causing Matt to jump. He ran the rest of the way. As soon as his door closed, Nedra stepped on the gas and they tore out of the driveway. Matt flew into the backseat, banging his shoulder against Miranda's car seat.

"Geeze, Mom, I don't even have my seatbelt on yet!"

"We don't have time. I told you I'd give you a ride to school if you hurried. Why weren't you hurrying?"

"I got distracted," Matt said, shrugging. He carefully pulled himself upright and buckled his seatbelt in place.

"Here you go," Nedra said as she pulled up beside the curb. "Love you. See you tonight."

Matt unclicked his seatbelt and jumped from the van. He barely shut the door when Nedra sped off once again. Matt pulled his hand back quickly to make sure she didn't take it with her.

"My interview is in ten minutes," Bryan said. "We're never going to make it."

"Oh, yes we are," Nedra said. Her eyes narrowed and her hands gripped the steering wheel so tight, her knuckles went white. "Hang on," she said.

Bryan's eyes widened as Nedra sped down the street, but he didn't dare say anything. She was determined to get there. "I'll drop you off first and then I'll take Miranda to daycare.

I'll swing back and grab you before I have to leave for work, okay?"

"All right," Bryan answered, staring at the digital clock on the dashboard. Nedra pulled up beside the curb of a tall, brown building filled with office suites. She left the engine running as she jumped out and ran around to the side of the van. She lowered his ramp before realizing Bryan was still strapped in. Nedra groaned as she hoisted herself back into the van's interior and loosened the thick, yellow straps. She climbed out and guided Bryan onto the track. Once he was in place, she pulled down on the lever and slowly lowered him to the ground. "Good luck, I love you, bye!" Nedra kissed him quickly before Bryan drove up to the building and disappeared inside.

"Okay, baby girl, just you and me left," Nedra said as she put the ramp away and climbed back into the driver's seat. "You ready for daycare?"

"No! No! No!" Miranda shouted.

Nedra sighed and pulled the van back onto the main road again, much more carefully this time. "I know, sweetie, but Mommy has to go to work. You get to go play with toys!" She tried to make her voice sound as chipper as possible.

It seemed to work this time. "Toys!" Miranda clapped her hands excitedly.

Nedra turned the key in the lock slowly. It had been a long day at the hospital, but she knew her day wasn't over yet. She had to go inside, make dinner, and then fight with Matt on his homework before she could finally relax. Taking a deep breath, she turned until she heard a click. She pushed the door open. Her ears were immediately assaulted by the sounds of screaming.

"MATTHEW MAYO CARROLL, YOU GET DOWN HERE THIS INSTANT! NO! STOP THAT!"

Nedra walked into the kitchen to find Bryan in front of the washing machine, his face purple and contorted with rage. Matt sat on top of the washing machine, squirting his dad in the face with a spray bottle. Miranda was beside her brother, making faces and taunting her father and then squealing when he yelled. Nedra dropped her large bag on the floor with a thud. Matt and Miranda both jumped when they saw their mother standing in the open doorway, a look of death on her face. Matt leaped from the washing machine and ran down the basement stairs, taking them two at a time. Miranda slid to the edge of the washing machine, her head hung down, not daring to meet Nedra's gaze. She held her arms out for Nedra to help her down.

"Get to your room NOW," Nedra threatened, each word coming out like ice. Miranda scurried as fast as she could, bawling loudly as she ran.

Nedra put her fingers to her temples, slowly rubbing them clockwise, willing the migraine that had formed to go away. "What happened?" she asked Bryan, falling into a kitchen chair.

"I told Matt he needed to turn off the TV and start on his homework," Bryan said, pulling up beside her. "He not only climbed on top of the washing machine again, but he found your squirt bottle up there."

"Yeah, I saw."

"He also taught Miranda how to climb up, so she could taunt me, too."

"Great," Nedra said sarcastically. "What are we going to do with them?"

"I don't know," Bryan said, still trying to calm himself. "All I know is it's a good thing I'm in this wheelchair or I would have killed that boy by now."

"He wouldn't be able to torture you the way he does if you weren't in a wheelchair." Nedra let out an angry breath. In a much calmer voice, she asked, "So how was the interview?"

"It was fine," Bryan said. "They said they don't have any full time positions open for me, but they offered me part time work."

"Not what we were hoping for, but that's good," Nedra said, nodding. "What's the part time job?"

"They need someone who can go to job fairs and computer conventions to try and sell their voice recognition software."

"Well that sounds like the perfect job for you," Nedra said. "After all, you use their program almost every day."

"Yeah, that's what they were thinking. Who better to sell it than one of their top customers?"

"That's great, Bryan." Nedra tried to sound enthusiastic. She bent down and gave him a kiss.

"It's not full time, though," Bryan said. "And it doesn't pay nearly enough to support us."

Nedra tried to hide the disappointment in her eyes. "Well, it's a good thing I still have my job."

"But I know your dream is to stay home with the kids. I want to make that dream come true for you."

Nedra shrugged. "You'll keep looking. You haven't given up on anything else yet, so I know you won't give up on this." Nedra gave his hand a squeeze. "Now I better go deal with our son."

Bryan gave her a weak smile before driving his wheelchair into the living room. After he left, Nedra picked up her purse from the floor and set it on the countertop. She stomped down the basement steps loudly so Matt would know how much trouble he was in. Nedra banged on his bedroom door with her fist. Matt opened it slowly, peeking his head around the door.

"Let me in."

Matt stepped back as Nedra pushed the door open the remainder of the way. "What were you thinking?"

"I don't know," Matt whispered, staring at his shoes.

"Look at me," Nedra said. Matt didn't move. "I SAID LOOK AT ME!"

Matt looked up, his lip trembling.

"I love your father very much. And if you can't be nice to him and learn how to be respectful, then one of you will have to go, and I can guarantee you, it won't be him." Nedra's eyes narrowed as she stared at her son, making sure the threat sank in. She turned and walked from his room, slamming the door.

Bryan tried not to show his excitement as they loaded the van for California. He didn't want to get his hopes up, or the hopes of his family, but he really wanted one of these jobs. Working the fairs and shows for the last year was fun, but he still needed full time work. When a full time position became available in San Jose, it took very little convincing for Nedra and the kids to agree to the trip. Once his first interview was set, Bryan found another job opening in Irvine, California, and scheduled an interview there as well. Bryan knew Nedra would love returning home to California.

The drive was long and slow, with Nedra having to drive the entire way. Even with stops and breaks, Matt and Miranda quickly grew restless. They were both fidgety and bored, fighting over having to stay in their seats, the amount of snacks they got, and anything else they could think of.

"Why don't you try counting semi trucks?" Bryan suggested.

Matt stared out his window for the next several hours, announcing to his parents when he reached one hundred.

When the van finally passed the 'Welcome to California' sign, Bryan blew out a breath of relief. They arrived at their hotel in Irvine well after dark. Nedra crashed onto the firm bed once Bryan, the kids, and all their belongings had made it safely inside. Matt and Miranda, who both napped on the way, were wide awake and wired. They bounced on the other bed, laughing and squealing, until Matt tried to jump from one queen to the other. He landed with both knees in Nedra's back. She yelled until her face turned purple. Both kids slipped under the covers and settled down very quickly after that.

The next day, Bryan came out of his interview feeling discouraged. "They said they don't know how to utilize the technologies I use," Bryan said. "Which is the polite way of saying they can't hire me, because they don't know what to do with me."

Nedra put her arm around him and kissed his cheek softly. "You will find the perfect job, where your skills will not only be utilized but will improve their company. It's out there. We just have to find it."

Bryan smiled. "You're right," he said. "Let's get out of here."

The next morning, the family made their way to Disneyland. Bryan couldn't go on any rides, but he enjoyed waiting in line with his family and then people watching while they rode. At last they came to the Enchanted Tiki Room, the one ride that Bryan could enjoy. When the crew members lowered their wheelchair lift, they discovered Bryan's chair was too wide to fit on the ramp, so he sat outside in the bright sunshine and listened to the music from the singing birds as it carried over the walls.

The next day, they packed their car back up again and traveled to San Jose for the second interview. Nedra sat in the waiting room, flipping through a magazine. She wasn't much of a nail biter, but she found herself chewing on her thumb nail as she waited anxiously for Bryan. She heard the elevator doors open, and her head whipped around. Bryan came driving toward her, but he didn't look happy. Not a good sign.

"How did it go?" Nedra asked, though she feared she already knew the answer.

"They said I'm qualified for the job. However, they just started a hiring freeze yesterday. So while we were standing in line and going on rides, our fate was already decided. I was never going to get the job." Bryan's face became red with anger. "They couldn't have called and given me a heads up before we spent all that money to drive out here?" Bryan's voice echoed through the corridor, and Nedra motioned for them to leave the building.

Once outside, in the bright, warm sunshine, Bryan's mood quickly softened. "I'm sorry," he said quietly.

"I don't think what they did to you is fair. However," Nedra said, "look at the kids."

Bryan drove forward and watched as Matt chased Miranda, tickling her to the ground. They both got up and Miranda took a turn chasing her brother across the grass. She caught up to him behind a big tree and they both fell to the ground, laughing again.

"You're right," Bryan said. "They have been having so much fun. They haven't stopped talking about Disneyland since we left. They needed this vacation, didn't they?"

Nedra nodded. Approaching Bryan, she wrapped her arms around his shoulders from behind and gave them a squeeze. "We all did."

CHAPTER TWENTY-SEVEN

"The only disability in life is a bad attitude."

- Author Unknown

"Okay, now add a little milk and whisk it into the eggs. Yeah, just like that. Check and see if the pan is warm enough yet."

"How do I do that?"

"Get your fingertips wet and flick them over the pan. If it sizzles, then it's ready."

Matt hopped off his stool, walked over to the sink and turned on the water, quickly dipping his fingers under the running faucet. He shut it off and then walked back over to where Bryan sat waiting for him by the stove. He climbed onto the stool and waved his hand above the hot surface, allowing the water to drip off his fingertips. It sizzled and melted away in a puff of steam. "Yup, it's hot," Matt said.

"Great, now pour the eggs in slowly. A little slower, little slower," Bryan guided him. "Now grab that spatula and scrape the eggs off so they don't stick to the bottom of the pan or burn. Yes, that's it," he encouraged. "Keep flipping the eggs so they can cook on all sides. You can chop them up with the spatula, too, to make the pieces smaller."

Matt tipped the pan so Bryan could see his progress. "How do they look?"

"Perfect," Bryan said. He could already feel the saliva building up inside his mouth. He was at a show all afternoon and didn't have anyone around who could feed him lunch, so he had to skip it. "Now sprinkle in some salt and pepper, but not too much. And add in some of that cheese we grated. A little more. A little bit more."

"Geeze, Dad, that's a ton!"

Bryan smiled. "It's perfect. Now stir it all up."

Matt stirred and flipped until the eggs were firm and the cheese had melted. He turned off the stove and dished the eggs onto two plates. He climbed down and carried the plates over to a tray set up in the living room. Bryan parked on the other side of the tray and Matt plopped into a chair. Bryan turned on the TV with the remote connected to his chair through the straw.

"What do you want to watch?" he asked.

"Cartoons?" Matt asked hopefully.

"You got it," Bryan said, flipping through the stations until they landed on Nickelodeon.

Matt scooped himself a large mouthful of eggs and then got a forkful for Bryan while he chewed. "Wow, these are really good!" Matt said. "Why haven't we ever had eggs like this before?"

"Because your mom hates eggs, so she just nukes them in the microwave." Bryan stuck out his tongue and scrunched his nose. "They taste awful!"

Matt laughed as he took another large bite.

"But don't tell her I said that," Bryan added.

Matt smiled as he gave his dad another bite. "Whatever happened to the idea of you getting a trained monkey to be your hands?" Matt asked. "I thought you and Mom were looking into that for a little while."

"We were," Bryan answered. "But why would I need a trained monkey when I have you?"

"Hey!" Matt said.

Bryan smirked and they both burst into laughter.

"So how's your job?" Matt asked. "Are you still looking for another one?"

"Yeah, it's the same problem with all the companies I temp for. They just don't know what to do with me, or how to utilize the technology I use. It's really frustrating."

"So it's not getting any better?"

"No. I'm so bored! I always just end up in the mailroom, looking through the mail and trying to figure out what to do with myself."

The front door opened. Nedra and Miranda came in from their shopping trip. "Hey, guys, what are you eating?"

"Dad taught me how to make eggs!" Matt beamed with pride.

"That's awesome! Now I won't have to touch that disgusting stuff ever again."

Bryan smiled at Matt, celebrating on the inside. "How was your shopping trip?" he asked. "Did you get everything you need for kindergarten?"

Miranda climbed onto Bryan's lap and curled up against his chest. "I don't want to go to school." She jutted out her bottom lip and looked up at Bryan with big, brown eyes.

"School will be fun! Your brother loved kindergarten."

"I just want to stay home and play," Miranda responded.

"Kindergarten is easy, and you get to play a lot," Matt said. "I'm in third grade this year. We only get to play at recess. The rest of the time it's really hard work."

"Well, you kids need to go get ready for bed. School starts early tomorrow and it's getting late."

Matt groaned as Nedra made him go down the stairs to change. Miranda screamed about not wanting to go to school as she changed into pajamas. He knew how she felt. Why couldn't it be summer all the time?

"You ready to go, big brother?" Jenny tossed her long, blonde hair over one shoulder as she walked up the driveway toward their house. Matt and Miranda had seen their aunt coming and quickly ran outside, assaulting her with hugs.

Bryan chuckled as he rolled down the driveway behind them. "Yes. Here are the keys," he said.

Jenny scooped up the car keys off his lap, where Nedra had put them, and unlocked the van just as the snow began to fall again. "Brrr, it's cold. I'll get the heater going. Are you doing okay?"

"I'm fine," Bryan said, from under his large, thick, blue poncho.

Matt and Miranda climbed in, settling into the backseat while Jenny got Bryan's chair loaded onto the lift. When everyone was seated and buckled, Jenny pulled the van into reverse.

"Where did you want to start?" she asked, glancing over in Bryan's direction.

"Let's head to the mall," Bryan said. "I have a couple of ideas, but I want to look around a little, too."

"Are you guys getting Christmas presents for your mom, too?" Jenny asked, trying to distract them from the slow moving traffic.

"Yes!" they yelled back.

Jenny stopped sharply, as the car in front of them slammed on their brakes. They drove about five miles an hour, creeping along State Street in the snow and slush as they made their way to the mall.

"Gotta love holiday traffic," Jenny said, glancing in her rearview mirror to find they were completely boxed in.

"It just means more time to hang out," Bryan said, smiling.

When they finally made it to the mall parking lot, Jenny drove slowly up and down each aisle, trying to find a parking place. "This is insane!" she said, looking around fruitlessly. Matt and Miranda began arguing in the backseat, which soon turned to Miranda wailing because Matt hit her. "Cool it, guys, and help me look for a spot," Jenny said.

Finally, a car backed out of a handicap stall and Jenny inched closer to take their place. Just as she was about to pull in, a small, sleek, sedan whipped into the empty spot. Jenny hit her fist against the steering wheel. "Wait a minute," she said. "He doesn't have a handicap sticker!"

The man got out of his car and jogged toward the building. He was obviously not handicapped. Jenny rolled down her window, ready to pitch a fit and yell at the selfish man for his actions. Bryan quietly stopped her.

"Don't worry about it," he said to her. "We'll find another spot. Besides, I remember what it was like trying to find parking in the crowds and the snow. I probably would have done the same thing twenty years ago."

Jenny looked at her brother and shrugged. She rolled her window back up and drove around a couple more times until another spot opened up.

Bryan watched as Miranda pulled her waist-length brown hair up into a high ponytail. Since when did his kids get so big? He could remember the times they used to tease and torment him, and now he had one teenager and the other not too far behind.

Miranda bent down and pulled a large, silver mixing bowl from under the cupboard. She stood and turned toward her dad, smiling. "What kind of cookies are we making?"

"My favorite."

Miranda's wide smile split her face. "Snickerdoodles!" She licked her lips. "I've always wanted to learn how to make those."

"Good, let's get started. Pull the recipe out and let's make sure we have all the ingredients first."

Miranda followed his instructions and found the correct recipe. She propped it up in a long, wooden stand and turned it for him to see. Bryan looked over the food items, listing each one aloud while Miranda opened the pantry and pulled everything out, setting them on the countertop. Miranda spoke animatedly about how crazy her life felt while Bryan listened patiently. He only spoke up when he needed to give a cooking instruction. Otherwise, he sat patiently and listened, nodding at the appropriate times.

"Tomorrow night is my choir concert. You're coming, right?" Miranda asked, glancing up as she stirred.

"Of course," Bryan said. "I wouldn't miss it for the world."

Miranda grinned and then paused. "I'm a little nervous about my solo," she admitted.

"Would you like to practice for me?"

"You wouldn't mind?"

"Nothing would make me happier. I love to hear you sing. You have a gift, Miranda. Don't ever stop using it."

Miranda cleared her throat and practiced the notes while she rolled the dough in cinnamon and sugar.

Nedra came into the kitchen, pausing in the doorway as Miranda finished her song. "That was beautiful, honey."

Miranda beamed. Nedra turned to Bryan, the smile dropping from her lips. "We need to talk."

"Uh-oh, that doesn't sound good."

"It's not. Can you come in our room for a second please?"

Bryan looked at Miranda. "Do you think you can finish?" he asked.

"Yeah." Miranda nodded. "How long do they bake for?"

"Ten minutes," Bryan read. "Call me if you need help." He followed Nedra around the corner and down the short hallway to their room. Once the door clicked behind them, Nedra sat down hard on the bed, sighing loudly.

"What's wrong, Ned?" Bryan asked.

"Matt is on his way home from scout camp," she said, looking down at her hands.

"Didn't we know that already?" Bryan asked, his eyebrows furrowed.

"Yes, but one of his leaders just called. It seems Matt got into a fight last night with another boy."

"What?" Bryan asked. He could feel the heat crawling up his neck, to his cheeks.

"Before you get really upset, the other boy was . . . well . . . he was making fun of you."

Bryan's demeanor calmed instantly. "I don't want him getting in fights for me," Bryan said quietly.

"I know," Nedra said. "But go easy on him." Bryan looked up into her emerald eyes. She held his gaze, her chin firm.

Bryan heard the front door open and close. "Send him in," he said.

Nedra climbed off the bed. She ran a hand along Bryan's shoulders as she passed him on her way out the door. "I'll go get him."

Matt trudged into their room a moment later. He tossed his backpack on the floor at Bryan's feet and remained looking down while he waited for Bryan to speak.

"Can you tell me what happened?" Bryan asked.

"I was chopping wood for our fire last night when Dylan came over and told me some kid was making fun of you. I ran towards him, the axe still in my hand."

"You chased a kid with an axe?"

"Not intentionally!" Matt looked up into his dad's face for the first time. "The axe was already in my hand. I wasn't bringing it as a weapon or anything. Dylan followed me and grabbed the axe out of my hands before I got to him anyway."

Matt didn't offer any more information, so Bryan had to prod him. "And then what happened?" he asked.

Matt huffed, his fists clenched tight. "When I found him imitating you, I just lost it. I knocked him to the ground and jumped on him, punching him in the chest until the leaders pulled me off." Matt looked down again, shuffling his feet. "The leaders didn't even get mad at me. They knew he deserved it . . ." Matt trailed off.

"I don't want you getting into fights for me," Bryan said. "Whether you feel it's deserved or not, fighting is never the way to handle a situation."

"But what was I supposed to do?" Matt raised his voice in indignation.

"Just ignore them. That's what I do."

"Do people ever make fun of you?" Matt asked, eyes wide.

"I get a lot of whispers and stares; you know that. When people don't understand something or someone, they tend to poke fun of it. I think it's a coping mechanism."

"Well, it's stupid! You're a person, just like they are!" Matt spat.

Bryan remained calm. "I know that and so do you, but people are scared of the unknown and they don't always react well to it. I love that you wanted to defend me, I really do, but fighting never solves anything."

Matt sighed. "Okay."

That night, after Matt and Miranda went to bed, Nedra sat beside Bryan in the living room. She reached for his hand, interlocking their fingers.

"Are you nervous for your interview tomorrow?"

"No. The only thing I'm afraid of is the bus not picking me up on time."

"I scheduled it myself, and I even called today to confirm, so you shouldn't have any problems. Once I get the kids out the door to school, I'll help you shave and look as sharp as possible." She smiled. "Are you sure you don't want to tell them?"

"Not yet. I want to be able to call the kids in one day and be able to tell them good news for once, not that another interview didn't work out."

"All right," Nedra said, resting her head on his shoulder. "Do you want to watch a movie or something?"

A few days later, Bryan got the phone call he had been waiting for since he graduated college several years ago. He had gotten the job! He would be working for the Utah Center for Assistive Technology, teaching people with disabilities how to use wind technology to bridge the gap between their disability and what it would take for them to be employed or improve their independence. He would mostly be working with alternative computer access and electronic aids to help people improve their lives and daily living.

Mark Ashman sat in his wheelchair, staring at the wall. It was filled with inspirational posters like 'You Can Do It' and 'Hang in There'. He felt like ripping them off the wall and tearing them into little pieces. He was so tired of everyone telling him he could live a normal life. Not having your legs anymore was anything but normal! Since that stupid motorcycle accident, his life was over. He should have just died in the crash. What good was a life spent in a wheelchair? He circled the room, waiting for some guy to come in and teach him how to live a 'normal' life. This was such a waste of time. What did this guy know, anyway? The last thing Mark needed was some jerk feeling sorry for him and pumping him full of false hope.

The door opened behind him and Mark turned in his chair. His eyes narrowed, his lips set in a firm line. He would listen to whatever bull this guy dished out and then he was out of here!

Bryan drove through the doorway, his lips blowing into his straw. Mark stared at him. Bryan's arms and legs were immobile, his fingers curled under, set on black armrests.

Mark looked down at his own arms, fully functional and becoming quite muscular from wheeling his chair around. *Well, if this guy could do it . . .*

Bryan stopped in front of Mark and smiled. "All right, let's get started."

EPILOGUE

"My dad has an engineer's mind. He doesn't see problems, just solutions waiting to be found."

- Matt Carroll

Bryan's cell phone rang loudly. With a few short puffs he muted the television and answered it. He could see from the caller ID that it was Matt.

"Hello?"

"Hi Dad! Guess what? We're at the hospital right now. Stacy is having the baby."

"Ha ha. April Fools."

"No, really, Dad. The ECV didn't work, the baby is still breech, and she's dilated to a four so they can't send her home. Stacy is having a C-section tonight."

"You're serious?"

"Yes, I'm serious, Dad," Matt chuckled. "I know the timing seems funny, since she's three weeks early and it's April Fools day, but really, truly, you're going to be a grandpa tonight."

Bryan smiled as Nedra walked into the room. "What's going on?" she asked.

"Matt and Stacy are at the hospital. It's time." Turning his attention back to Matt he asked, "Do you need us there now?"

"No, they said it will probably be a couple hours. Grab some dinner and then meet us here after. We'll call you if anything changes. We just wanted to give you a heads up."

Three hours later, Bryan wheeled into the delivery room of the hospital. He was all too familiar with hospitals, spending a good portion of his life in and out of them. Almost every year since the accident, he had to be hospitalized for one reason or another. Usually bed sores, urinary tract infections, and pneumonia were the most dangerous illnesses for a quad. Bryan always fought his way through them and recovered.

Now he was in the hospital for a good reason, the best reason. Matt stood by the hospital bed, cradling a small white bundle in his arms. Stacy lay on the bed, her blonde hair surrounding her head like a crown. She looked exhausted but very happy. They both waved Bryan and Nedra into the room. Matt approached his parents slowly, his face glowing with pride. "This is Kalianna," he whispered. "Meet your granddaughter." He handed her off to Nedra, who held her down for Bryan to see.

She was small, her face long and narrow like her mother's. Her small pink lips formed a perfect O as she yawned and cuddled further into her blankets. Bryan could feel a lump rising in his throat as he looked at the most beautiful baby he had ever seen. His mind raced back to that fateful day on the beach. The blistering sun beat down on him, his throat dry and raw, yet the thought at the forefront of his mind was not about survival. It was whether or not he would ever have children.

In the small hospital room, surrounded by everyone he loved most, he surpassed his wildest dreams. Not only had he become a father two times over, but he lived long enough to see his grandchildren.

Giving up on life would have been easy, but Bryan made a choice that day. He chose to live.

Family picture before Jenny's birth

Bryan getting his Eagle Scout award.
With his parents and Grandpa Carroll

Bryan and Nedra

Bryan and his sisters

Bryan with his dad and Grandpa Carroll

Bryan and Nedra's wedding

Bryan, Nedra, Matt, and Miranda

Bryan's graduation from the University of Utah

Bryan and his family today

Deleted Scene:

This scene was cut, simply because I wanted to keep the focus on Bryan and his story. But I still think it's a cute beginning to how his parents met, so here you go. Enjoy!

Winter 1959

The bell which hung over the small gas station door jangled, signaling a new customer had come in. Glenn was busy helping another patron behind the counter and didn't bother looking up. It had been a busy day, filled with angry people who wanted their cars fixed right away. The last thing he wanted to do was start on another job that would take several hours when he was supposed to be off work in twenty minutes. The stranger walked up to the counter and began tapping her fingernails impatiently on the laminate.

"My car won't start."

Glenn sighed, wiped his greasy hands off on his jeans, and finally looked up. His jaw dropped for a brief moment when his gaze fell upon the gorgeous redhead standing before him. She looked at him expectantly, her emerald eyes widening as she waited for a response. Glenn realized he had been staring a moment too long when her smile faded. He shook his head to clear it.

"What seems to be the problem?"

"I don't know. Isn't it your job to figure that out?"

Her words seemed sharp until he noticed the smile playing at her lips. Glenn smiled broadly and her grin widened in return.

"Can you take me out to where your car is?"

"Sure, it's just this way."

Glenn liked the way her blue skirt swished around her legs as she walked away from him. She had incredible legs to match the rest of her, and he had to refrain from whistling. He realized he had been staring again and quickly jumped forward to follow her out the door.

She led him straight over to a blue Cadillac and held her hand out in front of the car. Glenn circled the vehicle before taking a look under the hood.

"Listen, I'm going to be late for class." She gestured to the tall Westminster College buildings that stood across the street. "Can I just come back and pick it up?"

"Sure, give me a couple hours and I should have it all fixed up for you."

"Great, thanks!" She turned to leave when Glenn stopped her.

"I'm sorry, I never asked your name."

"No, you didn't." She looked at him with that teasing smile again.

"So what's your name?"

"I'm Carol," she responded.

"Glenn Carroll," he said, extending his hand over the hood.

"Your last name is the same as my first name?" she asked, taking his hand and shaking it gently.

"Imagine that. We already have something in common."

Carol looked at the grease that was now on her clean hand and made a little face.

"Oh! I'm so sorry!" He internally kicked himself for not checking his hands before touching her. "Here." He handed her the cloth that was in his front pocket.

She accepted it graciously and wiped the smear away. "I really better go," she added, returning the cloth.

Glenn watched helplessly as she began walking away. He could hear his heart pounding in his ears. He couldn't let her go. What if he never saw her again?

"Carol, wait!"

She turned and looked at him, surprised. "Yes?"

"Do you want to have dinner with me? After class?"

Carol hesitated, biting her lower lip as she considered his offer. "I actually have plans tonight. I'll take a rain check though."

She walked away from him, turning to wave one last time before she disappeared behind a building. Glenn hated watching her go, but he held on to the promise that she would return later to pick up her car. He remembered his shift was almost over. Frustrated, he kicked her car tire before trudging back inside. He kept staring at the building across the street, hoping she would magically reappear. No such luck. His replacement arrived right on time and, grumbling, Glenn drove home.

The following week, the little bell above the door jingled while Glenn stocked some shelves with an assortment of chips. It had been a slow day.

"I'll be right with you," he called. He shoved the last two bags on top of the pile and turned around.

"I'm not going anywhere." Her smile was even more enchanting than Glenn remembered.

"Hi! You're back!"

"I'm back!" she said, holding her hands up. "How are you, Glenn?"

He couldn't believe she remembered his name! "I'm fabulous, marvelous, and wonderful now that you're here," he said. "What can I do for ya?"

"My car is giving me problems again. Can you take a look at it, please?"

"Of course." He followed her outside, thanking the heavens for this second chance. "We didn't solve your problem last time?"

"I don't know what's going on, but I'm going to be late for work and the silly thing keeps stalling."

"How are you going to get to work?"

"Oh, I'll just have to walk."

"But if you're already late . . . can I just give you a ride?"

"Well," she glanced over at the building and back to Glenn again. "Sure, thank you."

Glenn ran around to the other side of the gas station and jumped in his own car. He tried to hurry, afraid she might leave before he drove around the building, but she still stood in the same spot beside her car. He jumped out and opened her door.

"Thank you," she responded politely. She glanced back at the station. "But are you sure you can leave?"

"I won't be gone more than two minutes, and it's been really slow today."

He pulled out onto the busy road and glanced over at her. He couldn't stand the idea of not seeing her again after this.

"Carol?"

"Yes?"

"Can I take you up on that rain check tonight, or do you have plans?"

She smiled. "I'd love to."

Acknowledgments

First and foremost I would like to thank Bryan for allowing me to write his story. Through all the many interviews, e-mails, texts, and late-night phone calls, I hope I was able to do his story justice. Bryan has been an inspiration and an example to countless people over the years. When his younger sister, Glenda, had both her legs amputated a few years ago because of illness, she did not wallow in self-pity or complain over her circumstances. Instead, she said, "Well, if Bryan can go through life without legs, then so can I."

I'd also like to thank the rest of Bryan's family for all their support! Glenn, Carol Jean, Becky, Jenny, Nedra, and Miranda for all the time they spent with me, answering questions and always being available when I needed something clarified.

Special thanks to my sweet, sweet husband, Matt, for always encouraging me to continue, even when I get frustrated and am ready to give up. Thank you for taking time off and allowing me to have writers' retreats, so I could focus on and finish this book. Thank you for playing with the kids while I furiously typed on Pinkie-Pie (yes, my laptop has a name) and thank you for providing me with caffeine when I needed to stay up to complete the next chapter. I also want to thank my three beautiful children: Kalianna, Magdalyn, and Daxton for allowing Mommy to have some writing time and for always asking when Grandpa's book was going to be done. I wrote this for you. May Grandpa's example always carry you through the hardships in your lives.

I'd also like to thank Steven Novak for taking a vague idea and turning it into a gorgeous cover. My beta readers for all their input and advice to make this book better: Charlene Hirschi, Jewel Adams, Lauri Schoenfeld, Sara Ebert, Jaime

Buckley, and J.R. Simmons. You were all so kind and encouraging! This book is truly better because of each one of you. Thank you Kim King for proofing, and for the boost to my ego. Roger, you are an incredible and generous friend! So glad I have you in my life! And to my editor, Juli Caldwell, who not only encouraged me, along with Mikey Brooks, when I felt this book would never come to light. But you truly were an amazing friend throughout the journey! You gave incredible advice and polished this manuscript until it was ready to meet the world. Thank you, thank you, thank you!

A special shout-out to my girls from the writing retreat: Kim King, Jill Pelton, and Jenny Rabe. Love you girls forever! Thank you for the break from daily life when I needed it most! This book never would have finished on time without that weekend away. Thank you! We definitely founded the start of a new tradition.

I'd also like to thank FotoFly for their professionalism and amazing job with our beautiful family picture, displayed in the back of the book. Kelsey was incredible to work with, especially for a family with four small children. I was extremely impressed with them, and will absolutely recommend them to anyone looking for a great photographer. I'd especially like to thank Eric and Marci Adams for allowing us to use the image for this book.

To the individuals who allowed me to use their quotes on each of my chapter headings, thank you! Thank you for letting me use your sage words to help set the tone for this book. And thank you for being examples in your own lives and for sharing your wisdom with the world. You took a chance on an unknown author and were gracious and kind, and for that I am truly grateful. These individuals are not endorsing this book, only allowing me to borrow their words.

And last, but certainly not least, I'd like to thank each and every one of you, for no book would exist without its readers. Thank you for picking this up and giving me the opportunity to share Bryan's story with you. May God bless you in your lives, to overcome the obstacles that are thrown in your way. Attitude is everything.

About the Author

Stacy Lynn Carroll has always loved telling stories. She started out at Utah State University where she pursued a degree in English. Go Aggies! She then finished her BA at the University of Utah (to be closer to her then boyfriend, now hubby) where she got an emphasis in creative writing. After college she worked as an administrative assistant, where she continued to write stories for the amusement of her co-workers. When her first daughter was born, and with the encouragement of a fortune cookie, she quit her job and became a full-time mommy and writer. It seemed like fate when Matt and Stacy married. She was a writer, and her father-in-law had a story that demanded to be written. She and her husband have three children, two Corgis, and a fish named Don.

If you enjoyed this book, Stacy would love and appreciate your reviews on Amazon and Goodreads! She also loves to make new friends. Follow her on:

Facebook: https://www.facebook.com/authorstacylynncarroll

Twitter: @StacyLCarroll

Or visit her website: www.stacylynncarroll.com